The

"The New Bhagavad-Gita will appeal to the younger generation that has generally been exposed to a liberal education."

M. R. SRINIVASAN, PhD

Former Member, Planning Commission, Government of India

"The Bhagavad Gita is not only a basic text of Hinduism – it also constitutes a most valuable piece of mankind's heritage. Each generation should therefore come up with its own version of Krishna's answers to Arjuna's questions. The new English version by Koti and Hari will gain international recognition in Century 21."

GABRIEL MINDER, PhD

Member, Swiss Academy of Engineering Sciences

"Human problems change with time, but what we call great works are precisely those that will always have something important to say in every age. I therefore welcome this translation by two authors of the new generation, and I applaud their decision to make the translation in simple, current English so that its message is directly absorbed."

RODDAM NARASIMHA, PhD

Aerospace Scientist and Fluid Dynamicist, JNCASR

"As a complete neophyte I read this translation of the Gita with great interest. It allowed me to access Indian philosophy and to get inspiration to more reading."

BALAZS SZELESS

Formerly Mechanical Engineer, CERN

"The translation is admirably readable and I hope it will bring many people closer to the profundity of India's ancient traditions."

ARUN PRASAD

Engineering Student, Stanford University

"A sincere and devoted effort in bringing up the English version of the Indian sacred work, without sacrificing the essence of message, at the same time retaining the colloquial nature of the friendly conversation between the charioteer and the archer sitting in despondency. The precise and exact nature of the work is commendable and deserves full credence."

V. PRASANNA BHAT, PhD

Former Advisor, Saudi Arabian Monetary Agency

"The New Bhagavad-Gita successfully attempts to translate the ancient writing into modern-day language, complete with interpretations making the book understandable to the international readership and illustrated with endearing drawings."

TANJA SCHULZE

Program Director, The Melton Foundation

"I enjoyed very much reading the translation. The efforts to bring the translation closer to the original are evident. In particular, the footnotes are clear and help the reader understand important details. This book is a welcome addition to the literature on Bhagavad-Gita."

M. G. PRASAD, PhD

Board Member, Hindu University of America

"The New Bhagavad-Gita not only gives the modern reader access to this ancient sacred Hindu text but also provides gems of wisdom for contemporary seekers and guidance for all of us on how to live in a world of turmoil. With the aid of the translators' illuminating commentaries throughout, I felt I was listening in on a private conversation between a supreme god and a mortal struggling with the same questions that confront us today, including what are best actions when confronted with danger, aggression, and violence. The New Bhagavad-Gita can be read through or opened to any page to receive your enlightening message for the day."

PATRICIA SMITH

Founder, Peace X Peace and Editor, *Sixty Years, Sixty Voices*

"I'm sure that The New Bhagavad-Gita will stand out among thousands of other translations. The New Bhagavad-Gita is indeed new, because it presents the eternal truth in modern language, so everyone can understand and learn from it. I highly recommend this book and congratulate the authors on their great achievement."

Dr. L. SUBRAMANIAM
Violin Maestro and Composer

"I was enjoying what I was reading and found almost no places I could add or erase a touch. This book seems to tell us that when we miss the good old days we actually miss great human wisdom as described in the Bhagavad-Gita."

HUILAN YING
Professor, College of International Studies, Zhejiang University

"If you thought Eastern philosophy was abstruse and tedious, prepare yourself for a delightful surprise. In this translation of the holiest of Hindu works, the authors present the most profound spiritual insights in a lucid, lively, and accessible language, while their helpful and witty asides help the reader navigate the text without ever feeling swamped. Scholars and laymen alike are in for a treat."

CHANDRA SHEKHAR, PhD
Science Writer

"This rendition of the Gita is very articulate. It puts forth the very essence of human existence in a language that is simple and unambiguous. It is a very good book, a pleasure to read, and worth having a copy."

SHANTI KARRI
Faculty, Galen College of Nursing

The New Bhagavad-Gita

Timeless wisdom in the language of our times

With Best regards to
Padma and Arun Cariappa

June 23, 2011

TRANSLATORS

Koti Sreekrishna

Hari Ravikumar

W.I.S.E.
WORDS

Published by W.I.S.E. (Wisdom In Simple English) Words Inc.
6692 Summerfield Drive, Mason, OH 45040, USA
+1-513-290-3064

FIRST EDITION, APRIL 2011

978-0-615-45952-3

TRANSLATION Koti Sreekrishna & Hari Ravikumar
ILLUSTRATIONS Ashok U., Shanti Karri† & Naethra Sreekrishna‡
EDITING Aditya J. DESIGN Hari Ravikumar
†for verses 4:32, 10:23, 10:30, and 15:2 ‡for verse 11:12

http://newbhagavadgita.in

Sthitaprajña

The greatest people I have met in my time and station
are those who seem common and ordinary;
quietly doing their work with focus and devotion,
not looking for any rewards or glory;
enjoying and cherishing every moment of their lives
with a smile on their lips and with a sparkle in their eyes;
not displaying talents or voicing opinions,
responding rather than reacting to situations;
observant, conscious, satisfied, tranquil,
unmoved by the forces of good or evil;
bearing no baggages of hate or envy,
holding no memories of pain or sorrow;
thankful for every single day,
unconcerned about tomorrow;
calm amidst chaos and crises,
untouched by hurdles and trifles;
harming none yet choosing not to beg or pray,
treating everyone in the same humble way;
unchanged in their spirit yet willing to cope,
unpertubed by despair, unattached to hope;
uninterested in belonging or identity,
eternally in resonance with the eternity;
respecting life yet unafraid of death or destruction,
not lusting behind any truths or seeking salvation,
yet find it impossible to tell a lie.

HARI RAVIKUMAR

Preface

From my childhood, I have been connected to the Bhagavad-Gita, one way or another. My father (K. S. Krishna Tatachar, Sanskrit scholar and author) taught me the recitation of the Gita in the traditional, rigorous way. He would recite a line; I would hear it, see it (Sanskrit verses written in Kannada script), and repeat it twice. He would correct any mistakes in articulation and make me chant it until I got it perfectly right. I had to be attentive, otherwise the session would be prolonged. Nevertheless, I was filled with thoughts of playing cricket, hoping it wouldn't rain and that my friend Lakshmisha would walk around so that my dad would let me go. But that wasn't too common; my friend got dismissed more often than the session!

After I mastered the correct way of recitation, using the text as a guide, I would repeat the verses over and over again until I memorized them completely. Within a matter of one year, I could consistently repeat any verse ad lib. And so, by the time I was 9, I had memorized the entire 700 verses of the Gita.

The most thrilling moment with this rote memorization, ever fresh in my memory, was when I won the first prize in 'Six Chapter Gita Recitation Contest' at my school (National Middle School, Bangalore) in 1963. One of the judges of the contest was apparently so impressed that he added ₹10 of his own to the actual award amount of ₹29. I consider that as the most valuable ₹10 ever earned in my life since it was a blessing from HSV (Prof. H. S. Varadadeshikachar, who was to be my Sanskrit professor in college; today he is better known as H. H. Sri Rangapriya Swamy).

Before I left to the US in 1978, I requested my father to say a few words about the Gita, which I promptly recorded. In his brief talk, he said that Gita is a *sarva anukoola shastra* (a scriptural guide convenient to everyone). That one phrase said it all. But I always wondered why even those who knew the Gita made life inconvenient for themselves and others. Was that because of 'something else' (divisive ideas and traditional dogma) coming in the way? I kept reading every book on Gita I could lay my hands on; I might have read 50 versions by now. I found some new insight as well as 'something else', which was not always the same, but was always there, and in disguise at times. All through, I was trying to intuitively make sense, especially of some tricky verses which could be understood in multiple ways; in a way, I was trying to read Krishna's mind.

In 1990, my brother K. Srinivas gifted me D. V. Gundappa's discourse on Gita in Kannada, *Jeevana Dharma Yoga* ('A manual for living'). This was a book first published in the '70s, bringing national recognition to the author. I was happy to see that some of my own intuitive understanding was also echoed in DVG's book.

My friend K. Vasudevan wanted to bring out an English translation of the Gita and asked me for a recommendation. I couldn't think of one that I wholeheartedly liked. So in 2005, I began working on a translation, trying to keep out the 'something else'. I had just completed a word-for-word translation to be published as a 'one verse a day, self-study manual' and shared the draft with a few, when the best happened. There came along my nephew, Hari Ravikumar, decades younger (only in age) as co-author with brilliant ideas, great depth, unique talents, insights, and style. He wanted to have a modern English version to make the book accessible to any person, from any culture, who wants to know about the Gita.

He put his mind, body, and soul to the cause with such great diligence and dedication that we have this book. I trust you will derive as much joy reading it as we have derived in putting it together.

I've always felt unexplainable joy even while simply reciting verses of Gita. As we celebrate my father's 108th birthday, certainly he couldn't have given me a better gift than this. I must thank my dear wife Shailini for putting up with this 'Gita-nut', a title accorded to me by my kids!

Koti Sreekrishna
Mason, Ohio, USA

In 2006 I wrote the poem *Sthitaprajña* ('the stable one') inspired by my grandmother. At that time, my uncle Koti Sreekrishna was visiting India and I had shown it to him. He read it and immediately said that he'd like to include it in his Bhagavad-Gita translation. Little did I realize at that point that I would become such an integral part of the project. Working on this book has been so much fun that it has nearly *yogi*fied me.

When I wrote that poem I hadn't read the Gita in detail and today when I look at it I realize that if I had to capture the essence of a text that I had never learned formally, it is because of a higher intuition, of which I am clueless. But certainly it is also because of the great people around me – my family, my *guru*s, my friends – who are always adding something, always inspiring, and always caring. They are, for me, the living Gita.

Hari Ravikumar
Bangalore, India

About This Translation

The translator's task is to translate and not to interpret. But in places where the meaning is unclear, some interpretation creeps in. So, every translation is stained by the translator's understanding and worldview. As translators our submission is that we have presented the Gita in the light of our own experiences, at the same time staying clear of the path connecting readers to the original text. We must mention, however, there is no equivalent to reading the Bhagavad-Gita in the original Sanskrit.

While we present just the translation in simple language, in some places we had to include additional notes at the bottom of the verse. We have put the verse number in superscript at the beginning of a verse for those who are familiar with the text and would like to compare with the original.

We have retained the original Sanskrit terms for words that we could not translate easily into English. Since those terms might be unfamiliar, we have explained them the first instance they appear in a given chapter. The Gita uses many names and epithets for Krishna and Arjuna. We have avoided translating those where we felt they did not add any value.

In the Gita, all pronouns are masculine. Our translation has retained that in places where it was not possible to have a neutral term. This should not be treated as gender bias but as a convention, just like how the moon is feminine in Spanish or the sun is masculine in French. So, for example, verse 3:21 could have well been: 'A great woman sets an example by her actions. The whole world follows the standard that she sets.'

After initial conflicts between British and American English spellings, we chose to go with the latter.

Acknowledgements

This book would not be in your hands but for the help, encouragement, advice, critique, blessings, and wholehearted support of many people – from our own family members and friends to complete strangers (who have now become good friends). Our sincere thanks to every one of them. It would be impossible to list out everyone who helped shape this work but we owe special gratitude to a few.

Twenty-six remarkable and diverse individuals from different cultures, age-groups, professions, and dispositions reviewed the manuscript and shared their wisdom and experience, which has made this book what it is. The complete list of reviewers appears at the end of this note.

Aditya J., our editor, spent endless hours (very often late into the night) reading, analyzing, simplifying, and reshaping the text.

Ashok U., our illustrator, toiled for months before we finalized the superb sketches that you see in the book. We were inspired by his patience and tenacity to ensure that he gave us only the best. Ashok illustrated most of the book, but Shanti Karri and Naethra Sreekrishna also contributed a few lovely sketches.

Shatavadhani R. Ganesh, PhD, a great Sanskrit scholar of our time, was so kind as to go through the final manuscript and check for any failings in our translation; we were delighted and reassured when he mentioned that we had captured both the letter and the spirit of the Gita in our book.

Kanchan B. A. enriched the book design and layout with her fresh ideas and great sense of aesthetics.

Narayanan Srinivasan, one of the reviewers, went beyond what we had requested him; he worked closely with us re-working some critical verses, helped manage our Facebook page, and brainstormed on issues that we raised in our blog, http://newbhagavadgita.in.

K. Vasudevan, Naresh Keerthi, M. S. Krishna, Arun Prasad, Malur Vasan, and Prateek Ranganathan gave us wonderful insights and suggestions for improvement. Though the Gita evokes different responses from each of them – ranging from rapturous love to mild contempt – they all helped significantly enhance this book.

Roy Prasad, Anshuman Borah, Divya Tyam, Anirudh Chandrakant, and Avishek Chakravarti offered lots of creative ideas for the book. Jyotsna Pattabiraman, Linda Spencer, Deepta Rangarajan, S. Swaminathan, and Jaikar Mohan enlightened us on the aspects of publishing, business, and marketing. Meeta Gangrade, Sartaj Singh Anand, Vinay Kumar, Siddarth Ramamohan, and Arun Ramanuj gave several tips on how best we can use the latest technology in connection with the book.

M. P. Ravindra, PhD and S. Revathikumari, PhD not only shared ideas but also gifted Bhagavad-Gita books by contemporary authors. Narayana Kulkarni, Hema Ravikumar, and Prathigna Poonacha helped with their contacts, shared their views, and often spoke about the book.

Corky and Holly Siegel, Patricia Smith, and Ashish and Elizabeth Khokar gave sage advice and motivation all through.

V. Krishnamoorthy of Repromen Offset Printers was the one who made this book possible, literally.

Special thanks to Dr. L. Subramaniam, Kavita Krishnamurti and their wonderful family for always inspiring, encouraging, and supporting.

Needless to say, amidst all the great things that others have contributed, any shortcomings in the book are solely our own and in no way reflect on our reviewers or advisors.

Koti Sreekrishna
Hari Ravikumar

List of Reviewers

B. Ranganayakamma, MS
Senior Mechanical Engineer and Production Planner, Science & Engineering Services
Formerly Scientist, Defence Research and Development Organization
Clarksville, MD, USA

Balazs Szeless, Dipl. Ing.
Rotarian, Rotary Club of Ferney-Voltaire
Formerly Mechanical Engineer, CERN, Geneva
Sopron, Hungary

Chandra Shekhar, PhD
Science Writer
Formerly Computer Scientist, University of Maryland
Princeton, NJ, USA

G. Sudesh Kumar, PhD
Director, SGS India Pvt. Ltd.
Green Technologies and Sustainability Expert
Gurgaon, India

Gabriel Minder, PhD
Member, Swiss Academy of Engineering Sciences
Liaison, WHO-Rotary Clubs against Avoidable Blindness
Formerly Head, Management Information Services, CERN, Geneva
Former UN Consultant for Trade Development
Geneva, Switzerland

Prof. Huilan Ying, MA
College of International Studies, Zhejiang University
Hangzhou, China

Javier Lorca Espiro, MS
Electronics Engineer and Physicist
Assistant Professor, Universidad de La Frontera
Jazz Pianist and Multi-instrumentalist
Temuco, Chile

Dr. Jwala Prasad, MD
Anaesthesiologist, The Christ Hospital of Cincinnati
Yoga practitioner and teacher
Student of Jainism, Patanjali's Yoga Sutra, and Umaswamy's Tattvartha Sutra
Cincinnati, OH, USA

K. Srinivas, BS
Retired Manager, State Bank of Mysore
Scholar and Critique of Hindu epics and scriptures
Bangalore, India

Prof. M. G. Prasad, PhD
Stevens Institute of Technology
Fellow, American Society of Mechanical Engineers
Board Member, Hindu University of America
Author and Playwright (Topics in Hinduism)
Hoboken, NJ, USA

Prof. M. K. Sridhar, PhD
Reader, Canara Bank School of Management Studies, Bangalore University
Executive Director and Member-Secretary, Karnataka Knowledge Commission
Bangalore, India

M. R. Srinivasan, PhD
Member and Former Chairman, Atomic Energy Commission, Govt. of India
Founder Chairman, Nuclear Power Corporation
Former Member, Planning Commission, Govt. of India
Ootacamund, India

M. V. Ravikumar, PhD
Management Consultant and Mentor
Member, Indian Management Association
Past President, Consortium of Electronics Industries in Karnataka
Bangalore, India

NARAYANAN SRINIVASAN, MS
Senior Manager, Accenture
Project Management Professional (PMP) with focus on Business Intelligence
Writer and Blogger (http://lokakshemam.blogspot.com/)
Dallas, TX, USA

PREETI SRINIVASAN
Book Reviewer
Thiruvannamalai, India

PROF. RODDAM NARASIMHA, PhD
Aerospace Scientist and Fluid Dynamicist
Engineering Mechanics Unit, JNCASR
Fellow of the Royal Society
Former Director, National Institute of Advanced Studies
Former Director, National Aerospace Laboratories
Bangalore, India

PROF. S. JAYARAMAN, MBA
Professor, Human Resources Management, International School of Business and Media
Former Group Head, Investment Research and Information Services
Formerly Divisional Manager, Tata Metaliks
Associate Member, Institution of Engineers
Pune, India

SHANA KALOYANOVA, MA
Senior Lawyer, Coeler Legal
Formerly Junior Lawyer, Ernst and Young
Formerly Stagiaire, German Construction Industry Federation
Sofia, Bulgaria

SHANTI KARRI, MA
Faculty, Galen College of Nursing, Cincinnati
Former Instructor, Department of Sociology, University of Cincinnati
Former Andhra Pradesh Public Service Commission Candidate
Painter, Writer, and Poet
Cincinnati, OH, USA

SHEKHAR BORGAONKAR, PhD
Senior Researcher, HP Labs India
Student of various new age spiritual movements across the world
Bangalore, India

SRIKANTH VASUDEVAN, MS
Manager, Aerospace Programs, Orbital Research Inc.
Senior Member, American Institute of Aeronautics and Astronautics
Cleveland, OH, USA

TANJA SCHULZE, MA
Program Director, The Melton Foundation
Member, Young SIETAR
Former Tutor, Institute of Intercultural Business Communication
Leipzig, Germany

V. PRASANNA BHAT, PhD
Independent Corporate Advisor
Certified Associate of Indian Institute of Bankers
Member, Indian Management Association
Winner of National Awards for Excellence in Organizational Research
Former Advisor, Saudi Arabian Monetary Agency
Former Managing Director, ITCOT
Chennai, India

VARUN PRAKASH, BE
Aerospace Engineering Student, University of New South Wales
Design Engineer, Virtual Logic Systems Pvt. Ltd.
Formerly Mechanical Engineer, Mahindra and Mahindra
Canberra, Australia

VASLAV MARKEVITCH
AMA Diploma - American Management, Dallas, Texas
Climate and Water Specialisation, Marco Vinci Research
Formerly Official Spokesman ICRC, International Committee of Red Cross
and Middle East Mission Delegate
Promotion Manager of Technicon Corp. International Division, Tarrytown, New York
Deputy to Director of Information, Dept. United Nations Geneva
Deputy to Director of IATA for Civil Aviation Development and Budget
Senior Associate Consultant, Technomic Marketing Consultants (Chicago)
in charge of Europe and Middle East areas for Aviation and Electronics
Member of American Association for the Advancement of Science
Geneva, Switzerland and Montepulciano (SI), Italy

PROF. VINAY KUMAR, PhD
Formerly Professor of Chemistry, Northern Kentucky University
Cincinnati, OH, USA

Introduction

Over the years, human beings have changed in significant ways. Even with our limited ability to see into our ancient past, we like to believe that we have evolved, refined our senses, heightened our aesthetics, and acquired exquisite tastes. However, we have also hunted, waged wars, spilled blood, destroyed the natural environment around us, and caused a whole lot of trouble to one another.

As we dive deep into this ocean of human activity – filled with astonishing achievements and abysmal atrocities – we are intrigued to observe that in spite of some seeming changes, few of the basic human qualities remain unchanged; for example, human emotions. The 'way we feel' has mostly been the same though it has taken different forms and characteristics.

It is both interesting and beneficial to who we are now to know what the ancient people 'felt' about life, growth, thought, awareness, death, and the universe. The quiet wisdom of our ancestors, often disguised as records of experiences or imaginative poetry, might give us some inspiration and insights into our own lives.

What we call as 'scriptures' is different from all other genres of literature, for they deal with a different kind of reality and operate at a different level of consciousness, often quite removed from our day-to-day life. They give us a completely different perspective on things and quite often awaken us to a broader realm of reality.

The Bhagavad-Gita is one such scripture from ancient India.

Hinduism

Hinduism is the major religion of India with a worldwide following of over a billion people. In its original and purest form, it is a *sanaatana dharma* (loosely translated as 'eternal truth' or 'timeless religion') that represents over 5,000 years of contemplation, tradition, and continuous development in the Indian subcontinent. One who follows Hinduism is called a 'Hindu' (the term originally referred to a person living in India).

Hinduism has no single founder. Many ancient seer-sages, both men and women, contributed to its scriptures. The Hindu scriptures are numerous and diverse. Most of them are written in the Sanskrit language. Sanskrit, like Latin, is the root language for several languages; both Sanskrit and Latin belong to the same language family.

The word 'scripture' comes from the Latin *scriptura*, meaning 'that which is written', but the equivalent terms in Sanskrit for Hindu scriptures are *shruti*, 'that which is heard' and *smriti*, 'that which is remembered'.

Rishis (the seekers of truth) of ancient India contemplated on creation, human nature, refining basic instincts, purpose of life, workings of the physical world, and the metaphysical dimensions of the universe. The collective consciousness of the *rishis* is called 'Veda'. The literal meaning of the word 'Veda' is 'to know' or 'knowledge'.

Vedas are the foremost revealed scriptures in Hinduism. Every Hindu ceremony from birth to death and beyond is drawn from the Vedas. There are four Vedas: Rig, Yajur, Sama, and Atharva. These comprise the ***shruti*** texts. Though any body of knowledge can be called a Veda, like Ayurveda (health manual), the term *shruti* applies only to the four Vedas.

The *rishis* taught this collected wisdom to their disciples, who in turn taught it to their disciples. Thus, this knowledge was passed on, intact, for many generations, without a single word being written down. Even today, traditional students learn Vedic hymns orally from a *guru* (teacher). A verse from the Rig Veda (10.191.2) poignantly captures the intellectual atmosphere of those times:

Come together, speak together,
let your minds be united, harmonious;
as ancient gods unanimous
sit down to their appointed share.

The final portion of the Vedas, called 'Upanishads' or 'Vedanta', contain anecdotes, dialogues, and talks that deal with body, mind, soul, nature, consciousness, and the universe. Of the several Upanishads, ten are very important: Isa, Kena, Katha, Prashna, Munda, Mandukya, Taittiriya, Aitareya, Chandogya, and Brihadaranyaka.

Post-Vedic texts form another set of scriptures, the ***smriti***, which were composed by a single author and later memorized by generations. These include Ramayana and Mahabharata (the epics), Astadhyayi (grammar), Manusmriti (law), Purana (old episodes), Nirukta (etymology), Sulba Sutras (geometry), Grihya Sutras (running a family), and a whole body of texts governing architecture, art, astrology, astronomy, dance, drama, economics, mathematics, medicine, music, nutrition, rituals, sex, and warfare, among others.

The Bhagavad-Gita (or simply 'Gita'), which is a small part of the epic Mahabharata, is an important and widely read scripture of Hinduism. It is one of the most comprehensive summaries of Hinduism.

The Sanskrit word for **Creation** is *srishti*, which means 'pouring forth'. It is not 'creation' but rather an outpouring, an expansion, a change. The idea of creation is discussed in different ways in the Vedas. One hymn (Nasadiya Sukta) proposes a brilliant conceptual model for creation while another (Hiranyagarbha Sukta) raises and answers many questions about god and creation. Yet another hymn (Purusha Sukta) describes in detail the process of creation. Amidst all these varied views, there is a single underlying idea: 'one became everything'.

Another contention is that the concept of god is subsequent to creation. Hinduism has many gods but only one Supreme spirit. The Vedas make a clear distinction between god and *brahman*, the Supreme spirit, which is beyond all creation and destruction.

Hindu timeline spans trillions of years and time is considered cyclical rather than linear; so we have eternal time cycles one after the other with no beginning or end. The Surya Siddhanta, a treatise of Hindu astronomy explains the staggering timeline:

...twelve months make a year
this equals a day and night of the gods (1.13)
360 days and nights of the gods make a divine year (1.14)
12,000 divine years make one *mahayuga*. (1.15)
A day of Brahma spans 1,000 *mahayuga*s
a night of Brahma also spans 1,000 *mahayuga*s. (1.20)
Brahma's life span is 100 Brahma years. (1.21)

A *mahayuga* (Great Age) is made up of four *yuga*s (Ages): Satya *yuga*, Treta *yuga*, Dwapara *yuga*, and Kali *yuga*. In human terms, a *mahayuga* is 4.32 million years.

A day of Brahma (the god of creation), spanning a thousand *mahayugas*, equals 4.32 billion human years, which is the time he is active and thus enables activity in the universe. During the night of Brahma, all creatures are dissolved only to be brought forth again at the beginning of the next day (this is also explained in the Bhagavad-Gita; see 8:17-19 and 9:7).

Hindu sects are many and they often follow their own set of traditions and customs. While they seem very divergent, they have an underlying unity. Hinduism has a lot of freedom and openness with regard to beliefs, practices, and philosophies of its followers. Take the example of belief in god: some Hindus believe in god with a form, some others believe in a formless god, while others are agnostics; some believe in one god and some others believe in many.

Hindu values include harmony, tolerance, righteousness, respect for nature, and respect for the supreme. Hinduism accepts other religions and modes of thought. Here are two verses from the Rig Veda that bring out these values very nicely:

May noble thoughts come to us from every side,
unchanged, unhindered, undefeated in every way;
May the gods always be with us for our gain and
our protectors caring for us, ceaseless, every day.
(1.89.1)

The truth is one; the wise call it by different names.
(1.164.46)

Hindu worldview emphasizes conduct more than creed. It celebrates the diversity of existence and embraces the world as part of a big family, as recorded in an ancient book of stories, the Hitopadesha (1.3.71):

"These are my own, those are strangers" –
thus the narrow-minded ones judge people.
But for those magnanimous hearts,
the world is but one family!

The Vedas call humans by a cheerful and hopeful name: 'the children of immortal bliss' (Rig Veda 10.13.1). We are born pure and perfect but over time we accumulate the dust of unhappiness and pettiness. The constant quest is to return to our true nature as children of bliss. A prayer from the Brihadaranyaka Upanishad (1.3.28) talks about the spiritual journey from ignorance to illumination:

Lead me from falsehood to truth,
lead me from darkness to light,
lead me from death to immortality.

Hinduism is perhaps the oldest, most diverse, and most sophisticated system of religious thought and practice, covering nearly everything that comes under the umbrella of religion and philosophy. A human lifetime is insufficient to exhaust the wisdom it has to offer, and accessing even a small portion of this vast treasure enthralls, enriches, and elevates!

Mahabharata: Story and Characters

Vyasa is a famous sage of ancient India. He is often called Veda Vyasa since he organized the Vedas. Vyasa composed several important works, including the Brahma Sutra, a collection of aphorisms on metaphysics and the Mahabharata, the world's longest epic. The Mahabharata is the great story of king Bharata's dynasty. Bharata was an important king of ancient India; the official name of India, 'Bhaarata', comes from his name.

Apart from composing Mahabharata, Vyasa appeared as a character in the epic. He was born to Satyavati, a fisher girl, before her marriage. She later married king Shantanu, a descendent of Kuru (of Bharata dynasty). They had two sons but both of them died young, thus leaving no heirs to the throne. And so, Vyasa fathered Dhritarashtra and Pandu for the sake of the dynasty.

THE AUTHOR

Kuru was a famous king of the Bharata dynasty and his descendents were the Kauravas (or the Kurus). However, the term 'Kauravas' often refers to the one hundred children of Dhritarashtra, while Pandu's five children are called the 'Pandavas'. It is the dispute between the Kauravas and the Pandavas that resulted in the Mahabharata war, which took place nearly five thousand years ago in Kurukshetra (the land of Kuru) in Northern India. Almost all major kings from the Indian subcontinent took part in this great war, which was fought for eighteen days.

THE GRANDFATHER

Bhishma was the son of king Shantanu from his first marriage. Bhishma took a great oath of celibacy for life and helped his step-brothers and their descendants rule the kingdom. He was, in a way, the 'grandfather' of the Pandavas and Kauravas. In the war, though he fought on the side of the Kauravas, his heart was always with the Pandavas because he felt they were the more righteous of the two.

THE TUTOR

Drona was a great archer and warrior, though he was born in a priestly family. Drona, who was extremely poor, came to the Kauravas seeking a job. Bhishma appointed him to teach the art of warfare to both Pandavas and Kauravas. Drona loved the Pandavas dearly and Arjuna was his favorite disciple. But Drona was indebted to the Kauravas for their patronage and fought the war on their side.

King Dhritarashtra was born blind and before the great war began, Vyasa offered him divine vision so that he could witness the war. But the blind king refused to see this terrible war between his sons and nephews.

Sanjaya was born in a family of raconteurs and he was Dhritarashtra's advisor and charioteer. When Dhritarashtra refused to witness the war, Vyasa gave Sanjaya divine vision in order that he might witness the events on the battlefield as they happened, without leaving the palace, and narrate them to the blind Dhritarashtra. In fact, the dialogue of the 'Bhagavad-Gita' is structured in the form of Sanjaya's narration to Dhritarashtra.

THE NARRATOR

Duryodhana, the eldest among the hundred sons of Dhritarashtra, was known for his exploits with the mace. His childhood jealousies towards the Pandavas and his greed for power made him plot against them.

THE AGGRESSOR

Teaming up with his maternal uncle Shakuni and his friend Karna, Duryodhana orchestrated many devious schemes to destroy the Pandavas. One such instance was when he got the Pandavas invited to a game of dice and defeated them by deceit; it had been decided earlier that the losers of the game would forsake their kingdom, retire to the forest for twelve years and live incognito for a year after that. Having lost the game of dice, the Pandavas went into exile for thirteen years. When they returned, Duryodhana refused to return their kingdom as promised; he wanted to wage a war to decide that.

THE RIGHTFUL HEIR

Yudhistira, eldest of the five Pandavas, was the personification of goodness. His wisdom and good conduct attracted the admiration of even his enemies. Yudhistira couldn't bear the thought of a war, so he pleaded for peace in the land of their ancestors. When the Kauravas showed no signs of compromise, he finally asked for five villages to be given to the five Pandavas, and all would be forgotten.

Duryodhana said in response, "I challenge the Pandavas to battle! Either I, killing the Pandavas, will rule over this kingdom or the sons of Pandu, killing me, shall enjoy this land. I will sacrifice everything but I can't live side by side with the Pandavas. I won't surrender to them even that much of land which is covered by the sharp point of a needle."

THE HERO

Arjuna was the third of the five Pandavas, known for his prowess in archery. He was a key player in the great war and spent years honing his martial skills and acquiring new weapons, knowing well that he will have to defend his family from the Kauravas. But just before the war began, he felt sympathetic towards his foes because they were his relatives and friends, and so refused to fight. At that point, Krishna, his old friend and mentor, spoke the Bhagavad-Gita to awaken him.

Krishna, a popular Hindu god, is an *avatara* (incarnation) of the supreme. He was related to both the Pandavas and the Kauravas. When war became inevitable, he declared that he won't raise a weapon. He allowed his entire army to fight on the side of the Kauravas, as Duryodhana wished. He became the charioteer to Arjuna and gave him the supreme guidance at the time of war. But before the war broke out, Krishna tried to broker peace between the cousins because he didn't want the dynasty to be destroyed.

THE MENTOR

Krishna went to Dhritarashtra's court and said, "Joy in the happiness of others, sorrow at the sight of another's misery – this has been the credo of the Kurus! Your race, O king, is so noble, that it will be a pity if its scion should do something so improper; and worse still if it were done by you. The evil Duryodhana's misconduct will lead to universal slaughter. Please do something!"

All the elders in the assembly, the many sages visiting the kingdom, and Dhritarashtra's counselors told Duryodhana that Krishna's words were appropriate for the situation and that peace was the best way forward.

Duryodhana shouted in rage, "Why me? I have done nothing wrong! But as long as I live, the Pandavas will not get a share of the kingdom. Out of ignorance or fear or some other reason, we had earlier given them the kingdom but now I will not give them even an inch of our land."

With anger in his eyes, Krishna said, "If you want a war, then you shall have it. In a short time, there will be terrible bloodshed. After so many devious acts, you claim that you have done nothing wrong! You are not willing to give them their share of the land even when they are begging for it! Ignoring the words of the wise and deriding the advice of friends, you can never achieve anything that is good. What you are set to do is dishonorable and sinful."

In an extreme fit of anger, Duryodhana tried to use violence against Krishna. A shocked Dhritarashtra tried to intervene. Krishna calmly said, "O king, if they wish to use violence, let them. On my part, I will not do anything that will bring disgrace."

In response to the violence, Krishna just showed a glimpse of his divine form to everyone present. Duryodhana left the place in a huff.

"If war is what they want, let them have it. Now, with your permission, I will return." So saying, Krishna calmly went out of the king's assembly.

The war had to be fought. Peace had lost.

(Appendix 3 of this book has a family tree that explains the relationships between some of the characters of the Mahabharata. It also has a map of ancient India that includes some relevant places.)

Bhagavad-Gita: History and Context

Krishna and Arjuna had the conversation on the battlefield, standing in the midst of the two armies. Sanjaya narrated it with visual detail to the blind Dhritarashtra. Vyasa wrote it down for posterity and taught it to his student Vaishampayana, who later narrated it to King Janamejaya, the great grandson of Arjuna.

As per the traditional accounts, the Kurukshetra war was fought between 22 November and 9 December, 3139 BCE and over 18 million warriors died; only a handful of them survived. The Pandavas won the war and ruled for about 35 years. Then with the death of Krishna the previous Age (the Dwapara *yuga*) came to an end. The present Age, Kali *yuga*, began on 18 February, 3102 BCE.

Many famous saints of medieval India wrote commentaries on the Gita as they considered it an important text. From what we know, the first of these commentaries was written by the 8th century CE philosopher and saint, Shankara. His work popularized the Gita and also standardized the number of verses in the text. Some of the other notable scholars who wrote commentaries on the Gita are Ramanuja, Abhinavagupta, Madhva, Nimbarka, and Vallabha.

Many leaders of the Indian Independence movement (late 19th century and early 20th century CE) translated and interpreted the Gita, including Tilak, Vivekananda, Gandhi, Aurobindo, Rajaji, Bharathiar, and Bhave.

The whole episode of the Kurukshetra war is so deeply engraved in the Indian mind that for most Indians 'Gita' refers to Bhagavad-Gita and 'the Great War' refers to the battle of Kurukshetra. This speaks a lot, given that there are many *gitas* in the Hindu canon like Anu Gita, Ashtavakra Gita, Avadhuta Gita, Devi Gita, Ganesha Gita, Ribhu Gita, Shiva Gita, and Uddhava Gita (or Hamsa Gita).

The influence of the Gita outside India has also been enormous. This is perhaps because the text has such a nice blend of everyday pragmatism and spiritual mysticism. It has something valuable for everybody.

(Appendix 4 of this book has a compilation of quotes about the Bhagavad-Gita by different eminent people from all over the world, spanning many centuries.)

Bhagavad-Gita: The Text

'Bhagavad-Gita' is made up of two words: *Bhagavat* (of the lord) and *Gita* (song) so it becomes 'song of the lord' in English. The chapters 25 to 42 of the sixth episode of Mahabharata contain the Gita.

The Gita has 700 verses divided into 18 chapters. Though it is structured thus, it is not a systematic manual but a conversation between two friends that is captured in poetry.

The Gita does not present arguments in a linear way; it is circular and often descriptive, with repetitions and clarifications all through. Krishna presents many ideas and opinions to inspire Arjuna to fight the war and in the course of the discussion, talks about many aspects of life. Finally, he gives the choice to Arjuna to decide for himself whether to fight or not.

Most of the verses in the Gita are set to the *anushtubh* meter, with 4 lines of 8 syllables each, like in 2.47:

ka-rma-ṇye-vā-dhi-kā-ra-ste
mā-pha-le-ṣu-ka-dā-ca-na
mā-ka-rma-pha-la-he-tu-rbhūḥ
mā-te-sa-ṅgo-'stva-ka-rma-ṇi

A few verses are in the *trishtubh* meter, with 4 lines of 11 syllables each, like in 2.20:

na-jā-ya-te-mri-ya-te-vā-ka-dā-cit
nā-yaṃ-bhū-tvā-bha-vi-tā-vā-na-bhū-yaḥ
a-jo-ni-tyaḥ-śā-śva-to-'yaṃ-pu-rā-ṇo
na-ha-nya-te-ha-nya-mā-ne-śa-rī-re

(Appendix 1 of this book has a transliteration guide, which will help in reading Sanskrit written in the roman script. Appendix 2 has the original text of the Bhagavad-Gita.)

Every chapter of the Gita ends with a colophon that includes the chapter number and name, along with a generic description of the Gita. Here is the colophon of the first chapter:

Thus ends the first chapter 'Arjuna's Despair'
from the Upanishad Bhagavad-Gita,
which is a dialogue between Krishna and Arjuna
on the knowledge of the supreme and
the art of union with the supreme.
That's the truth, *Om*!

Though the colophon refers to the Gita as an Upanishad, the Gita is not one of the Upanishads. The colophon is not found in the Mahabharata but by convention is used while reciting the Gita.

Bhagavad-Gita in Translation

The Bhagavad-Gita is the most translated Indian book. Saint Jnaneshwar composed one of the earliest translations of the Gita during the later part of 13th century CE; his Marathi language translation, along with elaborate commentary makes up the classic *Jnaneshwari*.

Even earlier, Abu-Saleh is said to have translated the Mahabharata into Arabic (11th century CE) and Abul-Hasan-Ali, into Persian (as *Modjmel-altevarykh* in 12th century CE). But the most popular Persian translation, *Razm nama*, was commissioned by King Akbar in 16th century CE. All these works contain the Gita either in part or in full.

Under the patronage of king Raja Raja Narendra, the poet Nannayya Bhatt (1000-1060) started translating the Mahabharata into Telugu but died after working on two episodes. Many years later, Tikkana (1200-1280) translated 15 episodes and Erra Pragada (1280-1350) completed the work.

The poet-philosopher Vedanta Desika (Venkatanathan) (1269–1370) did a Tamil poetic translation of the *Gitartha Sangraha*, a summary of Gita in Sanskrit, composed by philosopher-saint Yamunacharya (Alavandar) (916-1041).

Madhava Panikkar prepared a condensed Malayalam translation of the Gita in 14th century CE. The great classical poet, Kumara Vyasa (Gadag Naranappa), rendered the Mahabharata into Kannada in his *Karnata Bharata Kathamanjari*, which was finished in 1430. Orissa's 'first poet', Sarala Das, adapted Mahabharata into Oriya in *Sarala Mahabharata*, written during 15th century CE. It has portions of the Gita.

Kabi Sanjaya translated the complete Mahabharata into Bengali during the first half of 15th century CE.

During the reign of the Koch kings, Ram Saraswathi translated the Mahabharata into Assamese in 15th century CE. Later, king Lakshminarayan commissioned Govinda Misra to translate the Gita into Assamese verse.

The Gita has also been translated into other major Indian languages like Gujarati, Hindi, Kashmiri, Punjabi, Sindhi, Urdu, etc.

The Bhagavad-Gita was first translated into English in 1785 by Charles Wilkins, an orientalist and typographer. Very soon, his translation was translated into French and German.

Later, the German poet August Wilhelm Schlegel translated the Gita into Latin in 1823. Prussian minister and linguist Wilhelm von Humboldt translated the Gita into German in 1826. In 1846, orientalist Christian Lassen translated the work into French and in 1848, Dimitrios Galanos, an Indologist, translated it into Greek.

A conservative estimate is that the Gita has been translated about 2,000 times into over 75 languages.

Conclusion

In an ideal world, we don't need any religion by its brand name. We have enough collective wisdom that we use in various aspects of our life. Our true nature knows right from wrong. So we could easily light the fire and burn all religious books. But that would be inefficient. Why would we want to miss the opportunity to stand on the shoulders of giants?

We read and enjoy novels written by great authors without worrying about their religious backgrounds, but things change drastically when religion comes into the picture. We get crazy. We simply refuse to learn from each other when it is a matter of faith. In addition, we try to convince others that our brand of religion is the best.

Perhaps the world is not yet ready to absorb the collective wisdom from all religions and philosophies. Then, the best we can do is to present the most important book in each of our religions and cultures, and leave it at that; readers can draw their own conclusions.

People of a particular religion often take their books for granted and read them with minimal introspection beyond the dictates of their sectarian views. On the other hand, people from foreign cultures might not be very familiar with those books. Thus, revisiting such works might give fresh insights to adherents and a totally new inspiration to everyone at large.

The Bhagavad-Gita is a good place to start if one wants to know about India's grand heritage, religious traditions, philosophy, and spirituality.

May it protect both of us.
May it nourish both of us.
Let us work together.
Let our work be lit up by vigor.
Let us not hate each other.
May peace prevail, Om!

(from the Katha Upanishad)

The Bhagavad-Gita

Invocation

Salutations to the supreme lord,
the teacher of the world, and
the source of eternal bliss!

CHAPTER 1

Arjuna's Despair

Dhritarashtra

1 Sanjaya, tell me what is happening
in the sacred land of Kurukshetra,
where my people and the Pandavas
have assembled, eager to fight.

Sanjaya

[2]O King! Duryodhana saw the Pandava army
drawn up for battle;
then he went to his tutor Drona
and spoke these words.

[3]Respected sir,
look at the mighty Pandava army
arrayed in battle formation
by your talented student,
the son of Drupada.

[4]Their army has many great archers and heroes
who match Bhima and Arjuna,
such as Yuyudhana, Virata, and the mighty Drupada,
[5]Dhrishtaketu, Chekitana, and the valiant king of Kashi,
Purujit, Kuntibhoja, and the best of men, Shaibya,
[6]the courageous Yudhamanyu, the brave Uttamaujas,
Abhimanyu, and the sons of Draupadi.
They are all *maharatha*s.

A *maharatha* is one who is skilled in warfare and
can fight ten thousand warriors at once.

[7]Likewise, O best of men, also take a look at
the distinguished warriors on our side.

I shall briefly name the leaders in our army.

8 Besides yourself, Bhishma, Karna,
the victorious Kripa,
Ashvatthama, Vikarna, and Bhurishravas;
9 there are many other heroes armed
with a variety of weapons,
and each skilled in the art of war.
All of them are prepared
to give up their lives for my sake!

Selflessness has always been an important part of the Indian ethos.
Therefore, Duryodhana's 'my sake' is an aberration;
it is a reflection of his bloated ego.

10 Our army led by Bhishma seems inadequate,
whereas their force led by Bhima looks sufficient!

Duryodhana is envious of Bhima's strength and courage.
Thus, he sees Bhima as leading the Pandava army
although it is led by Dhristadyumna.

Duryodhana's grand description of the Pandava army implies that
he thinks they are stronger, although they are lesser in number.

This verse could also mean:
"Our army led by Bhishma seems unlimited,
whereas their force led by Bhima looks limited"
but given the context, we have preferred our version.

At this point, Duryodhana addresses his side:

11 Positioned in your designated places, in every move,
give maximum protection to Bhishma!

Having heard Duryodhana's words,

[12]to cheer him up,
Bhishma, the grandfather of the Kurus,
roared aloud like a lion and
blew his conch with full power.

The blowing of a conch shell signals the beginning of an event.

[13]At once, conches, kettledrums, cymbals,
soft-drums, and trumpets resounded
causing a lot of noise and tumult.

[14]Then, Krishna and Arjuna
seated in their mighty chariot
drawn by white horses,
blew their divine conches.

In those days, warriors would blow conch shells to announce the start of battle.
Each warrior had his own uniquely qualified conch shell,
which was either earned as a trophy or was obtained as a gift.

[15]Krishna blew his conch Panchajanya.
Arjuna blew his conch Devadatta.
Bhima, known for his terrifying feats,
blew his huge conch Paundra.
[16]King Yudhistira blew his conch Anantavijaya,
Nakula blew the Sughosha, and
Sahadeva blew the Manipushpaka.

[17,18]King of Kashi, the supreme archer,
Shikhandi, the mighty warrior,
Satyaki, the invincible,
Dhrishtadyumna, Virata, Drupada,
the sons of Draupadi, and
the strong-armed Abhimanyu –
each blew his conch one by one.

19 That dreadful sound echoed through earth and sky,
shaking the very spirit of the Kauravas.

20 Arjuna looked at the Kaurava army arrayed in battle
and lifted his mighty bow,
preparing himself for the clash of weapons
that was about to begin.
21 Then, Arjuna told Krishna:

Place my chariot
between the two armies
22 so that I may take a good look
at those with whom I must fight
among these battle hungry warriors.

The great warriors would choose to fight only with equals.

[23]I would also like to see all those
who have eagerly joined the battle
to please the wicked Duryodhana.

SANJAYA

[24]As per Arjuna's request,
Krishna placed their magnificent chariot
between the two armies,
[25]right in front of Bhishma, Drona
and all the kings of the world.

Then, he said:
Arjuna, look at the Kurus
who have assembled here.

26 There, Arjuna saw
grandfathers, teachers,
uncles, cousins, nephews,
sons, grandsons,
27 and friends in both armies.
When he took a closer look at
his relatives ready for battle,
28 Arjuna, the son of Kunti,
overcome by a sudden burst of pity,
spoke in despair:

Krishna,
when I see my own people
eager to fight us,
29 my limbs grow weak,
my body trembles,
my mouth turns dry,
my hairs stand on end,
30 my bow slips from my hand,
my skin burns,
my mind whirls, and
I can barely stand.

Arjuna's pity was misplaced sympathy that led to the weakening of his mind.
Interestingly, Arjuna refers to even his opponents as 'my own people'.
Compare this with Dhritarashtra's distinction between the two sides in 1:1 (page 43).

[31] I see only bad omens;
I can't see any good coming from
killing my own people.

32 O herder of cows,
I don't fancy victory, pleasure, or kingdom.
What is the use of this kingdom, happiness, or even life?

Krishna was the chief of the cowherds and
was called 'Govinda', the friend of cows.
Arjuna refers to Krishna as 'Govinda'
perhaps to highlight the latter's simplicity.

33,34 Alas! Teachers, uncles, sons, grandfathers,
nephews, and many relatives –
for whose sake we desire
kingdom, pleasures, and comforts –
the very same ones are standing here in battle,
risking their lives and riches.

35 O Madhusudhana,
I know they are eager to kill me
but I don't wish to kill them.

'Madhusudhana' is a title given to Krishna
because he killed a demon named Madhu.

I would not kill even for
the lordship of the three worlds,
let alone for this earthly kingdom.

The three worlds or the three 'realms of existence' are:
the earth, the heavens, and the skies.

[36]O protector of men,
what kind of happiness are we going to get
by killing the sons of Dhritarashtra?
Although they have incited the war,
we will only incur sin by killing them.

In a war, it is fair to kill the opponents.
Arjuna feels that this is immoral because
he is blinded by compassion for his relatives and friends.

In fact, it is against the code of a warrior to
run away from battle or refuse defending one's honor.

[37]O kind one,
it is not fair to kill our relatives.
How can we ever be happy
after killing our own people?

[38]Overcome by greed, they fail to see the evil
in killing one's own family and betraying friends, but
[39]we can clearly see the wrong in killing our kin.
Isn't it better to stay away from this evil?

[40]When a family is destroyed,
time-honored family values are lost.
When family values are lost,
chaos reigns in the family.

41 When chaos reigns,
the women of the family are violated.
When women are violated,
anarchy arises in society,
O Varshneya!

'Varshneya' is a name given to Krishna because he was born in the Vrishni clan.
Arjuna calls Krishna as Varshneya, perhaps to remind him
of the importance of a stable social order.

Arjuna's argument basically is:
with the men-folk killed, the women are vulnerable
to harassment by evil men; children born out of such unions
will have a confused lineage and are subjected to hardships.
When children have a chaotic life, the society will also be chaotic.

42 Anarchy paves the way to hell
for the destroyers of the family
as well as the family itself.
Deprived of post-death rites,
the ancestors of these people
meet their downfall.

The post-death rites include an offering of cooked rice and water to ancestors
after invoking their spirits with specific religious chants.
To perform the post-death rites, one must know
the past three generations of ancestors as well as specified protocol,
both of which may be difficult when there is chaos in society.
Arjuna laments that the ancestors,
bereft of post-death rites, will fall to lower realms.

Some sections of orthodox Hindus accept as authority this flawed logic of Arjuna
(that the actions of the current generation can affect the ancestors)
and ironically, quote this verse to support their argument.

43The age-old practices
of family and community are ruined
by the terrible deeds of these killers
who create anarchy in society.

44Further, we have heard that
those who have lost family values
are consigned to hell forever.

This is another fallacy of Arjuna;
there is no such thing as permanent stay in hell.

According to Hindu belief, 'hell' is a transient place
where people are punished for their immoral deeds;
they stay till they receive the full course of punishments.

45That being the case,
by getting ready to kill our own people,
we are on the verge of
making a terrible mistake
merely out of our greed
for royal pleasures.

46It would be better
if the armed Kauravas
were to kill me in battle
while I remain
unresisting and unarmed.

SANJAYA

47 Having said this,
Arjuna cast aside his bow and arrows
and sank down in his chariot,
overwhelmed by grief.

Religion is a mix of truth and tradition.
Truth is eternal, and therefore always relevant.
Tradition is contextual, and thus relevant for a particular place and time.

Arjuna ignored truth and was pursuing tradition.
This was perhaps the cause of his despair.

CHAPTER 2

Wisdom and Action

Sanjaya

1 To him, who was thus in despair,
overcome by pity, and in tears,
Krishna spoke these words:

2 How can you lose heart
in this hour of crisis?

This is disgraceful, ignoble, and
unworthy of higher realms.

3 Don't be a coward, Arjuna;
that's not right for you!

Arise, awake, and abandon your timidity,
O destroyer of enemies!

ARJUNA

4 How can I battle Bhishma and Drona?
How can I shower arrows on them?
They are worthy of my reverence.

5 If I kill these noble elders
for the sake of worldly gains,
my pleasures will be stained with their blood;
instead, I would rather beg for food.

6 Dhritarashtra's men are standing in front of us;
I don't wish to live at the cost of killing them.

Should we conquer them?
Should they conquer us?
I don't know which is better.

[7]I have become very sentimental.
I am totally confused about
what is right and what is wrong.
I surrender at your feet as your disciple.
Please show me the right path and
tell me for certain what is good for me.

[8]I don't see how
gaining absolute control
over this prosperous earth or
even lordship over the heavens
will drive away this grief,
which dampens my spirit.

SANJAYA

[9]Having said this to Krishna,
Arjuna – the destroyer of enemies – declared:
"I shall not fight!"
and became silent.

[10]In the midst of the two armies,
Krishna, with a smile,
spoke these words
to the grief-stricken one:

Krishna

11 You grieve for that which you should not,
yet you seem to speak words of wisdom.
The wise neither grieve for the dead
nor for the living.

12 There was never a time when
I or you or these kings did not exist.
There will never be a time when we cease to exist.

Here, 'we' refers to the soul.
Krishna goes on to explain how the soul is eternal and immortal.

13 The soul that lives in the body
passes through childhood, youth, and old age;
similarly, it passes through different bodies.
A wise person is not disturbed by these changes.

Here, 'it' refers to the soul.

14 When senses come in contact with sensates
we experience cold and heat, pleasure and pain.
These sensations come and go,
for they are not permanent.
Patiently endure them, Arjuna.

Senses (or sense organs) are ears, eyes, nose, tongue, and skin.
Sensates are sound, sight, smell, taste, and texture.
Sensations are what we experience when senses come in contact with sensates.

15One who is not affected by sensations
remains calm in pain and pleasure.
He is firm in his resolve and
he is ready for immortality.

By disconnecting oneself from materials and by subduing lower instincts,
one gets in touch with the immortal self.

16The Unreal doesn't exist.
The Real never ceases to be.
Those who know the ultimate truth
have indeed realized the nature of both.

Krishna refers to the soul as 'real' since it is imperishable;
he refers to the body as 'unreal' because it is perishable.
Indeed, the body is also real, but it appears unreal
in the face of a higher level of reality, the soul.

17The imperishable pervades everything
and no one can destroy the imperishable.

'Imperishable' refers to the soul.

18The body is perishable,
whereas the soul seated within
is eternal, indestructible, and infinite.
Therefore fight, O descendent of Bharata!

Arjuna was a descendent of king Bharata, the founder of the ancient Indian empire.
Krishna invokes the name of Arjuna's famous ancestor perhaps as a reminder
that one's character survives long after one is gone.

19 One who considers it as the killer
and one who thinks it is killed –
both of them do not know,
for it neither kills nor is it killed.

In this verse and in the following few verses, 'it' refers to the soul.

20 It is never born; it never dies.

It never came into being,
nor will it ever come into being.

Unborn, eternal, changeless, and primeval,
it is not killed when the body is killed.

The soul is always there – it is not bound by space or time.
The idea of 'birth' and 'death' is only for the body.

21 One who knows that the soul is
indestructible, infinite, eternal, and unborn,
how can he kill or incite another to kill?

22 Just as one discards old clothes
and puts on new ones,
the soul discards old bodies
and takes on new ones.

[23]Weapons do not cleave it,
fire does not burn it,
water does not wet it, and
the wind does not wither it.

[24]It cannot be cut or burnt
or drenched or dried.
It is everlasting, all-pervading,
stable, immovable, and primordial.

[25]It is beyond form, thought, or change.
Having understood it thus,
why should you grieve?

The soul is free from birth and death, growth and decay, existence and non-existence.

[26]Even if you believe that the soul is
perpetually subject to birth and death,
why should you grieve?

[27]Death is certain for those who are born.
Birth is certain for those who have died.
Why worry about the inevitable?

We go through cycles of birth and death until the soul is redeemed.

[28]Beings are formless in their beginnings,
they are formless in their ends, and
they acquire a form only in between.
What is there to lament in this?

Before birth and after death, beings are a part of the infinite.
It is only during bodily life that beings can be perceived by the senses.

[29]One sees it as a wonder,
another speaks of it as a wonder,
yet another hears of it as a wonder
and even having heard it all,
no one really knows.

30 The soul in everyone's body
is eternal and imperishable.
Thus, you should not grieve
for any living being.

31 Even from the point of view of
your own duty as a warrior
you should not hesitate to fight.
There is nothing superior for a warrior
than a war fought for preserving *dharma*.

Here, *dharma* refers to righteousness.
The Pandavas fought the war for the larger good
and not merely for their honor or for self-defense.

32 Fortunate are the warriors
who encounter a battle such as this
which comes of its own accord.
Indeed, it is an open door to heaven.

According to Hindu belief, 'heaven' is a transient place
where people are rewarded for their good deeds;
they stay till they receive the full course of rewards.

33 Now if you don't fight in this
battle sanctioned by *dharma*,
you will be making the mistake of
ignoring your own duty and reputation.

34 People will forever talk
about your dishonorable act
and for an honorable person,
disgrace is worse than death.

35 The great warriors will think that
you have run away from battle out of fear;
many who held you in high esteem
will no longer respect you.

36 Your enemies will ridicule your ability
and speak lowly of you.
What can be more painful than this?

Krishna tries to persuade Arjuna by presenting various perspectives on the issue. Earlier he spoke about how Arjuna's fundamental assumptions were wrong and here he speaks about the obvious problems of retreating from war.

37 If you are killed, then you will attain heaven.
If you are victorious, then you will rule over the kingdom.
Therefore arise, Arjuna, with a firm resolve to fight.

38 Gain and loss, victory and defeat,
comfort and discomfort –
treat them in the same spirit and fight;
then you will not incur any guilt.

[39]So far, I revealed to you the way of *sankhya*.
Now, understand the practice of *yoga*.

The way of *sankhya* is an approach based on reasoning.
'Practice of *yoga*' refers to *karma yoga*:
doing work without getting attached to it.

With this insight, you will break free
from the bondage of action.

Bondage of action refers to attachment to the results of an action.

[40]In this path, no effort is wasted
nor is there any bad outcome.
Even a little effort in this direction
will save you from misery.

[41]Those who follow this path
attain single-pointed focus.
But for those who are hesitant,
their decisions are multifold and endless.

[42]Those who lack proper insight
delight in the letter (and not spirit) of the Vedas;
they proclaim in flowery words:
"there is nothing else other than this."

The Vedas are the foremost revealed scriptures in Hinduism.

43 They are full of desires and
reaching heaven is their supreme goal.
They perform many elaborate rituals
to attain pleasure and power.
Their actions eventually result in rebirth.

See 2:49 (page 72) and 9:20-21 (pages 163,164).

44 Those attached to pleasure and power
are led astray by that flowery language.
They never attain the firm intellect of a
contemplative mind.

45 The Vedas deal with the three *guna*s;
free yourself from the influence of the *guna*s.

Guna refers to inherent tendencies of a human being. The three *guna*s are:
sattva (saintly goodness), *rajas* (restless activity), and *tamas* (deluded lethargy).

Go beyond the dualities and
give up the desire to acquire or hoard.

'Dualities' are relative opposites like hot and cold,
happy and sad, winning and losing, me and other, etc.
'Acquire' refers to pursuing what is yet to be attained.
'Hoard' refers to clinging on to what has already been attained.

Be a master of yourself and
be established in the eternal truth.

46 What is the use of a well when there is a flood
and water is flowing freely everywhere?
What is the use of all the Vedas
when one has realized the ultimate truth?

47 You have control only over your actions
but never over their results.
The expected results should not be
the motivation for action.
Also, don't shirk away from your work.

One is never in complete control over the outcome of an action.
See 18:13-14 (page 251).

It is pointless to worry about something that one cannot control.
Focus on work without fear of failure or greed for success.
At the same time, don't be lazy.

48 Work with a balanced mind
having given up all attachments;
such equanimity is called *karma yoga*.

49 Action guided by selfish interests
is far inferior to action guided by wisdom.
Seek refuge in that wisdom.
Pitiable are those
who have their eye on the result.

'Wisdom' refers to working with a balanced mind without attachments.

50 Endowed with that wisdom,
one remains unaffected by both
good and bad outcomes in this life.

Thus, act in the spirit of *karma yoga*,
which is a smart approach to work.

51 With a balanced mind,
the wise renounce
their interest in the results;
freed from the bondage of birth,
they reach a faultless state.

'Bondage of birth' refers to being caught in the cycle of birth and death.

52When your intellect transcends
the thickets of delusion,
you will go beyond what has been heard
and what is to be heard.

When the intellect becomes free of delusion,
it is able to view things objectively
and hence is not perturbed by external influences.

53Unmoved by confusing things
that you may hear,
when your intellect stands still
and is firmly fixed in meditation,
you shall attain *yoga*.

In this context, *yoga* is 'union with the supreme'.

ARJUNA

54How do you describe a man of steady insight?
How does a man of steady intellect speak?
How does he sit?
How does he go about leading his life?

KRISHNA

55When one abandons all selfish desires
and is satisfied within the true self,
he is said to be of steady intellect.

56 One whose mind is not agitated by adversity,
who does not crave pleasure,
who is free from
passion, fear, and anger,
is a sage of steady intellect.

57 He is detached in all matters, and
he neither rejoices nor hates
the pleasant and unpleasant situations
that he encounters;
his intellect stands firm.

58When he completely withdraws
the senses from the sensates,
just as a tortoise withdraws its limbs,
his intellect stands firm.

59When he abstains from feeding the senses
by turning away from the sensates,
the cravings for sensations still remain.

Even the cravings leave him
once he has realized the supreme.

60The turbulent senses
forcibly distract the mind
even of a wise person
who is sincerely striving
to control them.

61Having restrained the senses,
one should sit steady
seeking the supreme.

When senses are under control
one attains a steady intellect.

[62]When one is preoccupied
with sensations,
he easily gets attached to them.
From such attachment,
a desire to attain them is born.
Unfulfilled desires
lead to frustration.
[63]Frustration leads to confusion;
confusion impairs discretion.
Lack of discretion destroys reasoning.
Without the power of reasoning,
he is doomed!

[64]But a self-disciplined person,
who has subdued his senses and
is devoid of attraction or aversion,
remains peaceful even as
he encounters sensates.

[65]In that eternal peace,
all his pains are destroyed
for the intellect of the serene one
soon becomes firmly established in the Self.

66 One who is not disciplined
lacks wisdom and focus.
Without focus,
one cannot attain peace.
Without peace,
how can one be happy?

67 When the mind is led astray
by wandering senses,
then it carries away one's wisdom
just as the wind carries away a ship
off its chartered course.

[68]Therefore, he is of steady intellect,
whose senses are completely restrained
from the influence of sensates.

[69]The self-restrained person is awake
to which all other beings are asleep.
The seer-sage is asleep
to which all other beings are awake.

The self-restrained person is awake to the ultimate truth
and the seer-sage is asleep to mundane experiences
encountered by sense organs.

[70]Just as rivers flow into the ocean
which gets filled up and yet remains still,
so also, all desires merge in him
and yet he attains peace,
unlike the one who is driven by desires.

[71]He attains peace
once he overcomes all desires,
lives without cravings and
is free from ego
or any sense of ownership.

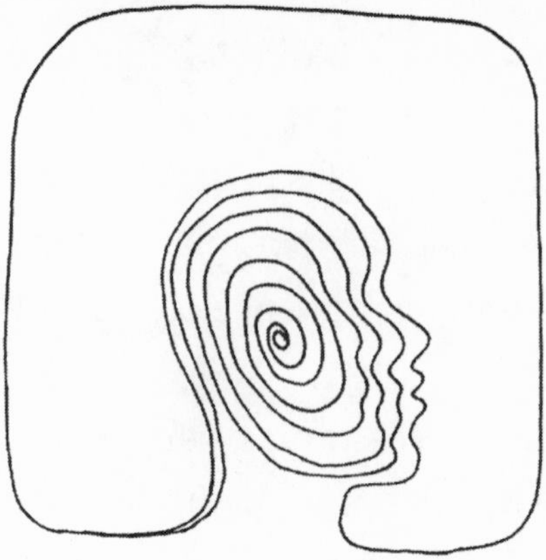

[72]This is indeed the state of *brahman*.
He who attains it is never deluded.
Being established in that state,
even barely at the hour of death,
he becomes one with the supreme.

CHAPTER 3

Selfless Action

Arjuna

[1]If you consider knowledge superior to action,
why do you urge me to commit this terrible deed?

[2]You confuse me with this conflicting message.
Tell me for certain just one thing
that will lead me to the greatest good.

Krishna

[3]O blameless one!
As I have proclaimed in the past,
there are two ways to lead a fulfilling life:
the path of knowledge and the path of selfless action.

The path of knowledge is best suited for the deep thinkers
who like to contemplate and reason.
The path of selfless action is best suited for those
who are active and like to work hard.

4 One cannot achieve freedom from action
by merely staying away from work.

One does not become serene
by merely giving up work.

5 Nobody can remain passive
even for a moment.
Everyone is helplessly drawn into action
by inborn, natural impulses.

6 One who sits idle
restraining the organs of action
yet mentally broods over sensations
is a hypocrite who has fooled himself.

Organs of action are:
mouth, hands, feet, genitals, and anus.
One who sits idle fools himself into thinking that he is not acting.

7 A person excels when
he disciplines the senses with the mind and
engages the organs of action in work
without getting attached to sensations.

A recurring idea in this chapter is 'working without attachment';
it refers to doing work merely as a duty and
being detached from the possible outcomes.

8Do the work you are supposed to do;
certainly it is better than laziness.
Even the basic maintenance of your body
is impossible without action.

9Humans are bound by their actions
except when they are performed
for the sake of *yajña*.
Thus, Arjuna, do your work,
free from attachments,
in the spirit of *yajña*.

Here, *yajña* means 'an act of self-dedication' or 'service above self'.
It is also an act of worship; so the message is 'do your work as worship'.

10Long ago, Prajapati, the lord of creatures
brought forth human beings
with the spirit of *yajña*, and said:
"By this, you shall grow!
May this grant you all your desires!
11By this, you nourish the *deva*s and
they will reward you in return.
By nourishing one another
you shall attain the supreme good.
12Pleased with your selfless service,
the *deva*s will fulfill your wishes."

One who enjoys those gifts
without giving back anything in return
is indeed a thief.

Here, 'this' refers to 'spirit of *yajña*'.
*Deva*s are divine beings that reside in heaven.
The elements and forces of nature such as wind, water, fire, earth, space, time, sun, moon, stars, planets, rain, oceans, mountains, plants, animals, etc. are also personified as *devas*.
We have to nourish and respect nature if we want to be nourished by it and more importantly, for natural goodness to prevail.
*Deva*s are the embodiment of natural infrastructure.
We cannot work without the infrastructure in place, so we should dedicate a portion of our gains for its maintenance.

13 Wise ones eat the food that remains
after being offered to *yajña*;
thus, they are released from all evils.
Wicked ones prepare food for their own sake
and indeed live on sin alone.

In the process of procuring our food, to some extent, we cause trouble to nature and also to other beings.
So we purify the food by offering it to the supreme and then eating it with a sense of gratitude.
Even if we eat a dry leaf that fell on its own accord, we must not do so with a sense of entitlement.

14 Living beings are sustained by food,
food comes forth from rain,
rain is caused by *yajña*, and
yajña is born out of action.

The idea of '*yajña* causing rain' is perhaps a reference to the maintenance of the natural cycle.

[15]This action originates from *brahman*,
which is the manifestation of the imperishable.
Therefore the all-pervading *brahman* is
always established in *yajña*.

Brahman is the supreme being.

[16]The wheel of life is thus set in motion.
Indulging in sensual pleasures,
one who violates this natural order
lives in sin, thus wasting his life.

Cosmic order of the universe is rooted in the principle of give and take.

[17]But for those who rejoice solely in the *atman*,
and are satisfied with the *atman*,
nothing remains to be accomplished.

Atman is the inner, higher self.
'...nothing remains to be accomplished' indicates that such people
don't work for any gains since they have already found satisfaction within.

[18]They have nothing to gain by performing action
and nothing to lose by renouncing action.
They are not dependent on anyone for anything.

[19]Therefore, do your work with a spirit of detachment
and you will attain the highest level.

[20]Janaka and others attained perfection
by just doing their work,
for the welfare of the world.
You too should work like them!

Janaka was a king of Mithila (a province in Northern India)
who was hailed as a *rajarishi*, who is both a king and a sage.
He appears in the Brihadaranyaka Upanishad and
also in the Ramayana (as the father of Sita).

[21]A great man sets an example by his actions.
The whole world follows the standard that he sets.

[22]There is nothing in the three worlds
that I have not yet achieved.
There is nothing to attain
that I have not yet attained.
Yet I continue to do my work.

The three worlds or the three 'realms of existence' are:
the earth, the heavens, and the skies.
The three realms may also refer to
the past, the present and the future.

23Indeed, if I fail to work tirelessly,
humans would blindly follow my example
and sit idle without working.
24If I did not work, these worlds would perish!
I would be the cause of confusion and chaos;
I would be the one to destroy these beings.

25The ignorant ones work for personal benefit
but the wise should work for the welfare of the world.

26The wise should not, however,
discourage the ignorant ones
who are attached to action.
The wise should inspire them
to learn detachment,
while they continue
to work selflessly themselves.

The wise should not be hasty in trying to correct the ignorant ones
but should allow them to relish activities in their own way;
sooner or later, they will realize the joy of working without selfishness,
either on their own or from looking at the wise.

27All actions are driven by the *gunas*.
One who is deluded by ego thinks:
"**I** am the one who is doing."

Gunas refer to the inherent traits of a person

28 One who has true insight into
the interplay of *guna* and *karma*,
and how they are influenced
by the collective nature of society,
does not get entangled.

Here, *karma* refers to the different spheres of action.

The world is always in motion and thus, always changing.
Most of us are a part of society and are influenced by it.
Our customs, mannerisms, and practices
adjust themselves to our surroundings
if we let them follow a natural course.
But if we are perturbed by changing times and
cling on to practices that are not applicable today,
then we are bound to be confused.

29 Those who are fooled by the *guna*s
are attached to the actions caused by them.
The wise should not disturb such fools.

They are deceived by the physical world into thinking that
the ultimate is what they can perceive through their senses.
The original has: "those with perfect knowledge should not perturb
the dull-witted ones who have imperfect understanding."

30 Dedicate all your actions to the supreme.
Focus your mind on the supreme.
Free yourself from possessions and desire,
cast off your mental fever, and
engage in the battle.

Dedicating work to the supreme basically refers to invoking
a higher purpose, a greater meaning for our seemingly mundane work.

31 Those who earnestly practice
my teaching without finding fault
are also released from actions.

The teaching here is: "Do your work and respect the greater purpose!"

32 But those who condemn my teaching and don't follow it
are utterly deluded, lost, and mindless.

33 People tend to follow their natural instincts.
Even the wise ones act within the
constraints of their natural instincts.
What is the use of superficial restraint?

34 When senses encounter sensates
indeed Likes and Dislikes arise.
One should not be swayed by them
for they are obstacles in the path.

35 Excelling in one's own *dharma*,
even if it is less glamorous
is better than trying to excel
in another's *dharma*.

Here, 'one's own *dharma*' refers to 'work in tune with one's inherent nature'.
One should be natural, free from deceit, and true to oneself.
By staying close to what we are intrinsically good at, we attain personal success
and also become valuable to society; see 18:45-48 (pages 264,265).

It is better to die
upholding one's *dharma*;
following the *dharma* of others
is worse than death.

Leading a life doing things against our true nature
and imitating other people, is worse than death.

ARJUNA

36 What is that powerful force
which compels a man to sin
though he doesn't want to be sinful?

KRISHNA

37 It is Desire,
leading to anger;
it arises from *rajas*.
Unquenchable and corrupting,
it is an evil enemy indeed!

'Desire' indicates selfishness, lust, and greed.
Unfulfilled desires lead to frustration and anger.

38 As fire is enveloped by smoke,
mirror is covered by dust, and
embryo is enclosed in the womb,
wisdom is veiled by Desire.

39 The insatiable fire of Desire,
indeed a perennial enemy,
veils the wisdom of even the wise.

40 Desire is seated in
the senses, mind, and intellect.
Through them it deludes people
by eclipsing their wisdom.

Desire leads to delusion and ruin; see 2:62-63 (page 76).

41 Thus, control the senses first
and then shatter Desire,
the sinful destroyer of knowledge and reason.

42 Senses are superior to the body,
mind is superior to the senses,
intellect is superior to the mind,
but *atman* is superior to the intellect.

43 Thus, knowing that
atman is higher than intellect and
subduing the outer self by the *atman*,
defeat that formidable foe
appearing in the form of Desire.

CHAPTER 4

Wisdom in Action

Krishna

1 I taught this eternal *yoga* to Vivasvat.
Vivasvat taught Manu and
Manu taught Ikshvaku.

Vivasvat is the patriarch of the famous solar dynasty;
Manu and Ikshvaku are his descendents.

2 Thus handed down
in regular succession,
the *rajarishi*s knew this.

A *rajarishi* is one who is both a king and a sage.

But over the long course of time
the *yoga* seems to be lost in the world.

Over time, the eternal *yoga* gets cluttered by tradition and
complicated by excessive scholarship; thus, it is practically lost.

3I have now told you the same ancient *yoga*,
because you are my friend and admirer.
This *yoga* is a supreme secret indeed.

ARJUNA

4Vivasvat was born long before you.
How could you have taught him?

KRISHNA

5You and I have passed through many lives, Arjuna.
I remember them all but you do not.

6I am the lord of beings,
unborn and imperishable,
yet restraining my basic nature
I incarnate myself by my own *maya*.

The Supreme is inherently beyond space and time.
Through *maya*, the divine power of illusion,
the Supreme veils its own inherent nature to assume a role and form
that is relevant to a particular situation.

[7]Whenever there is a decline of *dharma*
and a rise of *adharma*,
I manifest myself in this world.

Dharma is that which sustains everything;
it is the harmony in the universe that sustains the greater good.
By definition, *dharma* protects one who protects it.
Adharma is the opposite of *dharma*; it is that which hinders sustainability.

[8]To protect the good, to destroy evil,
and to firmly establish *dharma*,
I manifest myself time and again.

Here, 'good' not only refers to sages but also to
ordinary, helpless folk, who are exploited by the wicked.
History has shown that during a great crisis,
someone rises to the occasion,
assumes leadership, and brings about change.
Krishna presents the concept of incarnation (*avatara*)
without limitations of space or time.

[9]He who truly knows the scheme of
my divine birth and deeds,
is not reborn when he leaves the body;
he comes to me, Arjuna.

This verse perhaps implies that one who fully comprehends life is liberated.

[10]Freed from attachment, fear, and anger,
thinking of me, dedicated to me, and
cleansed by the fire of wisdom,
many have attained my state of being.

11 Everywhere, humans pursue a path to attain me.
In whatever manner they approach me,
I reward them accordingly.

[12]Those who work craving for worldly success
offer ritualistic worship to the gods;
indeed, in the world of humans,
one attains material success quickly.

Rituals often arise from the prevailing geographical conditions and culture.
They help achieve short-term gains and inculcate basic discipline.
Rituals are the means to spiritual progress; they should not become the ends.

Material success is more readily achieved as compared to true knowledge.
There is no short-cut to knowledge.

[13]I have brought forth the four basic traits,
a classification based on *guna* and *karma*.

'Basic traits' refers to the inherent aptitudes of a person.
The four basic traits of humans are explained in 18:41-44 (pages 263,264).
Guna refers to the inherent qualities of a person
and *karma* refers to work, which is attuned to *guna*.

Although I am their cause,
I am unchanged and
beyond all action.

It is like a catalyst that causes change but itself remains unaffected.

[14]I am not bound by actions
because I don't crave for rewards.
One who knows me thus
is also not bound by action.

'One who knows me' refers to identification with the soul within
and the relation of the soul to the supreme.

15 With this understanding,
ancient seekers of liberation did their work
without being attached to its outcomes.
Therefore, I suggest that you too should act
just as the ancient seekers did in the past.

16 What is action?
What is inaction?
Even sages are puzzled.
Let me explain about the true nature of action.
Once you know this, you will be liberated from evil.

Here, 'evil' refers to continued circulation in the cycle of *karma* due to one's attachments. See 9:20-21 (pages 161,162).

17 The nature of action is hard to grasp.
One should correctly know:
What is right action?
What is not right action?
What is inaction?

18 One who can see Stillness in the midst of Activity
and Action in the midst of Inertia is indeed wise.
He acts sensibly at all times.

'Stillness in the midst of Activity' is explained in the following verses. 'Action in the midst of Inertia' is explained in 3:6 (page 82).

[19]The pursuits of the wise
are not motivated by desire;
their actions are purified by the fire of wisdom.

The wise don't have any personal agenda; they work for the welfare of all.

[20]They are ever-satisfied and independent.
Even while engaged in action, they do nothing
because they are not attached to the outcome.

The wise realize that they are not Doing the work,
but rather that the work is getting Done.

[21]Just by doing activities with discipline,
not expecting anything from it,
and free from a sense of possession,
you can stay away from evil.

[22]Satisfied with what comes on its own accord,
even-minded in success and failure,
rising above the dualities,
and free from envy,
one is not affected
even when involved in action.

'Dualities' are relative opposites like pain and pleasure,
attraction and aversion, gain and loss, me and others, etc.

[23]One who is wise, unattached, and liberated
acts in the spirit of *yajña*.
All his actions are indeed absolved.

'Spirit of *yajña*' refers to a spirit of service or offering.
'Absolved' means that he is not bound by those actions.

Ideally one should perform all actions in the spirit of *yajña*;
in other words, work in a dedicated manner.

It might not be possible to do every activity in the spirit of *yajña*
but we should try to do at least some activities in that spirit;
not doing so is as good as wasting one's life; see 4:31 (pages 105,106).

The next ten verses describe the various *yajña*s
and how every aspect of our life –
both voluntary and involuntary activities –
is rooted in the Supreme.

[24]*Brahman* is the offering,
brahman is the oblation,
brahman is the fire to which
brahman makes the offering;
brahman indeed is attained by
one who is absorbed in action,
which is also *brahman*.

Yajña is a Vedic ritual in which fire is raised in an enclosed altar
and several deities are invoked. Clarified butter (the fuel for the fire),
medicinal herbs, twigs of Peepul tree, and other offerings are put in the fire,
accompanied by chanting specific hymns from the Vedas.

Every component of a *yajña* is presented as a metaphor for
brahman, the supreme being. See 9:16 (page 162).

[25]Some aspirants perform *yajña*
to lesser gods,
while some others perform *yajña*
in the fire of *brahman*
offering the *yajña* itself.

When performing a *yajña* dedicated to a lesser god,
one can offer something that the god likes.

But when performing a *yajña* dedicated to *brahman*,
the only thing left to offer is the *yajña* itself.
Such aspirants perform every action in the spirit of *yajña*.

[26]Some aspirants submit hearing
and other senses
to the fire of restraint.
Some others subdue sound
and other sensations
in the fire of senses.

Some aspirants block their senses
to avoid coming in contact with sensates.
Some others block their sensations itself,
in spite of their senses being in contact with sensates.

[27]Some offer the *prana* and
all actions of the senses
in the fire of self-control,
which is kindled by knowledge.

Prana refers to the 'vital force' of an organism, its life energy.
It is also known as the 'vital breath', for without breathing, there is no life.

28 Some aspirants offer their wealth,
some offer their *yoga* expertise,
some offer austerities, and
others offer learning –
they are true ascetics.

Any action performed with dedication counts as a *yajña*.

29 Others, solely engaged
in the art of breathing,
having regulated
inward and outward breaths,
offer their inward breath to
their outward breath
and vice-versa.

The art of breathing or breath control involves the regulation of the course of inhalations and exhalations.

30 While others, restraining their diet,
offer their inhalations to their inhalations.
They all know the way of *yajña* and
their sins are cleansed by doing *yajña*.

31 Relishing the remnants of *yajña*, which is elixir,
they attain the eternal *brahman*.

'They' refers to those who perform *yajña*.

Those who don't perform any *yajña*
are unfit even for this world;
how can they enter the other world?

Some people devote their life doing what they love
without worrying about any rewards.
One must pursue at least some activities with this spirit of *yajña*;
otherwise, life will be dull and mechanical.
Such dullness never leads to perfection or happiness.

32 Thus, many kinds of *yajña*
are described in the scriptures.
All these *yajña*s are rooted in action;
know this, and you will be free.

Once we grasp the larger scheme of things,
we begin to do all our actions with a spirit of selflessness.
That breaks all bonds and leads us to true freedom.

[33]Pursuing knowledge is superior to
any ritual with material offerings
because all activities find their
fulfillment only in knowledge.

[34]Learn that knowledge from
those who have realized the truth.
Approach them with
a spirit of sincere enquiry
and serve them with humility.
They will impart that knowledge to you.

In ancient India, students would live with a *guru* (teacher) for many years and over time, learn the path to the ultimate truth. They would serve the *guru* and attend to all his mundane needs, which taught them how the *guru* handled daily life situations and not just the intellectual or spiritual quests.

[35]Having learned it, Arjuna,
you will never be deluded again
because with that knowledge
you will perceive all beings
in yourself and in me.

[36]Even if you were the gravest of sinners,
you will cross the ocean of sin
with the raft of knowledge.

37 Just as the blazing fire reduces firewood to ashes, the fire of knowledge reduces all *karma* to ashes.

Karma refers to all spheres of action. So it encompasses normal day-to-day work, selfless action, lethargy, inappropriate action, rituals, inevitable action, working for greater good, etc. All *karma* is cleansed by understanding the basis of *karma*.

38 Nothing is as pure as knowledge in this world.
One who reaches perfection by *yoga*
will eventually find it within.

39 A sincere person gains knowledge
through focus and mastery of senses.
Once he has acquired knowledge,
he soon attains supreme peace.

40 But a person who is
ignorant, insincere, and indecisive
gets destroyed.

'Indecisive' indicates hesitation as well as suspicion.

One who remains
hesitant and confused
finds no happiness
in this world or beyond.

41 Actions do not bind a person who
engages in *yoga* with clear understanding
and is always watchful over himself.

Here, *yoga* refers to the path of selfless action.

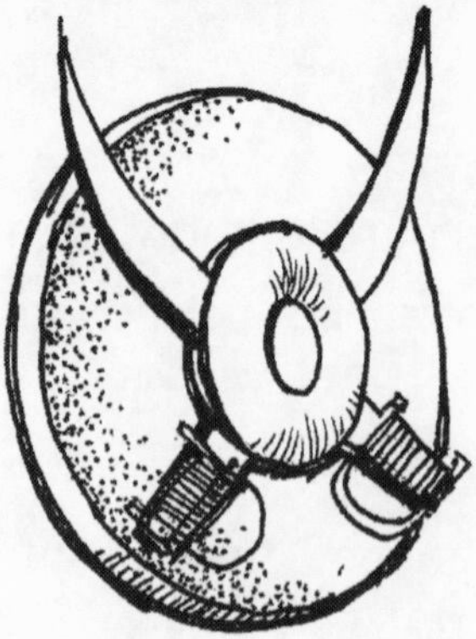

[42]With the sword of wisdom,
cut through this doubt born of ignorance
residing in your heart.
Arise Arjuna and resort to *yoga*!

CHAPTER 5

Renunciation

Arjuna

[1]Krishna, you praise *sanyasa*
and also *karma yoga.*
Tell me for certain,
which of the two is better?

While the literal meaning of *sanyasa* is 'giving up action',
in this context it perhaps refers to *sankhya,* the path of knowledge.
Karma yoga refers to the path of selfless action.
See 3:3 (page 81).

Krishna

[2]Both *sanyasa* and *karma yoga*
lead to matchless bliss;
of the two, however,
karma yoga is superior.

Work is the prerequisite for *karma yoga*;
detachment is the prerequisite for *sanyasa*.
It is easier to work and progress on the path of *karma yoga*.
The path of detachment easily drifts towards laziness rather than realization.

3A true *sanyasi* harbors no hate or desire.
Free from duality, he is free from bondage.

Sanyasi is a person who is on the path of *sanyasa*.
'Duality' refers to relative opposites like success and failure, hot and cold, etc.
'Bondage' refers to any sort of clinging.

4Only the ignorant, not the wise,
speak of *sankhya* and *yoga* as different.
One who earnestly pursues either
will reap the benefits of both.

Sankhya is the 'path of knowledge' and *yoga* is the 'path of action'.

[5]A *sankhya yogi* and a *karma yogi*
reach the same state ultimately.
One who sees the truth
sees *sankhya* and *yoga* as same.

Yogi is one who is steadfast on the path of *yoga*.

[6]It is difficult to achieve *sanyasa*
by simply avoiding work.
But one who works with diligence
readily attains supreme bliss.

[7]One who controls his senses
and masters himself
is steadfast in *yoga*.
He relates to everyone
as he relates to himself.
He is pure within and is not tainted
even as he engages in action.

[8,9]For even while
seeing, hearing, touching, eating, or smelling;
walking, sleeping, breathing, or speaking;
letting go or grasping; opening or closing the eyes –
one who knows the truth, thinks:

"It is not I who is performing action;
it is simply the Interplay of
the senses with the sensates."

10 Just as water doesn't stick to a lotus leaf,
sin doesn't stick to a person
who works unattached and
dedicates the work to the supreme.

One who works without selfish motives and has true humility has a lesser chance of committing sin.

11 Giving up attachments,
a *yogi* engages in action
with his body, senses, mind, and intellect
merely for purifying himself.

When there is absolute focus on work, there is no craving for rewards. This is self purification of the highest order and also the ideal of *karma yoga*.

12 Endowed with determination,
a man of poise doesn't care for rewards
and attains lasting peace.

Driven by selfish desires,
a man who lacks self-control,
craves for rewards, and lives in bondage.

[13]Mentally renouncing all actions,
the inner master lives happily
in the city of nine gates,
neither acting nor causing action.

The body is considered as a city of nine gates (the nine gates being: two eyes, two ears, two nostrils, a mouth, a genital organ, and an anus).

14 God does not command people to act.
God does not create activities
or its associated rewards.
All these arise from Nature.

15 God is not responsible
for good or evil in this world.

People are deluded because
their knowledge is clouded by ignorance.

Good and evil are merely results of actions that people perform.
It is foolish to think that god is responsible for this.

16 For those who have
destroyed ignorance using Knowledge,
that Knowledge, like the shining sun,
illuminates the supreme within.

17 With thoughts absorbed in that,
with the self immersed in that,
with faith in that, and
finding fulfillment in that,
a self-realized person
attains liberation.

Here, 'that' refers to the supreme within.

18 A wise person treats everyone equally –
a scholar endowed with modesty, a cow, an elephant,
a dog, and one who eats a dog.

A scholar is generally held in high esteem in society and
a person who eats a dog is considered to be at the lowest level.
The wise see the same inner spirit in all these beings
irrespective of their external characteristics;
see 4:35 (page 107) and 6:29-30 (page 129).

19 Those who are always impartial
overcome rebirth in this world.
Brahman is flawless and impartial;
so are those established in *brahman*.

Brahman is the supreme being.

20 They are not overjoyed when good things happen.
They are not dismayed when bad things happen.

With stability of mind and freedom from delusion,
those who know *brahman* are established in *brahman*.

21 One who is not attached to external objects
finds happiness in one's own self.

One whose self is united with *brahman*
attains a state of everlasting bliss.

22 Sensory pleasures are the cause of sorrow
as they are short-lived.
The wise do not rejoice in them.

In the original, the expression for 'sensory pleasures' is 'pleasures that are born from contact (of senses and sensates)'. Sensations of pleasure are short-lived and one is often disappointed when they come to an end.

23 In the midst of daily life,
if one can endure the turmoil
caused by selfish desire and anger,
then he is truly happy.
Indeed, he is a *yogi*.

24 A *yogi* finds comfort, joy, and radiance within himself.
He is liberated and becomes one with *brahman.*

25 He has cleared his doubts,
he is free from flaws, and
he has subdued his senses.
Involved in the welfare of all,
the seer attains supreme bliss.

26 He lives in supreme bliss
who is self-disciplined,
self-knowing, and
free from greed and anger.

27,28 Keeping away all external contacts;
fixing the gaze between the two eyebrows;
having made equal the inward and outward breaths;
having controlled the senses, mind, and intellect;
free from desire, fear, and anger;
with liberation as the highest goal
the sage is free from all bondages.

'...fixing the gaze between the two eyebrows' denotes concentration at one point,
which helps us elevate our focus to a greater objective.
To get the bigger picture, we cannot just look at something,
but rather we have to look beyond everything.

[29]One attains peace
when he realizes that
the purpose and the beneficiary
of all forms of worship
is the Supreme,
the sole lord of the universe,
and the true friend of all beings.

CHAPTER 6

MEDITATION

KRISHNA

[1]One who works without seeking rewards
is both a *sanyasi* and a *karma yogi*;
one who merely avoids work is neither.

In the original, the expression for avoiding work is:
"one who lights no fire and does nothing",
indicating someone who neglects his responsibilities.

A *sanyasi* is one who renounces the rewards of action and not the action itself.
The idea of a *sanyasi* here is different from the typical image of an old man
who has given up everything and has fully retired from active life.

A *karma yogi* is one who works without attachment to results.

[2]Arjuna, *sanyasa* is indeed *yoga*.
One can't become a *yogi*
without giving up selfish motives.

Sanyasa refers to 'renunciation of rewards'
and *yoga* refers to 'selfless action'.

3Work is the path for one
who wants to advance in *yoga*.
Serenity is the path for one
who has already attained *yoga*.

If we want to climb to a high level, we have to work hard;
once we reach the top, we have to remain calm.

4One ascends to *yoga* when
he renounces selfish thoughts and
is not attached to actions or to sensations.

5One should advance by one's own efforts;
one should not degrade oneself;
for the self alone
is one's true friend or enemy.

6When one has self-control
one's own self becomes a friend.
When one lacks self-control
one's own self becomes a hostile foe.

7One who has conquered the self
is united with the supreme.
He is always at peace – in cold or heat,
in pleasure or pain, and in honor or dishonor.

8 A *yogi* is one who is steadfast in *yoga*.

He has conquered his senses and
his mind doesn't waver.

He has equal regard for
gold, mud, or stone.

He has attained fulfillment
through knowledge and wisdom.

9 He behaves in the same way
with his family, friends, foes,
a mediator, a bystander,
a saint, or a sinner.
Thus, he attains excellence.

10 With mind and body under control,
free from ownerships and desires,
a seeker of *yoga*
should go to a secluded place and
steadily meditate on the *atman* in solitude.

'...free from ownerships and desires' indicates
a reasoned disregard towards possessions.

Atman is the inner, higher self.

11 In a clean place,
one should set up a firm seat,
neither too high nor too low,
covered with *kusha* grass, deerskin, and cloth.

Kusha grass is a kind of Bermuda grass; it is a sacred grass for the Hindus. The cloth is put above the deerskin, which in turn is placed over the grass.

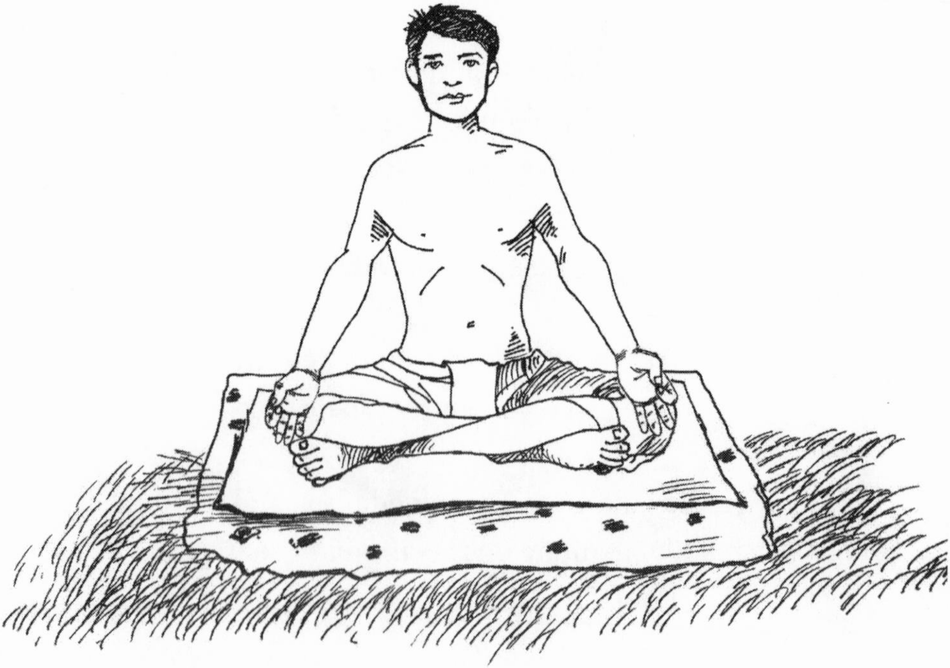

12 One should sit on that seat,
control the senses and thoughts,
direct the mind to a single object, and
practice meditation for self-purification.

13 Keeping the body, head, and neck
straight, steady, and still,
looking at the tip of the nose,
not letting the eyes wander,
14 remaining calm and fearless,
sticking to principles of *brahmacharya*,
with the mind under control,
one should sit resolute,
thinking of me as the supreme goal.

We cannot see the tip of our nose
however wide we keep our eyes open,
so the idea is merely to look at
no external thing in particular.

Brahmacharya (following the path of *brahman*)
refers to leading a life of purity and
not letting the mind wander around trivial things.

15 Thus, a seeker of *yoga* –
constantly disciplining himself
with a steady mind –
attains the supreme blissful peace
that abides in me.

16 Indeed *yoga* is not for one
who eats too much or too little.
It is also not for one
who sleeps too much or
stays awake for too long.

17 Whereas, *yoga* destroys all sorrows for one who
takes the right measure of food,
is moderate in sleep and in staying awake,
works in a disciplined manner, and
enjoys moments of recreation.

18 With the mind under control,
freed from desires, and
absorbed in the *atman*,
one attains *yoga*.

19 A *yogi* who has mastered Thought
by meditating on the *atman*
is like a lamp that does not flicker
when sheltered from the wind.

20 With thoughts restrained and mind silenced
by the regular practice of *yoga*,

the *yogi* sees the *atman* through the *atman*
and rejoices in the *atman*.

See 2:55 (page 73).

21A *yogi* will never stray from Truth
once he attains infinite bliss
that transcends the senses and
can be perceived only by intuition.

22Upon gaining infinite bliss,
he knows that there is no greater attainment.

Once he is established thus,
he is not moved by even the deepest sorrow.

23He should practice *yoga*
with undaunted determination
for it is a blissful state of being.

24He should renounce, without exception,
all desires born of selfish motives.

He should completely control his senses
with the power of the mind.

25 Little by little,
thinking of nothing else,
he should attain
stillness of mind and
focus it firmly on the *atman*.

26 Whenever and wherever
the unsteady, restless mind
tends to stray away,
then and there
he should pull it back
and bring it under his control.

27 A *yogi* attains supreme joy
once he overcomes restlessness,
keeps his mind calm,
breaks free from evil, and
tunes himself to *brahman*.

28 Free from all sin and
ever in unison with the self,
a *yogi* at once feels boundless joy
that comes from merging with *brahman*.

[29]In that state,
the *yogi* sees the *atman* in all beings
and all beings in the *atman*;
everywhere he sees the same *atman*.

[30]He who sees me everywhere
and sees everything in me,
I am never lost to him
nor is he ever lost to me.

31 The *yogi* who is aware of this oneness
worships me as the one who lives in all beings;
he abides in me, regardless of his way of living.

Such a person is always connected with the supreme,
regardless of where he is, what he does, or how he is treated by society.

32 He is indeed a *yogi*, Arjuna,
who sees true equality of all beings and
thus relates to the joy and sorrow of others
just as he relates to his own.

A true *yogi* doesn't discriminate between himself and others;
he knows that he is one with the rest and feels their joys and sorrows.

ARJUNA

33 You have taught me that *yoga* is,
in essence, equanimity of the mind.
But I don't think it's possible
because the mind is so fickle.

34 The mind is restless, Krishna.
It is turbulent, powerful, and unyielding!

Controlling the mind
seems as difficult as
controlling the wind.

KRISHNA

[35]Without doubt, O mighty one,
the mind is restless and tough to restrain.
But the mind can be controlled
by practice and by detachment.

[36]In my opinion, *yoga* is hard to attain
for one who lacks self-restraint.
But one who has self-control
can attain it by proper practice.

ARJUNA

[37]What happens to him
who is sincere but lacks self-control,
when he strays from the right path and
fails to attain perfection in *yoga*?

[38]Having fallen from both,
gone astray on the path to *brahman*,
with no place to stand,
will he not perish
like a cloud scattered and lost in the sky?

Here, 'both' refers to self-control and proper practice. Alternatively, it may refer to the material and the spiritual: "by giving up the material and improperly following the spiritual, won't he miss out on both?"

39 Only you can completely dispel my doubt, Krishna!
Who else is better suited to answer my question?

Krishna

40 One who strives to do good
never ends up in misery.
Whether in this world or beyond,
he never perishes, my son.

Liberation is the ultimate goal; but those who fall short are not condemned.
There is no urgency for liberation either; each can work at his own pace.
What truly matters is one's sincerity of purpose.

41 One who falls short of perfection in *yoga*
reaches the world of the righteous,
dwells there for a very long time, and
is reborn in the house of the pious and the wealthy;
42 or he may be born into a family of *yog*is
who are endowed with wisdom;
but such a birth is rare in this world.

Those who fall short of liberation are reborn in this world.
Rebirth bears imprints from previous life, and this influences
not only the inherent tendencies and aptitudes
but also the lineage or the family in which one is born.

'...the house of the pious and the wealthy' refers to a good home
that provides a healthy atmosphere to enable spiritual growth.

After all, birth and death are happening all the time:
the previous moment is dead, the next one is born;
what we did in the previous moment
impacts what we do in the next.

[43]In the family of *yogi*s,
he regains the knowledge
that he had in his previous life.
From there,
he strives once again
for perfection.

We are not born with a clean slate.
The soul carries experiences from previous births,
which to some extent influence the present life
(for better or worse, depending on the nature of the experiences).
Birth is a new opportunity but has roots in the past.
See 15:8 (page 228).

[44]All that past experience
guides him on the path of *yoga*.
He transcends the rewards
gained by performing rituals
by just being on this path of *yoga*.

45 Striving with great effort over many births,
a *yogi* cleanses himself of his defects
and attains the ultimate goal.

The ultimate goal is to attain *brahman*,
which is the same as liberation from the cycles of birth and death.

46 A *yogi* is superior to an ascetic,
he is also superior to the learned, and
is far superior to a ritualist.
Therefore (aim to) be a *yogi*, Arjuna!

An 'ascetic' is one who practices severe penance,
'learned' refers to one who is well-versed in the scriptures, and
'ritualist' is one who performs religious rites merely seeking favors.
All these people are entangled to some extent,
so Krishna advises Arjuna to be a *yogi*.

47 Among all *yogi*s,
the most dedicated ones
sincerely worship the supreme
with true humility.

CHAPTER 7

Knowledge and Wisdom

Krishna

[1]Practice *yoga* with focus,
fix your mind on me,
and take refuge in me;
without doubt
you will know me
completely.

Here, *yoga* refers to contemplation and
'me' refers to the supreme.

[2]I will fully teach you this knowledge
as well as how you may apply it.

Once you know this,
nothing remains to be known.

3 Among thousands of humans,
hardly a few strive for perfection.
Among the few striving for perfection
barely one will realize the supreme.

4 Earth, fire, wind, water, space,
mind, intellect, and ego –
such is the eightfold division of my nature.

5But this is just
my lower nature, Arjuna.
Beyond this, I have a higher nature,
which is the life-force
that sustains the universe.

Here, 'this' refers to the eightfold divisions.

6All beings originate from
my higher and lower states.
I am the source and the dissolution
of the entire universe.

7There is nothing beyond me!
Everything in the universe is strung on me
like a row of pearls on a string.

The supreme one sustains everything in the universe,
like a string that holds together pearls in a necklace.

8Know me as the essence in the waters,
the light of the sun and moon,
the '*om*' in all the Vedas,
the sound in space, and
the manhood of men.

Om is a single syllable word that denotes *brahman*, the supreme being.
It is the most sacred sound according to Hindu belief.

9 I am the sacred scent of earth,
the radiance in fire,
the life in the living, and
the austerity of the austere.

10 I am the eternal seed of all beings,
the wisdom of the wise, and
the splendor of the splendid.

11 In those who are strong
I am pure strength,
devoid of lust and passion.
In all beings
I am the desire
that doesn't violate *dharma*.

Dharma refers to a moral law or principle.

12 The traits of
sattva, *rajas*, and *tamas*
come from me alone.
They are in me
but I am beyond them.

Typically, humans have three inherent tendencies (*gunas*):
sattva (saintly goodness), *rajas* (relentless activity),
and *tamas* (deluded lethargy).

13The whole world is governed by
the interplay of these *gunas*.
People are fooled by the *gunas* and
fail to recognize my true nature.

The supreme is imperishable and above the *gunas*.

14It is difficult indeed to overcome
the influence of my *maya*,
which is caused by the *gunas*.
But those who have true humility
go beyond *maya*.

Maya is the divine power of illusion.

True humility is the recognition that a greater force governs the cosmic order in the universe.

15The wicked, the foolish, and the demonic,
languishing at the lowest level of humanity
are not endowed with that humility
as their minds are carried away by illusion.

16Four kinds of sincere people worship me:
a seeker of wealth,
a person in distress,
a seeker of wisdom, and
a wise person.

[17]Among the four,
the wise one is ever-steady;
he is devoted to the supreme and he excels.
I am dear to him and he is dear to me.

[18]While all these devotees are noble,
I consider the wise one to be my very self.
Having realized his true self
he looks upon me as the supreme goal
and abides in me.

[19]At the end of many cycles of birth and death,
the wise one realizes that Vasudeva is everything
and connects with the supreme.
Indeed, such great souls are hard to find.

Vasudeva refers to the soul of the universe, which pervades everything.
Vasudeva is another name for Krishna.

At the end of many births, the wise man exhausts all options
and comes to realize that there is nothing beyond the supreme.

[20]Those who are distracted
by desires for this or that
turn to other deities,
following this or that rule
of their own making.

[21]But, in whatever form one chooses
to worship god in good faith,
I strengthen his faith further.
[22]Endowed with that steady faith,
he gets his desires fulfilled.
Those desires are indeed granted by me.

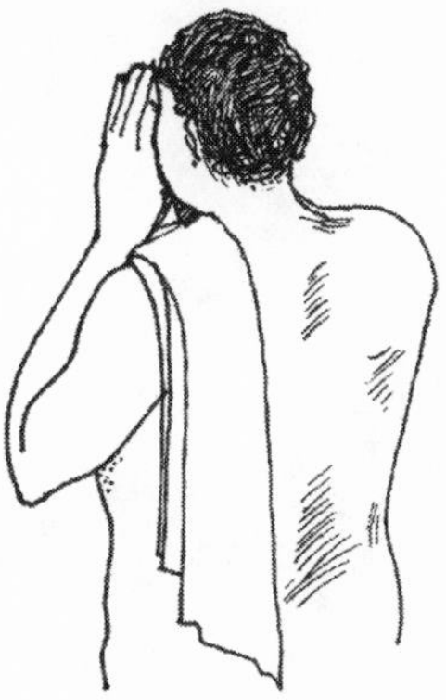

[23]But these are men of limited learning;
the rewards that they get are temporary.
People who worship other deities
go to the deities they worship
but my devotees surely come to me.

We become what we think we will become.
People who worship a particular deity will attain that state of being.
Those who worship the supreme will attain the supreme.

[24] Ignorant people think of me only as having a form.
They are unaware of my mysterious higher existence,
eternal and incomparable.

25 Hidden by my own *maya*,
my glory is not revealed to all.

The deluded ones do not know me
as the unborn and the unending.

26 Arjuna, I know all the beings
of the past, present, and future
but no one knows me!

27 All beings are ignorant
due to the illusion caused by duality,
arising from love and hate.

At a basic level, our thinking is dualistic – it is governed by likes and dislikes. Due to these opposing emotions, we fail to examine things objectively.

28 But as people do good and put an end to evil,
they are freed from the illusion caused by duality;
they worship the supreme with intense devotion.

29 Those who take refuge in the supreme and
strive for freedom from old age and death –
they will know about
brahman, *adhyatma*, and *karma*.

[30]Those who know me as the
adibhuta, *adidaiva*, and *adiyajña*,
truly know me.
They are controlled in their thoughts;
they are aware of me
even at the moment of their death.

In the next chapter, Krishna goes on to explain the terms *brahman*, *adhyatma*, *karma*, *adibhuta*, *adidaiva*, and *adiyajña*.

CHAPTER 8

The Imperishable

Arjuna

[1]What is *brahman*?
What is *adhyatma*?
What is *karma*?
What is *adibhuta*?
Who is the *adidaiva*?

[2]Who is the *adiyajña*?
Who resides in this body?

In a *yajña* (traditional fire ritual) several deities are invoked,
like Soma, Varuna, Rudra, Indra, and Mitra.
Arjuna wishes to know the real recipient of the prayers and offerings;
in other words, he is asking "who is truly venerated in a *yajña*?"

How does a man of self-restraint
attain the supreme state of mind
at the time of his death?

KRISHNA

3*Brahman* is the imperishable, supreme being.
Adhyatma is the essence of one's unique qualities;
it is an individual's real identity.
Karma is every activity associated with
origin, sustenance, and destruction.

Karma refers to all activities, including the creative impulse that brought all creation into existence and keeps it going.

4*Adibhuta* refers to the body,
the perishable aspect of all beings.
The *adidaiva* is *purusha*, the supreme spirit.
Indeed, I am the *adiyajña* and
I am the one who resides in the body.

See 9:16 (page 162) and 16:18 (page 238).

5At the moment of death,
those who depart from their body
thinking of me alone,
will surely be united with me.

6The state of mind prevailing at the time of one's death
is the very state one will attain
because those thoughts are a true reflection
of the kind of life one has led.

7 So remember me at all times,
even during combat.
Fix your mind and intellect on me
and you will surely come to me.

8 One who meditates on the supreme
with steady focus and discipline
becomes one with the supreme.

[9,10]*Brahman* is all-knowing,
primeval, timeless, and
beyond one's imagination.

Brahman is the primal cause,
the sovereign ruler,
the primordial poet, and
the supporter of all.

Brahman is subtler than the subtlest
and mightier than the mightiest.

Brahman is radiant like the sun
and beyond all darkness.

At the time of death,
one who fixes the *prana*
in the middle of the eyebrows
with the power of *yoga*
and meditates on the
magnificent *brahman*
with sincerity and steadiness,
certainly attains the *brahman*.

Prana refers to 'vital breath'. It is the source of our energy.
For without breathing, from where else do we get energy?

[11]The seers call it the eternal state.
Those who hope to reach that state
lead a life of *brahmacharya* and
sages who are rid of passions attain it.
I will briefly tell you how one reaches there.

Brahmacharya is following the path of *brahman*, leading a life of purity, and not letting the mind wander around trivial things.

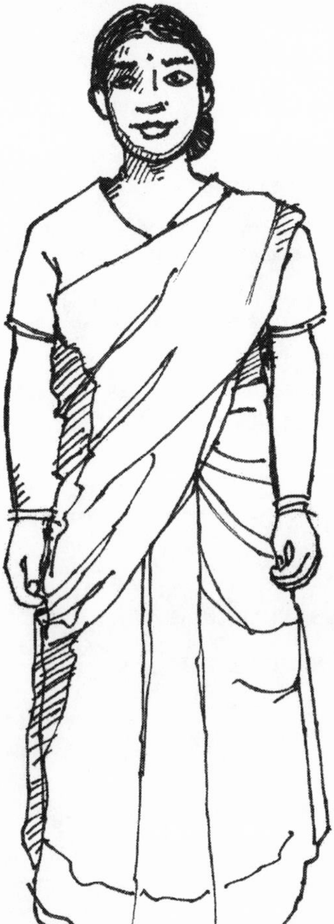

[12,13]Closing all the gates of the body,
focusing the mind inward, and
drawing the *prana* to the forehead;
invoking the supreme by
chanting '*om*', the one-syllable *brahman*;
and thus being established in *yoga*
while departing from the body,
he attains the supreme state.

The body is considered as a city of nine gates
(the nine gates being: two eyes, two ears,
two nostrils, a mouth, a genital organ, and an anus).

'Closing all the gates...' refers to holding back the senses
from being attracted to the outside world.

Prana is distributed all over the body as it energizes all the cells;
'...drawing the *prana* to the forehead' means 'focusing all energy upward'.

Om is a single syllable word that denotes *brahman*, the supreme being.
It is the most sacred sound according to Hindu belief.

[14]Arjuna, the *yogi* who is steadfast and
constantly contemplates on the Supreme
easily attains the supreme state.

[15]Great souls who have attained the supreme
have reached the state of highest perfection.

They are spared from rebirth,
which is impermanent and sorrowful.

[16]All the realms from the earth
up to that of lord Brahma
are subject to rebirth.
But on reaching the supreme,
there is no rebirth.

According to the Hindu belief of afterlife, there are many
intermediate abodes between earth and the supreme state
like Pitr loka, Deva loka, Yama loka, Brahma loka, etc.
All these in-between realms are impermanent.
The supreme state of no return is eternal.

Lord Brahma has a life span of 100 Brahma years (around 300 trillion human years)
He arises from *brahman* and performs the function of creation.
At the end of his tenure, he is absolved and another Brahma emanates.

Note that lord Brahma is different from *brahman*.

[17]A day of lord Brahma spans a thousand *yuga*s and
a night of lord Brahma also spans a thousand *yuga*s.

Only those who know this fact truly understand
the cosmic meaning of day and night.

A *yuga* is equal to 4.32 million years.
So, a day or night of lord Brahma spans 4.32 billion years.

[18]When Brahma's day begins,
all forms emerge from the hidden state.

When Brahma's night begins,
all forms disappear from the visible state.

[19]Indeed, the countless beings
that come into existence again and again
are inevitably dissolved at the arrival of night.
They come forth again at the arrival of day.

This process goes on throughout the life of lord Brahma, spanning 100 Brahma years.
After that, Brahma also dies, and is born again.

[20]But higher than this,
there is a formless eternal state of being
that remains untouched by cosmic cycles.

A cosmic cycle, spanning 8.64 billion years,
equals a day and a night of lord Brahma.
The eternal state of being doesn't get destroyed
even when all beings perish.

[21]What is spoken of as
the unseen and the indestructible
is considered the highest state.
Those who reach it, stay on forever
for that is the supreme domain.

[22]*Purusha* is the supreme spirit
who pervades the entire universe
and in whom all beings abide.
One can attain the state of *purusha*
by wholehearted devotion.

DRESS

23 When a *yogi* dies,
either he comes back
or he stays on forever.
Let me explain.

When a *yogi* dies, either he returns to earthly existence
or he lives forever in the supreme domain.

24 The *yogi* who dies during *uttarayana*,
the symbol of dazzling white daylight
goes forth to reach *brahman*.

Uttarayana is the period of six months following winter solstice.

During *uttarayana*, the days grow longer and
hence it is regarded as the 'bright-half' of the year.

25 The *yogi* who dies during *dakshinayana*,
the symbol of hazy dark night
attains the lunar light
and is born again.

Dakshinayana is the period of six months following summer solstice.

During *dakshinayana*, the nights grow longer and
hence it is regarded as the 'dark-half' of the year.

The period of *uttarayana* is equal to one day for the gods
and the period of *dakshinayana* equals one night;
hence the mention of 'lunar light' with respect to *dakshinayana*.

This suggests that only some of the realized people get liberated.
The rest of them are perhaps among us, guiding us towards liberation.

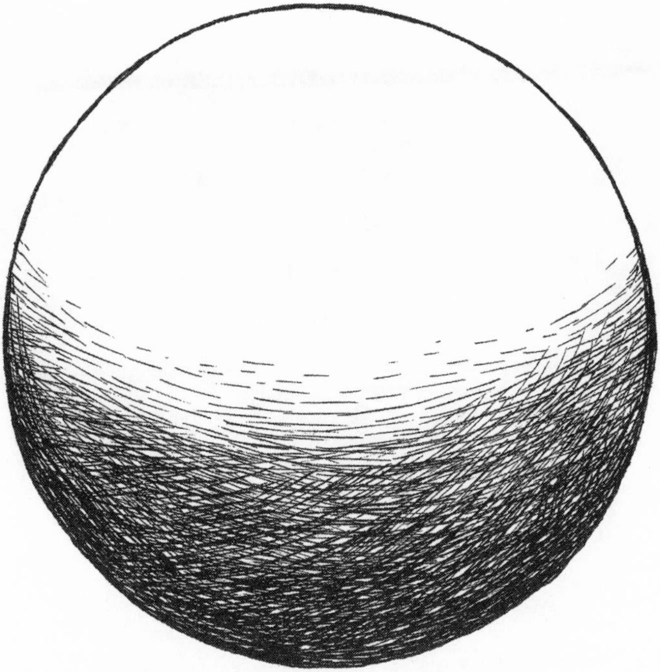

[26]Indeed, the bright and the dark
have always been the two paths of this world.

By one, the *yogi* goes to stay on forever,
whereas by the other, the *yogi* returns again.

[27]Knowing these two paths,
a true *yogi* is never deluded.
Thus, be established in *yoga* always.

[28]Knowing this truth,
a *yogi* goes beyond all the merits
of studying the Vedas or
yajña, *dana*, and *tapah*;
he truly attains that
foremost supreme state.

Yajña is the traditional fire ritual. In a broader sense,
it refers to worship and a sense of dedication to one's work.
Dana is charity, but bordering on philanthropy.
Tapah refers to austerity, penance, and single-minded focus on work.

CHAPTER 9

Best of Secrets

Krishna

1 Arjuna, you are interested in my words
so I shall reveal to you the best of secrets:
it is practical knowledge guided by wisdom.
Know this and you will be free from sorrow.

2 This is the deepest of all mysteries
and the greatest of all studies.
It is the purest of the pure
and the best of the best.
It follows the rules of *dharma*
and it is eternal.
It is easy to practice and
one can experience it directly.

Dharma refers to a moral law or principle.

3 Those who reject this doctrine
fail to attain the supreme.
They are born again and again
in the endless cycle of death and rebirth.

4 I pervade the entire universe but I am invisible.
All beings depend on me, but I don't depend on them.

Here, 'I' is a reference to *brahman*, the supreme being.
Brahman is the source and the sustainer of the entire universe;
there is nothing beyond *brahman*.

[5]Though I bring forth and sustain all beings,
I am not dependent on them.

In a way, even they don't depend on me.
Such is my magnanimity, Arjuna!

[6]The mighty wind arises in space and
moves freely in all directions,
yet it is always confined to the space.

In the same way,
all creatures arise from me
yet they always remain within me.

[7]At the end of a cosmic day,
all beings return to my
unmanifest state.

Again, I bring them forth
at the beginning of the
next cosmic day.

A cosmic day spans 4.32 billion years and is followed by
a cosmic night that spans another 4.32 billion years;
this together forms a cosmic cycle.
See 8:17-19 (pages 151,152).

8Again and again,
controlling my own nature,
I bring forth these myriads of beings
and subject them to the laws of nature.

9These actions don't bind me because
I remain unconcerned and unattached.

10Under my supervision,
nature brings forth all beings –
animate and inanimate –
and sets the universe in motion.

11When I appear in human form,
the foolish people disregard me
because they don't recognize my higher state
as the great lord of all beings.

They fail to look beyond physical appearances.

12They lack insight.
With unreal hopes,
trivial knowledge, and
insignificant deeds,
they resort to wicked ways.

13 But the great souls who abide in divinity
are aware that I am the eternal source of all beings.
They worship me with singular focus.

14 Further, those great souls glorify me,
honor me with intense devotion, and
worship me with firm resolve.

15 And there are some others,
engaged in the cultivation of knowledge,
who worship me as the One, the distinct,
and as the supreme presence
that is manifested everywhere.

16 I am the ritual,
I am the *yajña*,
I am the *mantra*,
I am the offering
that nourishes and heals,
I am the fuel and
I am the fire.

The *yajña* is a Vedic ritual in which fire is raised in an enclosed altar,
typically a square-shaped structure made of bricks,
with the top portion open to air.
The sacred fire is both a deity as well as the medium
to deliver offerings made to other deities.
The deities to be worshiped are invoked during the *yajña*.
Clarified butter (the fuel for the fire), medicinal herbs,
twigs of Peepul tree, and other offerings are put into the fire,
accompanied by chanting specific hymns from the Vedas.
Mantra refers to the formative thought behind the chanted hymns.

All the distinct elements of a *yajña* are recognized here
as embodiments of the supreme. See 4:24 (page 103).

17 I am also the father, the mother, the grandfather,
and the protector of this universe.
I am the purpose of knowledge,
I am the one who purifies,
I am the sacred syllable '*om*', and
I am the Rig, Sama, and Yajur Vedas.

The Rig, Sama, and Yajur are the three principal Vedas.
Rig Veda is the foremost one and the other Vedas were developed from it.
A wholesome Vedic *yajña* involves the three principal Vedas.

18 I am the lord, friend, and witness.
I am creation, dissolution, and existence.
I am the everlasting seed and the sustainer.
I am the goal, the abode, the refuge,
and the final resting place.

19 I radiate warmth.
I send forth and also hold back rain.
I am both immortality and death.
I am what is and what is not.

20 Well-versed in the three Vedas,
they relish *soma* and are cleansed of sin;
they honor me through *yajña*s
with the desire to go to heaven.

By the merit gained they reach heaven –
the domain of Indra – and enjoy celestial pleasures.

Rig, Sama, and Yajur are the three Vedas
that are required to perform a *yajña*.
Soma is the brew of the *soma* plant, which the Vedic seers
used to drink as an instant reward of performing a *yajña*.

This verse talks about those who follow Vedic rituals
and refrain from doing bad deeds.

21 Having enjoyed the wide world of heaven,
they return to earth once their merit is exhausted.
Again impelled by desire for heavenly pleasures,
they resort to meritorious rites prescribed in the Vedas
and are thus caught in the cycle of birth and death.

The duration and level of enjoyment in heaven is
proportional to the merit earned in one's life;
once the merit is exhausted, one returns to earth.

22 But those who are eternally devoted to me
and think of me alone,
I provide them with what they lack and
preserve what they already have.
I will completely look after their welfare.

In this verse and the following verses, 'I' and 'me' are references to the supreme.

23 Arjuna, even those who faithfully worship other gods
in essence, are worshipping me, though unaware of it.

24 I am the recipient and the goal of all worships.
But those who are unaware of my true nature
are caught in the cycle of birth and death.

25 Those who worship *devas*
go to the *devas* they seek;
those who worship the *pitrs* go to the *pitrs*;
those who worship elemental spirits,
attain those spirits;
those who worship me, attain me.

Devas are divine beings.
Pitrs are the spirits of dead ancestors.
See 8:16 (page 151).

26 I happily accept whatever one offers me –
a leaf, a flower, a fruit or just water –
with love, devotion, and a pure heart.

27 Whatever you do,
whatever you eat,
whatever you offer in worship
or give as charity
or give up in austerity,
dedicate that to me.

28 Living in the spirit of dedication to me,
you will be freed from the bondages of actions.
Then the results of your action – good or bad –
will not impact you in any way.
Thus, you will be liberated
and will come to me.

29 I am equally present in all beings;
none is hateful or dear to me.

But those who worship me with devotion –
I am in them and they are in me.

30 Even if a man steeped in evil
takes on to my worship with undivided devotion,
he must be considered as noble
because he has taken the right decision.

31 Readily, he becomes righteous and
attains everlasting peace.
Arjuna, know this:
no devotee of mine is ever lost.

32 Whoever takes refuge in me –
even men of sinful birth, women, traders, or laborers –
will attain the supreme goal.

Societies typically look down upon certain sections of people.
Krishna clarifies that whoever submits to the supreme attains liberation,
irrespective of their birth, gender, or occupation.

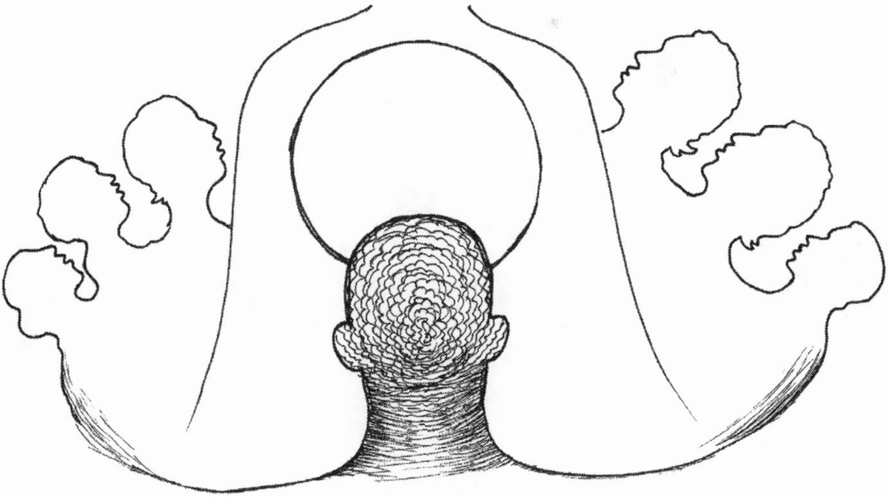

33 What more to say of
the pure and wise ones,
the devotees, and the royal seers,
who take refuge in me?

Having come into this fleeting
and unhappy world,
engage yourself in my worship
for the sake of liberation.

34 Fix your mind on me, be devoted to me,
worship me, bow down to me;
seek me as the supreme goal with all your heart,
and you shall certainly be united with me.

In verses 30-34, Krishna explains the path of devotion leading to liberation.
Even an evil person can instantly attain goodness and peace.
One can be liberated regardless of birth, gender,
learning, occupation, or position in society.

CHAPTER 10

Divine Splendor

Krishna

[1]Arjuna,
listen to more
of my supreme words,
which I speak for your good
because you are dear to me
and you are interested
in what I have to say.

[2]Even *devas* and *maharishis*
don't know my origin
because in every way,
I am the source of them all!

Devas are divine beings.
Maharishis are great seers.

3 I am the supreme lord of the universe
without birth or beginning.

One who knows this
has understood me correctly
and is free from evil.

Recognizing a greater force that governs
the cosmic order in the universe,
such people have attained true humility
and are thus freed from evil.

4 Intellect, wisdom, clarity, forgiveness,
truth, self-control, calmness,
joy, sorrow, birth, death, fear, courage,
5 benevolence, equanimity, fulfillment,
austerity, generosity, fame, infamy –
all these arise from me alone.

6 The seven *maharishi*s,
the four ancient ones and the *manu*s
are projections of my thought
and have powers like mine.
The creatures of the world
came forth from them.

The seven great seers, the four ancient ones, and the fourteen *manu*s
are the ancestors of the human race.

[7]One who understands my yogic powers
and my manifold manifestations
becomes steadily established in *yoga*.
There is no doubt about this.

In this context, *yoga* means 'union with the supreme'.
When one perceives the cosmos as divine force at work,
he can no longer distance himself from the supreme –
just as the waves have no independent existence from the ocean;
they arise from ocean and merge into ocean.

[8]I am the origin of all and
everything evolves out of me.
Knowing this, the wise worship me
with all their heart.

[9]Their focus is totally on me.
With their senses absorbed in me,
they enlighten one another.
Forever they speak of my glory
and find immense peace and joy.

[10]I grant the power of discretion to those
who love me and are always devoted to me,
so that they may unite with me.

The 'power of discretion' is the ability to
discriminate between right and wrong
(higher and lower states of truth).

[11]Out of my kindness, I,
residing in their hearts,
destroy the darkness of ignorance
by lighting the lamp of wisdom.

ARJUNA

[12-14]Krishna! All the rishis
including Asita, Devala, Vyasa, and
the divine seer Narada,
describe you as
the supreme *brahman*,

the ultimate refuge,
the greatest purifier,
the supreme spirit,
the lord of lords,
the eternal, the divine,
the unborn, and
the all-pervading one.

The 'unborn' refers to something that is always there.
The idea of 'birth' and 'death' is only for mortals. See 4:6 (page 96).

Besides, you have confirmed it yourself.
I take this as true.

Neither the gods nor their enemies
can truly know your infinite grandeur,
15because only you know your true self,
O lord of lords,
O supreme person,
O lord of the beings,
O source of all beings,
O master of the universe!

16You are the only one who can tell me in detail
about your boundless divine manifestations
with which you pervade the universe.

[17]O master of *yoga*,
how may I know you?

O blessed lord,
which of your forms
should I meditate upon
so that I will always be aware of you?

[18]Tell me more about your power and glory!
I feel that I can never hear enough
of your immortal words.

KRISHNA

[19]There is no end to my divine manifestations
so I will share with you just a few prominent ones.

[20]I am the true self,
seated in the heart of all beings.
I am the beginning, the middle,
and the end of all creatures.

Here, the 'beginning, middle, and end' refers to 'birth, growth, and decay'.

[21]I am Vishnu among *aditya*s;
of the lights, I am the radiant sun;

I am Marichi among *maruts*;
amidst stars, I am the moon.

Adityas are the twelve children of sage Kashyapa and his first wife Aditi.
Vishnu is one of the *adityas* (not to be confused with lord Vishnu).
The five lights (or luminaries) are: sun, moon, stars, fire, and lightening.
Maruts are a group of wind gods;
Marichi, the breeze in the vicinity, is the chief of *maruts*.
'...amidst stars, I am the moon' indicates that
the moon is the most prominent object in the night sky.

22 I am Sama Veda among Vedas;
I am Indra among *devas*;
of the senses, I am the mind and
in living beings, I am consciousness.

Vedas are the foremost revealed scriptures in Hinduism.
There are four vedas – Rig Veda, Yajur Veda, Sama Veda and Atharva Veda
Indra is the king of the *devas*.

23 I am Shankara among *rudra*s;
among *yaksha*s and *rakshasa*s I am Kubera;
I am fire among *vasu*s;
among mountain peaks, I am Meru.

*Rudra*s are a group of storm gods, Shankara being the foremost among them.
*Yaksha*s and *rakshasa*s are spirits with special powers;
while *yaksha*s are semi-divine and benevolent,
*rakshasa*s are notorious and often disturb the harmony.
Kubera is the god of wealth and the king of *yaksha*s and *rakshasa*s.
*Vasu*s are divinities presiding over the elements of nature.
Meru is the golden mountain at the center of the cosmos.

[24]Of high priests,
I am their chief, Brihaspati,
of war generals, I am Skanda;
among the waters, I am the ocean.

Brihaspati is the principal priest of the *deva*s.
Skanda is the general of the army of gods.

[25]Of *maharishi*s,
I am Bhrigu;
among words,
I am the single syllable '*om*';
among *yajña*s,
I am *japa*;
among stationary objects,
I am the Himalayas.

Om is a single syllable word that denotes *brahman,* the supreme being.
It is the most sacred sound according to Hindu belief.
Japa is the chanting of divine names or sacred verses mentally or in a low voice.
It is the simplest and the best form of all *yajña*s (worships).

[26]Of trees, I am Ashvattha;
I am Narada among divine seers;
of *gandharva*s, I am Chitraratha;
I am sage Kapila among *siddha*s.

Ashvattha is the sacred fig tree (*Ficus religiosa*).
Narada is the seer among gods.
*Gandharva*s are a group of divine artists and musicians; Chitraratha is their king.
*Siddha*s are people who have attained a high degree of perfection.

27 Among horses,
I am Uchchaishrava, born of *amrita*;
of mighty elephants, I am Airavata;
among men, I am the king.

Uchchaishrava is the great horse of Indra and
Airavata is his famous white-colored elephant.
The legendary cosmic ocean was churned for *amrita*, the nectar of immortality,
and it was during that time both these animals arose.

28 I am Vajra among weapons;
I am Kamadhenu among cows;
of instincts for procreation,
I am Kandarpa;
of *sarpa*s, I am Vasuki.

Vajra is the thunderbolt weapon of Indra.
Kamadhenu is the cosmic cow that fulfills all wishes.
Kandarpa is the god of love;
perhaps the best way to fulfill the instinct of procreation
is through mutual love rather than mere physical interaction.
Vasuki is the king of the *sarpa*s, a group of serpents that live on land.

29 I am Ananta among *naga*s;
I am Varuna among water creatures;
I am Aryaman among ancestors;
I am Yama among the enforcers of law.

*Naga*s are a group of multi-hooded snakes.
Ananta is the infinite snake on which lord Vishnu reclines.
Varuna is the water god.
Aryaman is the noblest of all ancestors.
Yama is the god of death. He accords punishments to people
during afterlife for sins they committed in their lives.

30 Among *daityas*, I am Prahlada,
of all measures, I am time;
among animals, I am the lion;
among birds, I am Garuda.

Daityas are the children of sage Kashyapa and
his second wife Diti (who was the sister of Aditi).
Daityas are typically of demonic nature.
Prahlada was born in a family of *daityas* but was very virtuous.
The lion is the king of the jungle.
The eagle Garuda is the king of birds.

31 Among things that purify, I am the wind;
of the wielders of weapons, I am Rama;
among the fish, I am the crocodile;
and of rivers, I am Ganga.

Rama is the hero of the epic Ramayana.
'...among the fish, I am the crocodile' indicates that the crocodile, which lives among the fish, is more powerful than them.
Ganga is a river that flows in Northern India;
it is a sacred river for Hindus.

32 I am the beginning, the middle,
and the end of all manifestations;
among all the branches of knowledge,
I am the knowledge of the supreme self;
among all arguments and opinions,
I am the logic that leads to the truth.

33 I am 'a' among letters;
I am *dvandva* among *samasa*s;
I am the ever-lasting time;
I am the omnipresent sustainer.

Samasa is a system for formation of compound words.
The three main *samasa*s are *tatpurusha*, *bahuvrihi*, and *dvandva*.
The *dvandva* elegantly combines two words.

34 I am death that destroys all
and I am the origin of beings yet to be born;

of women, I am fame, fortune, eloquence,
memory, intelligence, firmness, and forgiveness.

35Of hymns of the Sama Veda,
I am those that uniquely govern the mind;
among poetic meters, I am the Gayatri;
I am Margashirsha among months;
I am spring among seasons.

Gayatri is a popular poetic meter found in Vedic hymns;
it has the least number of syllables per line.
Margashirsha is the month just before winter solstice.
Early on, the Hindu calendar used to start with Margashirsha.

36Among all deceptions, I am gambling;
I am the splendor of the splendid;
of success, I am the effort;
I am goodness of the good.

Among deceptions, gambling is the most honest
since everyone has an equal chance at winning.

37I am Krishna among Vrshnis;
I am Arjuna among Pandavas;
I am Vyasa among sages;
I am Ushanas among poets.

The Vrishnis were an ancient clan.
Pandavas were the sons of king Pandu.
Vyasa was the sage who organized the Vedas.
Ushanas was the teacher of the *daityas*.

38Of law enforcements, I am punishment;
of the paths to victory, I am statesmanship;
of secrets, I am silence;
of the wise, I am wisdom.

The traditional methods of law enforcement are: gentle persuasion, offering incentives, manipulating behavior, and if all fails, punishment. Of these, punishment is perhaps the one that is sure to work for all. A secret is best kept when silence is maintained.

39Whatever is the source of all beings, I am that.
Nothing animate or inanimate can exist without me.

40Arjuna, what I have told you
is simply a brief illustration of my countless attributes,
because there is no end to my divine manifestations.

41All that is endowed with glory, grace, and grandeur,
has sprung from a mere flare of my radiance.

42But what is the use of all this information, Arjuna?
Just remember that I stand holding the entire cosmos
with a fraction of my divine splendor.

Krishna mentions all these things because Arjuna asked him for the ways in which he could relate to god. It is evident that Krishna uses the examples already known to Arjuna. Finally, he reminds Arjuna that the focus should be on the sublime and not the mundane.

CHAPTER 11

UNIVERSAL FORM

ARJUNA

[1]You have graciously taught me
the grand spiritual truth
of the supreme self.
Your words have cleared my delusion.

[2]You have taught me in detail
about the origin and dissolution of everything
and also about your own imperishable majesty.

[3,4]O magnificient lord and master of *yoga*!
Now I wish to see you with all your divine splendor
just the way you have described it.
If you think that it is possible for me
to see your divine form,
then please show it to me.

KRISHNA

5Arjuna see my divine forms
by the hundreds or by the thousands
of many colors and shapes.
6Behold many marvels never seen before!
Look at all the *adityas*, the *vasus*, the *rudras*,
the *ashvins*, and the *maruts*.

Adityas are the twelve children of sage Kashyapa and his first wife Aditi.
Vasus are divinities presiding over the elements of nature.
Rudras are a group of storm gods.
Ashvins are the divine twins who are the physicians of the gods
and are believed to witness all religious ceremonies.
Maruts are a group of wind gods.

7Now, you can see in my body
the assembly of the entire universe,
with every animate and inanimate being
and whatever else you wish to see.

8I grant you divine vision;
else, you won't be able to see
my universal form.

SANJAYA

9Having said this, O king,
the great master of *yoga* revealed
his majestic universal form to Arjuna.

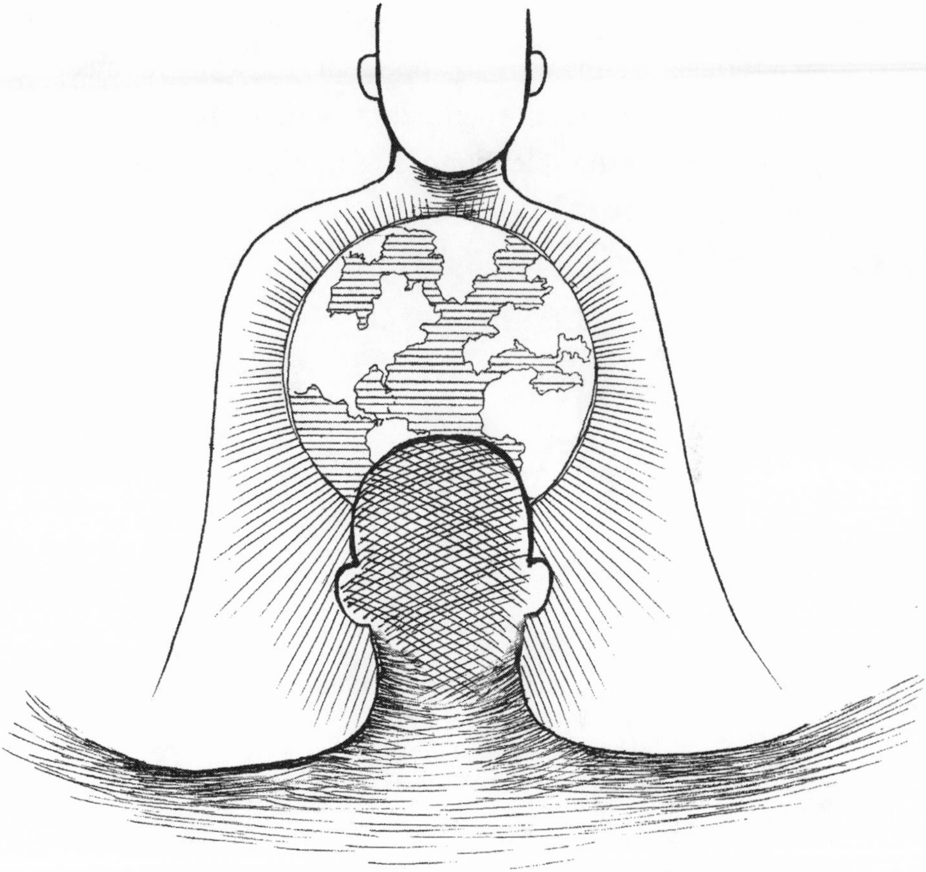

[10,11]With countless mouths and eyes,
sporting many divine ornaments, garlands, and garments;
anointed with heavenly fragrances and
armed with divine weapons ready to strike,
the infinite and all-pervading god is full of wonder.

12 If a thousand suns were to appear in the sky all at once,
the brilliance of their light would perhaps
resemble the splendor of this glorious being.

[13]Within the body of the lord of lords,
Arjuna saw the entire universe
with its countless elements
gathered together as one.

[14]Wonderstruck, with his hair standing on end
and hands folded in salutation,
Arjuna bowed down to the lord, and said:

ARJUNA

[15,16]O lord of the universe
and essence of the cosmos!
In your body, I see the *deva*s,
the *rishi*s, the divine snakes,
lord Brahma seated on his lotus throne,
and beings of all forms and shapes.

*Deva*s are divine beings, *rishi*s are seer-sages, and
divine snakes are serpents with special powers.

I see you everywhere,
with countless arms, bellies, mouths and eyes;
but I see neither your beginning nor middle nor end.

The universal form is a seamless joining of space-time pieces;
due to the sheer magnitude of the universal form,
Arjuna is unable to see any boundaries.

17 I see you wearing a crown
and holding a mace and a discus.

The mace and the discus are two of Krishna's divine weapons.

Your brilliance spreads in all directions
with the radiance of the sun and a blazing fire.

It is difficult to fathom
your immeasurable form.

18 You are the imperishable, supreme being
worthy to be known.
You are the purpose of all knowledge.
You are the ultimate abode of the universe.
You are the guardian of the eternal law and order.
You are the primeval spirit.

19 You are without beginning, middle, or end.
You have countless arms with infinite power,
with the sun and the moon as your eyes.

Your face glows like the burning fire,
whose radiance warms the whole world.

[20]You pervade the entire space
between heaven and earth
and all the quarters.

The three worlds tremble
upon seeing your intimidating form.

The three worlds or the three 'realms of existence' are:
the earth, the heavens, and the skies.
Looking at it in another way, the three realms may also refer to
the past, the present and the future.

[21]Hordes of deities are entering your body;
some of them, out of fear, are greeting you reverently.

Many great *rishi*s and *siddha*s are singing your glory
with lofty hymns, chanting: "may all be well!"

*Siddha*s are people who have attained a high degree of perfection.

[22]The *rudra*s, *aditya*s, *vasu*s, *sadhya*s,
*vishvedeva*s, *ashvin*s, *marut*s, *ushmapa*s, and
several *gandharva*s, *yaksha*s, *siddha*s and *asura*s –
all of them are looking at you with awe.

*Sadhya*s are a group of accomplished ancient seers who are not bound by time.
*Vishvedeva*s are a group of Vedic gods.
*Ushmapa*s are ancestors. *Gandharva*s are a group of divine artists and musicians.
*Yaksha*s are spirits with special powers; they are semi-divine and benevolent.
*Asura*s are a demonic group, opposed to the *deva*s.

23 O mighty-armed one!
Seeing your immense form
with countless mouths and eyes,
with numerous arms, feet, and thighs, and
with several bellies and dreadful tusks,
the whole world is terrified, and so am I.

24 I shudder seeing your body glow in different colors,
stretched as far as the sky,
with wide-open mouths and large fiery eyes;
I am terrified when I look at it.
I find neither courage nor calm.

25 Seeing your mouths with terrible tusks
blazing like the fire at the end of time.
I lose sense of direction and find no peace.
Have mercy on me, O refuge of the universe!

26,27 I see all the sons of Dhritarashtra and
kings such as Bhishma, Drona, and Karna;
I see our own chief warriors and hosts of others
rushing into your dreadful mouths with fearful teeth.
Many of them are getting stuck between your teeth and
their heads are getting crushed to powder.

[28,29]Just as rivers having many torrents
swiftly flow into ocean and
as moths are drawn into the blazing fire
only to be burnt,
so do these heroes of the world
rush into your mouths
for their own destruction.

[30]You are hungrily licking up and devouring
all the worlds from every side
with your fiery mouths.

Your brilliance is scorching
the entire universe!

[31]I bow to you,
O foremost among gods!

Have mercy on me and
tell me who you are,
in this dreadful form.

I don't understand your
true nature or purpose.

Krishna

32-34 I am death, the mighty destroyer of the world!
I am engaged now in the destruction of all creation.
With or without you, all these warriors shall die,
for I have already killed them.
Therefore, arise and be victorious!
Fight merely to show the world your skill in archery.

Do not hesitate; kill Drona, Bhishma, Karna,
Jayadratha, and other brave warriors,
whom I have already killed.
Conquer your enemies and
enjoy the bountiful kingdom.
Be fearless! Fight!
You will win!

SANJAYA

35 Hearing Krishna's words, Arjuna, trembling
and with palms joined in prayer, offered salutations.
Overwhelmed with fear,
he prostrated over and over again,
and spoke in a choked, faltering voice.

ARJUNA

36 Demons run away from you in all directions,
while the rest of the world
is truly delighted to sing your glory and
hoards of saints are bowing to you with respect.

37 And why would they not bow to you, O great one?
You are the primeval cause,
greater than even lord Brahma.

You are infinite and imperishable,
the abode of the universe and the lord of gods.
You are what all there is, what there isn't, and beyond that.

38 You are the primal god, the primordial person;
you are the ultimate refuge of the universe.

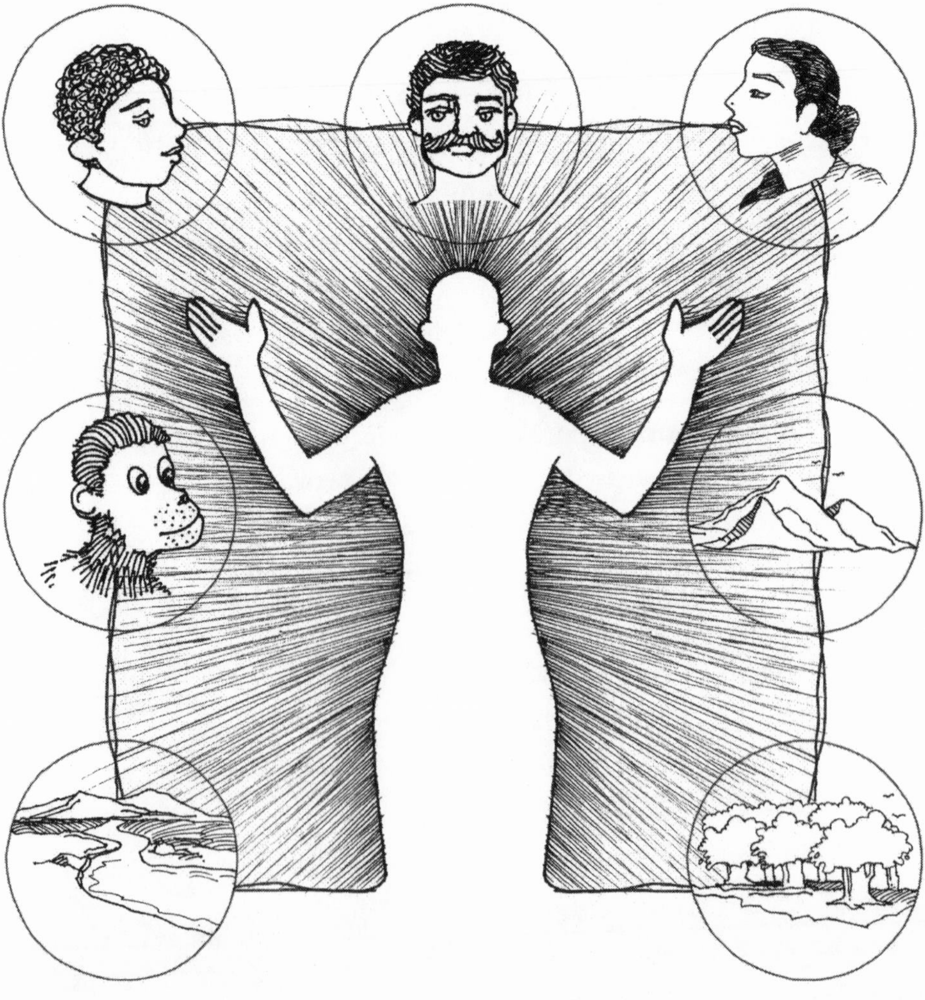

You are the knower and the goal of knowledge.
You are the supreme abode and
you pervade the universe
with your infinite form.

39You are Yama, Vayu, Agni, Varuna,
Shashanka, and the grandsire Prajapati.
I salute you a thousand times,
and over and over again.

Yama is the god of death. He accords punishments to people
during afterlife for sins they committed in their lives.
Vayu is the wind god, Agni is the fire god,
Varuna is the water god, and Shashanka is the moon.
Prajapati is the lord of the creatures and the progenitor of the universe.

40I salute you from every direction!
You have unfathomable energy
and immeasurable courage.
You pervade everything;
therefore you are everything.

41,42Taking you for granted as a mere friend
and unaware of your greatness,
I have arrogantly addressed you as
"hey Krishna", "hey Yadava", and "hey friend"
perhaps out familiarity or sheer carelessness.

In whatever other ways
I may have jokingly offended you,
while at play or at rest,
during conversations or at meals,
either alone or in the company of others –
please forgive me for everything.

43 You are the father of the universe,
of the animate and the inanimate;
you are the object of worship and the greatest teacher;
there is no one equal to you in the three worlds.
You are of incomparable greatness!
How can any other be greater than you?

44 Therefore, I offer my respects and
plead you to have mercy on me;
just as a father pardons his son,
a friend forgives another,
or a lover is kind to his beloved,
you be merciful to me!

45,46 O thousand-armed one!
I am delighted to have seen this rare form,
never seen before and yet I am trembling.

I wish to see you as before;
Please assume that four-armed form,
wearing a crown and holding a mace and discus.
Be kind to me and show me your familiar form.

KRISHNA

47With my yogic power and grace
I have revealed to you my universal form –
infinite, unique, and full of splendor.
Apart from you, no one has seen this form before.
48Neither by worship nor by scholarship
nor through charitable or pious activities
and not even by severe austerities
can anyone else see me in this form.

This form was shown for the sake of Arjuna; Sanjaya saw it by default.

49Don't be afraid having seen my dreadful form.
Free from fear and with a light heart,
see my gentle form, which is familiar to you.

SANJAYA

50Saying thus, Krishna revealed his previous form.
The terrified Arjuna was reassured
once Krishna took on his pleasant form.

ARJUNA

51 I now feel at ease,
having seen your familiar form.

KRISHNA

52 The universal form of mine
that you have seen is very rare.
Even the *deva*s are always longing
to see me in that form.
53 Neither by study of the Vedas
nor by *yajña*, *dana*, and *tapah*
can anyone see me the way you have.

Yajña refers to worship and a sense of dedication to one's work.
Dana is charity, but bordering on philanthropy.
Tapah refers to austerity, penance, and single-minded focus on work.

54 But I may be known, seen, and attained
through single-minded devotion.

55 One who is truly devoted to me
dedicates all actions to me
and looks upon me as supreme;
he is free from attachments
and he does not hate anyone.
Without doubt, he attains me.

CHAPTER 12

DEVOTION

ARJUNA

[1]There are people who worship you
(as a personal god with form and attributes)
with their mind fixed on you.
There are others who contemplate on
the eternal and formless.
Who among them knows *yoga* better?

Arjuna wishes to know who is better established in *yoga* (union with supreme) – those who worship Krishna as he just described (11:55 - page 198) or those who follow his earlier statement (7:24 - page 142).

KRISHNA

[2]In my opinion,
those who always worship me
(as a personal god with form and attributes)
with focus and faith
are better established in *yoga*.

[3]Yet those who worship
the all-pervading,
the eternal, the formless,
the changeless, the inconceivable,
and the immovable,
[4]with complete control over their senses,
balanced in all situations, and
rejoicing in the welfare of all,
also reach me.

[5]Greater is the trouble
for those who contemplate
on the formless
for it is only through much pain
that they succeed in the path
to the invisible, formless god.

[6,7]Those who worship me
by dedicating their actions to me,
considering me as the supreme goal,
and meditating upon me
with single-minded concentration,
I liberate them from
the deadly ocean of worldly life.

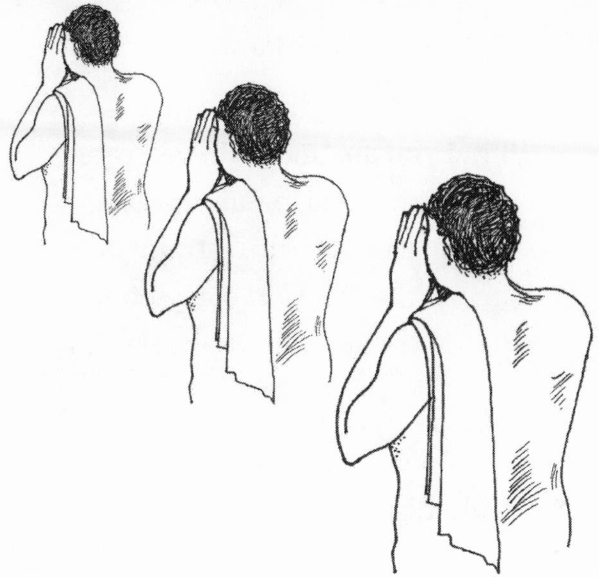

[8]If you fix your mind on the supreme
you will certainly reach the supreme.
There is no doubt about this!

[9]If you can't focus on the supreme,
then try to reach the supreme
through diligent practice.

Often, it is easier to focus on our work
than to meditate on an unseen, supreme being.

[10]If you are incapable of regular practice
then try to dedicate all your actions to the supreme.
This way, you will attain perfection.

If we realize that our work is part of the grand cosmic design,
it brings a greater purpose to the activities that we look upon as mundane.

11 But if you are unable to dedicate
all your actions to the supreme
then act with self-restraint,
giving up the Fruits of your actions.

'Fruits' of action are the rewards or results of our work.
One should ideally focus on the Work and not on the Fruits.

12 Knowledge is better than
blindly following routines.

'Routines' refers to mechanically performing an action
without understanding the underlying principles.

Contemplation is better than knowledge.

Renouncing the Fruits of one's actions
is better than contemplation
because soon after this,
one attains peace.

13 One who harbors no hatred,
who is gentle and friendly to all,
who is beyond the feeling of 'I' or 'mine',
who is poised in pain or pleasure
and is endowed with forgiveness
(is dear to me).

14The *yogi* who is self-controlled,
always content, and of firm resolve,
with single-minded devotion to me,
is dear to me!

15He is dear to me
whose peace is not shaken by anyone,
who is at peace with everyone, and
who is free from fear, restlessness,
envy, and reckless joy.

16One who is pure and expects nothing,
one who is diligent, impartial, and calm,
one who works without selfish motives
and is devoted to me,
is dear to me!

17He neither revels nor hates
nor complains nor craves,
he has given up fortune and misfortune,
and he is truly devoted.
He is dear to me!

The outcome of a process may be favorable or unfavorable;
but it makes no difference to such a person because he has given up reacting to both.
Generally we tend to enjoy good fortune and complain about misfortune
but such a person does neither; he just does his work.

18He is the same to friend and foe,
in honor and disgrace,
to heat and cold,
in pleasure and pain;
he is free from attachments!

19Praise and criticism are the same to him,
he is contemplative and contented,
he does not care for a home,
he is steady-minded, and
he is full of devotion.
He is dear to me!

'He does not care for a home' indicates that he doesn't consider any place as home, yet he feels at home everywhere.

[20]Those who regard me as the highest goal
and practice with sincerity and faith
the immortal wisdom that I have declared
are indeed very dear to me!

CHAPTER 13

MATTER AND SPIRIT

ARJUNA

*Krishna, I wish to learn about:
prakriti and *purusha*,
kshetra and *kshetrajña*,
knowledge and its purpose.

Prakriti refers to 'material nature'.
Purusha refers to 'indwelling spirit'.

Kshetra means 'field', 'domain', or 'realm';
in different contexts, it also means body, matter, or world.
Kshetrajña is 'one who knows the field' or 'domain expert';
it can also mean soul, spirit, or lord.

*This verse is not found in all versions and hence is not numbered.

KRISHNA

1 The wise refer to this body as the *kshetra*;
one who knows the *kshetra*
is called *kshetrajña*.

2 I am the *kshetrajña* in every *kshetra*.
In my opinion, true knowledge is
knowledge of the *kshetra* and the *kshetrajña*.

True knowledge comprises knowledge of matter (organic and inorganic) and spirit.

3 I shall briefly explain about the *kshetra*,
its attributes, its origins, and how it changes.

I will also tell you about
the *kshetrajña* and his powers.

4 Seers have revealed this in many distinct ways
in the sacred hymns of the Vedas.
It is also conclusively stated
in the Brahma Sutra.

Here, 'this' refers to knowledge of matter and spirit.
Brahma Sutra is a collection of aphorisms that Vyasa compiled,
drawning from the Vedic philosophy.
It is an authoritative text that concisely presents
the nature of *brahman* (supreme being) and how to attain *brahman*.

5 The five great elements,
the five sense organs,
the five sensations,
the five organs of action,
the unseen, mind, ego, intellect,

[6]desire, hatred, pleasure, pain,
awareness, courage, and the body –
these together constitute the *kshetra*.

The five great elements are earth, fire, water, air and space/ether.
The five sense organs are ears, eyes, nose, tongue, and skin;
the five sensations are sound, sight, smell, taste, and touch.
The five organs of action are mouth, hands, feet, genitals and anus.

[7]Humility, freedom from hypocrisy,
non-violence, patience, honesty,
reverence towards one's teacher,
purity, steadiness, self-control;
[8]absence of egoism,
reasoned disregard towards sensates,
insight into the limitations and tribulations
of birth, death, old-age, sickness, and pain;
[9]freedom from selfishness,
devoid of undue love for family and community,
constant equanimity towards
desirable and undesirable events;
[10]unwavering and single-minded devotion to the supreme,
seeking solitude and avoiding sordid crowds;
[11]sincere persistence in knowing the supreme,
and the quest for the truth –
these numerous factors constitute true knowledge;
anything contrary to these is ignorance.

12 Next, I shall explain about that
which ought to be known.
Once you know it,
you will be immortal.
It is the supreme *brahman*
that is without beginning;
it is spoken of as neither real nor unreal.

Brahman, the supreme being, transcends existence and non-existence.

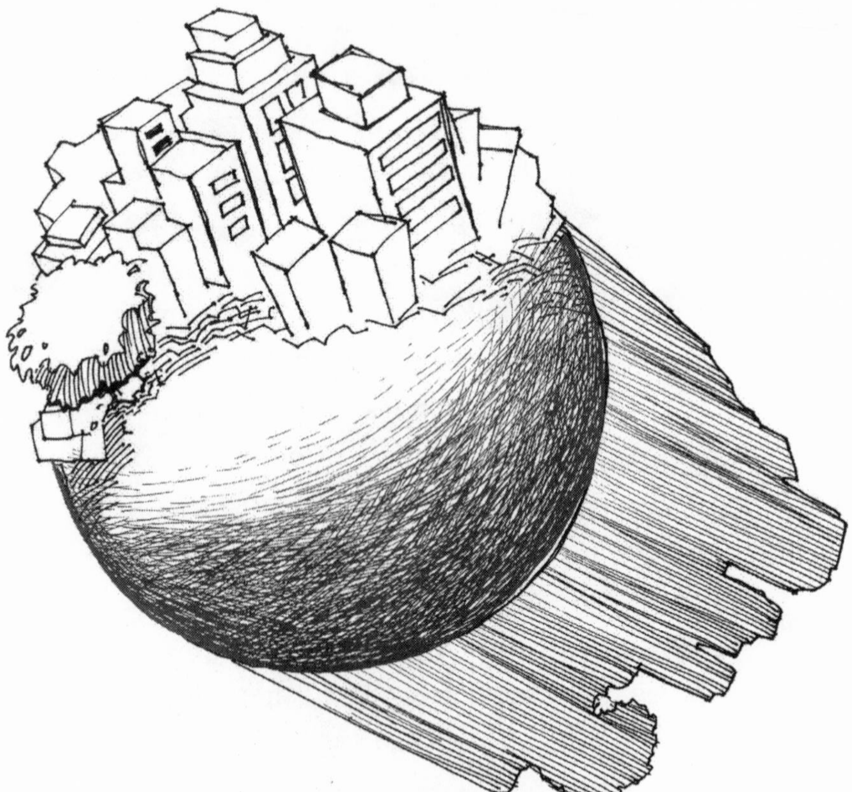

[13]With heads, hands, legs,
eyes, ears, and mouths everywhere,
brahman abides in the universe
encompassing everything.
[14]It is free from the influence of the senses
and yet is fully aware of all sensations.
It supports everything but remains unattached.
It is free from *guna*s and yet enjoys them all.

Here, 'it' refers to *brahman*.
*Guna*s are inherent tendencies of a human being.

[15]It is outside, yet within all beings;
motionless, yet always moving;
far away, yet nearby;
it is too subtle to grasp.
[16]It is the undivided whole
yet it appears divided among beings.
It supports all the creatures,
consuming them as well as creating them.

[17]It is the knowledge,
it is the knowable subject,
it is the purpose of knowledge;
it is seated in the heart of all beings.
It is the light of lights, beyond all darkness.

[18]I have briefly told you about the *kshetra* and
also about Knowledge and its purpose.
Having learned this,
my devotee is united with me.

[19]*Prakriti* and *purusha*
are both without beginning.
Change arises from *prakriti*
and so do the *gunas*.

Everything in the universe constantly undergoes change because everything arises from *prakriti* (nature), which is always changing; whereas *purusha* (spirit) is beyond change.

[20]*Prakriti* is the material basis
of the body and
associated activities.
Purusha is the cause
of the experiences of
pleasure and pain.

Prakriti is the source of the five elements and the body, including the five senses, mind, ego, and intellect. *Purusha* is the cause of one's feeling of being alive and the associated experiences of pleasures and pains.

[21]When associated with *prakriti*,
purusha experiences the *gunas*
that arise from *prakriti*.

Attachment to the *gunas* is the cause of one's rebirth, for the better or for the worse.

Any attachment, good or bad, leads to bondage (rebirth). The type of experiences to which one is most attached in this life determines the type of person one is going to be in the next.

22 The indwelling *purusha* is said to be
the witness, the approver, the supporter, the enjoyer,
the supreme lord, and the supreme self.

23 One who thus understands
purusha, *prakriti*, and the *gunas*,
although engaged in worldly activities,
will not be born again.

24 Some people perceive the *atman*
through meditation,
some realize it through wisdom, and
others through selfless action.

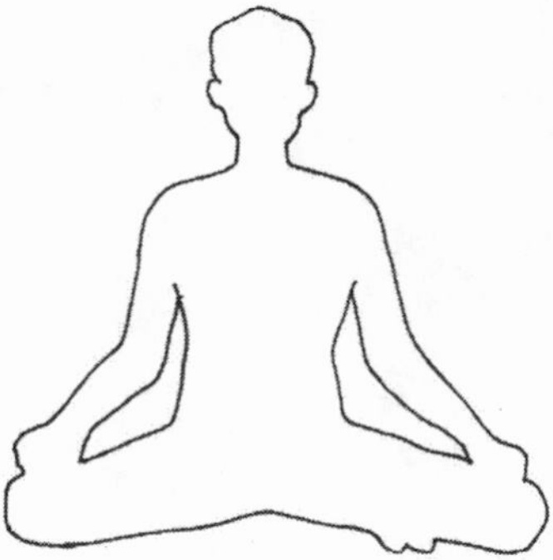

[25]Those who don't know these paths
pursue the *atman* by hearing it from others;
they too transcend death by faithfully following
what they have learned from others.

[26]Every being that exists – fixed or moving –
is born as a result of the interaction
between *kshetra* and *kshetrajña*.

[27]He truly sees who sees
the same Supreme
living in all beings and
undying within the dying.

[28]He doesn't degrade himself
for he sees the same lord
established everywhere.
He attains the supreme state.

He recognizes the same supreme spirit in himself and in others.
See 6:29-30 (page 129).

[29]He truly sees who sees that
all actions are performed by *prakriti* alone
and the *purusha* is a mere witness.

[30]When one observes the diversity of existence
as having a common source in the Supreme and
all manifestations arising from that alone,
then he becomes one with *brahman*.

[31,32]Arjuna, the supreme self is imperishable,
without beginning, and beyond attributes.
Though it resides in the body,
it does not act and it is not tainted;
just as the all-pervading space
remains pure because of its subtlety.

Space is the unlimited expanse that is within and outside everything.
Though all events occur in space, nothing happens to it
because it is far too subtle and ethereal.

33 Just as a single sun illuminates the whole world,
so also the *kshetrajña* illumines every *kshetra*.

In the original, the word *'kshetrin'* – the owner of the field or the lord – has been used instead of *'kshetrajña'*.

34 Those with spiritual insight
recognize the difference between
kshetra and *kshetrajña*;
they know how all beings are liberated
from the bondages of *prakriti*;
they reach the supreme!

The wise see a distinction between the lower (*kshetra*/*prakriti*) and higher (*kshetrajña*/*purusha*) levels of reality.

Krishna starts with, 'true knowledge is knowledge of *kshetra* and *kshetrajña*'. He concludes by pointing out the difference between the two.

It is important for us to learn in total and then distinguish the important from the trivial. There is no short cut to true knowledge.

CHAPTER 14

Natural Tendencies

Krishna

1 I shall tell you more
about this supreme wisdom,
which transcends all knowledge.
By knowing this, the sages have
attained the highest perfection.

2 Contemplating on this wisdom,
they have reached the supreme state.
They remain unaffected by creation or destruction.

Having reached the supreme state,
they are not born again at the time of creation
nor are they disturbed at the time of dissolution.

3 Primordial nature is my womb,
in which I plant my seed;
all creatures are born from that.

4Whatever life forms develop in any womb,
primordial nature is their mother
and I am their seed-giving father.

5*Sattva*, *rajas*, and *tamas*
are the three *guna*s.
These *guna*s are born out of *prakriti* and
they bind the imperishable soul to the body.

Guna refers to the inherent tendency of a person.
Prakriti refers to nature or environment.

6*Sattva*, which is pure, luminous, and free from distress
binds one by attachment to knowledge and comfort.

7*Rajas*, marked by passion,
the source of thirst and anxiety,
binds one by attachment to relentless activity.

8*Tamas*, born of ignorance and delusion,
makes one careless, lethargic, and sleepy.

The states of *sattva*, *rajas*, and *tamas* are temporary;
all of them are merely different kinds of bondages of the soul.
The objective is to go beyond the *guna*s.

Interestingly, in 2:23-25 (page 65), there is no mention of 'the soul can't be bound'.
Perhaps, attachment is the one thing that affects the soul.

9 *Sattva* brings happiness;
rajas gives rise to action;
tamas shrouds knowledge and
binds one to laziness.

10 *Sattva* predominates,
subduing *rajas* and *tamas*;
or *rajas* prevails,
overpowering *sattva* and *tamas*;
or *tamas* sets in,
masking *sattva* and *rajas*.

Among the three *guna*s,
one dominates over the other two.

11 When the glow of wisdom
emanates from all the gates of the body,
indeed *sattva* is dominant.

The body is considered as a city of nine gates
(two eyes, two ears, two nostrils, a mouth,
a genital organ, and an anus).

12 When *rajas* predominates,
one is governed by greed, vigor, desire,
unrest, and constant activity.

Such a person takes up many activities out of greed
and with an eye on the rewards.

13Darkness, delusion, lethargy, and negligence arise
when *tamas* is predominant.

14When the soul departs a body
while *sattva* is predominant,
the soul attains the pure worlds of the wise.

15Departing in the state of *rajas*,
one takes birth among those attached to action;
likewise dying in the state of *tamas*,
one is born among the deluded.

The state of mind that prevails at the time of one's death
is often a reflection of the kind of life one has lived. See 8:6 (page 146).

16The fruit of *sattva* is purity and goodness;
the fruit of *rajas* is pain;
the fruit of *tamas* is ignorance.

17Wisdom is born from *sattva*,
greed from *rajas*, and
distraction, ignorance, and delusion from *tamas*.

18Those who live in *sattva* advance upwards;
those in *rajas* are stuck in the middle,
ever caught up in activity;

those in *tamas*,
the lowest state of quality,
sink downward.

The 'upward', 'middle', and 'downward'
are references to spiritual advancement.

19 One who has realized that
*guna*s are the driving force (in every activity)
and also knows what exists beyond *guna*s,
attains the supreme state.

He realizes that the Self is not the cause of action and activities, but it is *guna*.

20 When one has risen above these *guna*s,
which are associated with the body,
he is liberated from birth, death, old age, and pain
and becomes immortal!

ARJUNA

21 What are the traits of one
who has gone beyond the three *guna*s?

What is his way of life?

How does he go beyond the *guna*s?

KRISHNA

[22]One who has gone beyond the influence of the *guna*s
is not moved by the illumination of *sattva*,
the activity arising from *rajas*,
or the delusion caused by *tamas*;
he neither dislikes them when they are present
nor desires for them when they are absent.

[23]He is never distracted and he stands firm;
he remains calm and unaffected by the *guna*s
for he understands how the *guna*s work.

24 He is the same towards pleasure and pain;
gold, mud, or stone make no difference to him;
with the same courage he faces
reward and punishment or
the pleasant and the unpleasant;
25 he regards alike:
praise and criticism,
friend and foe, and
honor and dishonor;
he is above selfish pursuits;
and he is established in the *atman*.
He has truly gone beyond the *guna*s.

'Established in the *atman*' refers to
a sense of self-satisfaction and self-sufficiency.

26 One who sincerely worships me
through the path of devotion,
crosses the barriers of *guna* and
is ready to attain *brahman*.

27 For I am the *brahman* –
the immortal, the imperishable,
the eternal *dharma*, and the absolute bliss.

The 'eternal *dharma*' refers to
the natural law that governs universal welfare.

CHAPTER 15

SUPREME SPIRIT

KRISHNA

[1]The wise speak of the perennial Ashvattha tree,
which has roots above and branches below.
The leaves protecting it are the Vedas.
One who knows this tree, truly knows.

Ashvattha is the sacred fig tree (*Ficus religiosa*); it is used as a metaphor for existence. The roots above show our spiritual dimension, whereas the branches below depict our material bondages. Material existence is rooted in the spiritual. The perennial nature of the tree represents cycles of birth and death. Just as the leaves nourish the tree, knowledge (the Vedas) nourishes human life. One who understands this metaphor truly understands both the spiritual and material dimensions of life.

[2]The tender sprouts of this mighty tree
are the senses nourished by the *gunas*.
The branches extend both above and below.
The secondary roots going downward represent actions
that bind the individual soul to earthly existence.

Guna refers to the inherent tendency of a person.

[3]The true nature of this tree –
its basis, beginning, or end –
is not readily perceived.

It is difficult for us mortals to be a part of life and understand it too.
The only thing we know for certain is that life goes on.

Cut down this firmly-rooted tree
with the sharp axe of detachment.

[4]Then seek that eternal goal –
attaining which one is liberated –
by submitting yourself
to the supreme *purusha*,
the primal cause of
this ancient universe
and its relentless activity.

[5]Free from false pride and delusion,
overcoming the burden of attachment,
renouncing desires entirely,
always conscious of the *atman*, and
unaffected by pairs of opposites
such as pleasure and pain,
the wise reach that eternal goal.

Atman is the inner, higher self.

6 Neither sun nor moon nor fire
can illuminate that state;
it is verily my supreme abode and
having gone there, you will not return.

Here, 'that state' refers to the state of *brahman*, the supreme being.
The supreme abode is self-luminous, beyond all light.
'...you will not return' indicates that no force can dislodge you from there.

7 A fragment of my own self becomes
the soul in the world of mortals.
It attracts towards itself
the five senses and the mind,
which are a part of the body.

8 When one acquires a body or departs from it,
the master within carries these senses,
just as the wind carries scents
from one place to another.

We acquire a body when we are born; we depart from it when we die.
Here, 'the master within' refers to the soul, the eternal witness
which carries the *vasanas* (past baggage).

9 Through the mind, the ear, the eye,
and the organs of touch, smell, and taste,
the *atman* experiences the sensations.

'Sensations' are the experiences of sound, sight, smell, taste, and touch
but in a broader sense, it refers to the worldly pleasures and pains that one feels.

[10]The deluded ones fail to perceive the *atman*
residing, entering, or departing the body.
They also fail to see the *atman*
enjoying the sensations
as well as being impacted by the *gunas*.

See 13:21 (pages 212,213).

But those with the eye of wisdom perceive this.

They sense the *atman* at all times.

[11]Those who strive with discipline
can see the fraction of the lord
situated in their own self.
But those who are selfish and insensitive
fail to see, however hard they try.

The selfish ones are too full of themselves and fail to see anything else. Preoccupied with lower motives, they miss out on the higher ideals.

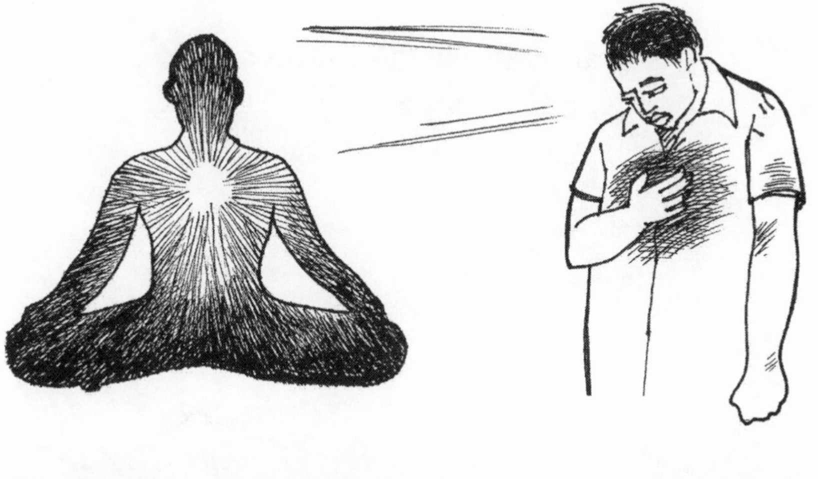

12 The radiance of the sun which lights up the world,
the radiance in the moon and in fire –
I am the source of all that radiance.

13 Entering the earth,
I support all creatures with my energy;
becoming the life-giving sap,
I nourish all plants and herbs.

14 Having entered the bodies of creatures as the digestive fire
and working along with inward and outward breaths,
I digest the four kinds of food.

Foods that are chewed, foods that are sucked, foods that are eaten by licking,
and foods that are gulped/drunk are the four kinds of food.

15 I am seated in the hearts of all;
I grant memory and knowledge,
and I also make them disappear!

Perhaps a part of our memory and knowledge
should recede if we want to function coherently.
For example, we know death is certain, yet we are able to live
without being troubled by that idea every day.

I know all the Vedas and
I am the author of the Upanishads
I am the one who is to be known in them.

Upanishads are the concluding portion of the Vedas.
Vedas are the foremost revealed scriptures in Hinduism.

The initial portions of the Vedas largely comprise contextual knowledge,
while the Upanishads mainly contain universal wisdom.

One needs to know both and use them appropriately.

16 There are two entities in this world:
ksharam and *aksharam*.
Ksharam consists of all beings
(yet to be liberated).
Aksharam refers to those
that are immutable
(the liberated beings).

Ksharam refers to something that is changing
while *aksharam* refers to something that is beyond change.

Another way of looking at this verse is by considering
ksharam as a reference to all beings, and
aksharam as a reference to the individual soul.

17 But above these two entities,
there is a higher principle:
the supreme soul, the ultimate person,
known as the eternal god
who sustains and pervades the universe.

18 I am beyond *ksharam* and
I am superior to *aksharam*.
So I am respected as the supreme spirit
by the people and in the Vedas alike.

The idea of a higher power is shared by the laity and the learned.

19 One who is free from delusion
knows me as the supreme spirit;
indeed, he knows all there is to know
and he wholeheartedly worships me.

20 Arjuna, I have taught you a great truth.
He who learns this will become enlightened and
will have accomplished everything.

CHAPTER 16

Good and Bad

Krishna

1 Courage, purity of heart,
pursuit of knowledge,
generosity, self-control,
spirit of sacrifice, study of scriptures,
austerity, simplicity, righteousness,
2 benevolence, honesty, freedom from anger,
a sense of renunciation, serenity,
not finding fault with others,
kindness, gentleness, modesty,
absence of greed and fickleness,
3 radiance, patience, strength, cleanliness, and
absence of malice and false pride –
these are the qualities of a person
of divine nature.

4Hypocrisy, arrogance, vanity, anger, cruelty, and ignorance
are the traits of a person with demonic nature.

Here, 'ignorance' refers to lack of perseverance in the path of knowledge.

In a strict traditional sense, divine and demonic qualities
belong to one who is 'born with' a divine or demonic nature.
Actions performed in one's previous lives determine future births
with divine or demonic qualities.

5The divine qualities lead to liberation.
The demonic qualities lead to bondage.
But don't worry Arjuna,
you are endowed with divine qualities.

6There are two types of people in the world:
the divine and the demonic.
I have spoken about the divine ones in detail.
Now, hear from me about the demonic ones.

Krishna has explained divine attributes in
12:13-20 (pages 203-206) and 13:7-11 (page 209).

[7]Demonic people don't understand
what should be done and what shouldn't.
They are neither pure nor honest;
even their behavior is not good.

[8]They proclaim:
"The universe has no basis and no abiding truth.
There is no greater force governing it.
Life is merely a product of mutual union, driven by lust!"

Here, 'basis' refers to *dharma*, that which supports and sustains everything.
Such people claim that the universe has no meaningful order;
they also fail to see a larger purpose for any activity.

[9]Rigidly holding on to such views,
these lost souls of limited understanding
commit many cruel deeds.
They are indeed enemies of the world,
bent upon its destruction.

These people neither perceive a grander cosmic order of the universe
nor recognize a greater social order of the world and
disturb the overall harmony for satisfying momentary pleasures.

[10]Clinging on to unquenchable passions,
drunk with pride and hypocrisy,
they live in delusion with false notions,
and act with impure motives.

11 Till their last breath
they are lost in
boundless wishes and anxieties.
Gratification of desire is their highest aim,
as if that is all there is to one's life!

12 Bound by a hundred chains of vain hope and
driven by lust and anger,
they amass wealth by unjust means
for sensual enjoyment.

13 "I have gained this today and
I shall attain that tomorrow.
All these riches are mine, and
soon I shall have more!
14 I am the lord.
I have killed this enemy and
I will also destroy all other enemies.
I am successful and I am powerful;
I am healthy and I enjoy life.
15 I am noble and I am rich.
Who is my equal?
I will perform elaborate rituals,
I will give alms and
I will rejoice as per my will" –
thus they boast out of sheer ignorance.

16 Carried away
by countless fanciful thoughts,
they get caught in the web of illusion
and are addicted to
gratification of the senses.

Thus they plunge into the hell
of their own making.

17 They are arrogant and stubborn.
Intoxicated by wealth and pride,
they engage in worship
only in name (and not in spirit)
focusing more on pomp and show,
without regard for rules or regulations.

18 Clinging on to egoism and vanity,
exhibiting force, lust, and rage,
these malicious people
undermine the divine presence
in their own bodies and
in the bodies of others.

[19]I constantly throw these
cruel, hateful, and worst of men,
into demonic wombs
in the vast cycles of birth and death.

Here 'demonic womb' signifies rebirth with demonic qualities.

[20]Again and again
these deluded people are born
with demonic traits
and fail to attain the supreme;
they sink to the lowest of depths.

[21]Lust, anger, and greed
are the three gates to hell
that degrade the self.
One should renounce them!

Lust, anger, and greed are impediments in the path of self-realization.
In this context, 'hell' is a confused state of mind that degrades the self.

In the literal sense, hell is an after-death transient place
where one is punished for their sins.

[22]One who is liberated
from these three gates of darkness
elevates his inner self and
attains the ultimate goal.

[23]One who ignores the established rules
and follows his own preferences
driven by selfish desires
does not attain perfection, happiness, or liberation.

The wise have given us practical guides and principles to lead a good life.
Krishna is advising Arjuna to engage in battle
but Arjuna has to use his own knowledge and skill of warfare.

Texts like the Bhagavad-Gita suffice for eternal aspects,
but we still have to know the rules for the roles we play in daily life.

[24]Therefore, let the words of the wise
be your guide in determining
what should be done and what should not.
Having understood the eternal wisdom,
you should act accordingly.

CHAPTER 17

Attitudes at Work

Arjuna

[1]When a person sincerely engages in worship
but fails to follow the prescribed rules,
is that an act of
sattva, *rajas*, or *tamas*?

Sattva (saintly goodness), *rajas* (relentless activity),
and *tamas* (deluded lethargy) are
the three inherent basic qualities (*gunas*).

Krishna

[2]Human attitudes are of three kinds:
sattva, *rajas*, or *tamas*;
they are born of one's own nature.
Listen, as I explain further.

In any individual, the three *gunas* prevail to varying extents.
'...one's own nature' refers to the
innate and untutored aspect of the personality.

3 Each one's faith conforms with his inborn nature.
A man is made up of his faith.
He is what his faith is.

4 People with the nature of *sattva* worship the gods;
those of *rajas* worship demons and demigods;
those of *tamas* worship evil spirits and ghosts.

5 Those who perform austerities
motivated by false pride and ego,
driven by the force of lust and passion
indeed violate the sayings of the scriptures.

6 They foolishly torture the body
and also the divine spirit within.
Know them to be of a demonic resolve!

Some people feel that it is a noble thing to
subject oneself or others to torture in the name of religion.
Krishna reminds Arjuna that exaggerated austerities or
mortifications of the body are unwarranted, to the point of being demonic.

[7]Food that is dear to a person is also of three kinds,
just as with the ways of *yajña*, *dana*, and *tapah*.
Let me explain the differences to you.

Yajña is the traditional fire ritual.
In a broader sense, it refers to worship and
a sense of dedication to one's work.
Dana is charity, but bordering on philanthropy.
Tapah refers to austerity, penance, and single-minded focus on work.

[8]Foods that promote longevity, vitality, stamina,
health, happiness, and contentment and
foods that are tasty, mild, nourishing, and pleasant
are dear to those of the nature of *sattva*.

[9]Foods that cause pain, sorrow, and sickness,
and foods that are bitter, sour, salty,
excessively hot, spicy, dry, and pungent
are dear to those of the nature of *rajas*.

[10]Foods which are insipid, stale, rotten,
left-over, filthy, and unhygienic
are dear to those of the nature of *tamas*.

In verses 7-10 describing the kinds of food that people like,
'...dear to those of the nature of *sattva* (or *rajas* or *tamas*)'
is perhaps just an indication of what they don't mind eating.

It is likely that a person who relishes stale food
will also relish fresh food, but not the other way round!

11 The *yajña* that is carefully performed,
according to the scriptures,
without any thought of reward, and
with the sense that it must be performed
is of the nature of *sattva*.

12 The *yajña* that is performed
for the sake of reward or merely for show
is of the nature of *rajas*.

13 The *yajña* that is performed
contrary to the scriptures –
without sincerity,
without offering food,
with no sacred texts recited,
with no respect to guests, and
without paying the officiating priest –
is of the nature of *tamas*.

[14]Simplicity, self-restraint, purity, benevolence, and
respect for gods, priests, *gurus*, and the wise –
this is austerity of body.

This leads to the refinement of the body.

[15]Speaking words that are truthful, pleasant,
beneficial, and not causing distress or anxiety,
as well as the study and recitation of scriptures –
this is austerity of speech.

This leads to the refinement of speech.

[16]Silence, serenity of mind, self-control,
gentleness, and purity of thought and being –
this is austerity of mind.

This leads to the refinement of the mind.

[17]This threefold austerity,
diligently practiced with utmost faith
and without desire for reward
is of the nature of *sattva*.

[18]Austerities practiced merely out of pride and hypocrisy
for the sake of gaining temporary rewards
such as praise, respect, and special treatment,
are of the nature of *rajas*.

19 Austerities performed
with foolish notions
by torturing oneself or
by injuring others,
are of the nature of *tamas*.

20 Giving with the feeling that
it is one's duty to give,
without expectation of anything in return,
and offering it at the right place
and at the right time
to a worthy person,
who cannot make any favor in return,
is of the nature of *sattva*.

21 Giving something reluctantly or
with the aim of getting something in return,
is of the nature of *rajas*.

22 Giving with contempt and disrespect,
offering it at the wrong place
and at the wrong time
to an unworthy person,
is of the nature of *tamas*.

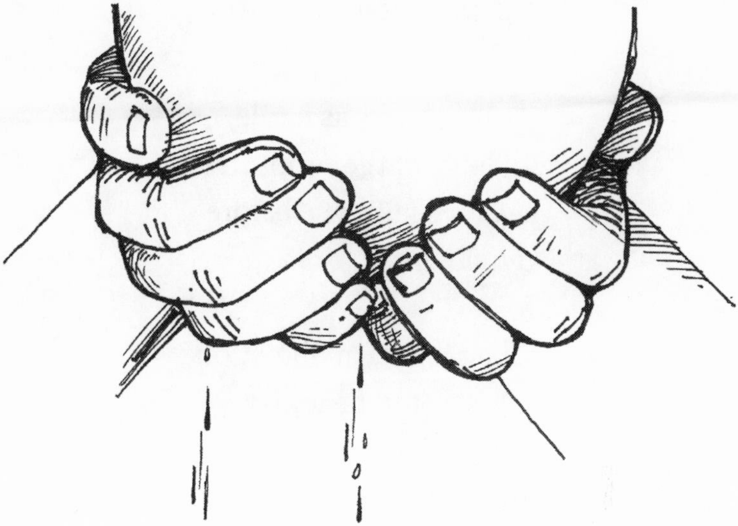

23 '*Om*', '*tat*', and '*sat*' –
each word is a reference to *brahman*;
The Vedas, *yajñas*, and priests
were established in them
from ancient times.

Brahman is the supreme being.
The Vedas are the foremost revealed scriptures in Hinduism.

Doing *yajña*, *dana*, and *tapah* with the attitude of *sattva* is best.
But there is a tinge of impurity associated with them and so,
invoking '*om*', '*tat*', and '*sat*' helps to cleanse those activities.

Om is a single syllable word that denotes *brahman*.
It is the most sacred sound according to Hindu belief.

Tat means 'that' or 'it' and refers to *brahman*.
It serves as a reminder that 'we are not doing the work'
and helps overcome our ego.

Sat means 'real' or 'good' and refers to *brahman*.
It inspires an overall attitude of goodness in action.

24 Therefore, as a rule,
students of the scriptures
always chant '*om*' before
yajña, *dana*, or *tapah*.

25 The seekers of liberation
say '*tat*' prior to
yajña, *dana*, and *tapah*,
with no desire for rewards.

26 '*Sat*' refers to goodness and reality.
Thus, the word '*sat*' is also used
to denote any act worthy of praise.

27 Doing *yajña*, *dana*, and *tapah*
with dedication is *sat*.
Any action we perform
to support that is also *sat*.

28 Doing *yajña*, *dana*, or *tapah*
without dedication is *asat*
and has no value
in this world or beyond.

Asat means 'unreal', the opposite of reality and goodness.
Compare this verse with 6:40 (page 132).

CHAPTER 18

LIBERATION

ARJUNA

1 Krishna, what is the real difference
between *sanyasa* and *tyaga*?

Arjuna asks this question because both the words – *sanyasa* and *tyaga* – have the same literal meaning: 'to give up'.

KRISHNA

2 *Sanyasa* is giving up actions driven by selfish desire.
Tyaga is giving up attachments to the results of all actions.

3 Some thinkers declare that
every action is tainted and should be given up;
others say that *yajña*, *dana*, and *tapah*
are not to be given up.

Yajña is the traditional fire ritual. In a broader sense, it refers to worship and a sense of dedication to one's work.
Dana is charity, but bordering on philanthropy.
Tapah refers to austerity, penance, and single-minded focus on work.

[4-6]Arjuna, I shall reveal to you
the ultimate truth about *tyaga*.
First of all, one shouldn't give up
yajña, *dana*, and *tapah*
because they can sanctify life
when followed wisely.

However, one should do these actions
by giving up attachment and desire for rewards.

Without doubt,
this is the best way to act.

Further, note that *tyaga* is of three kinds.

[7]It is not right to abandon work
that is meant to be done.

'Work that is meant to be done' refers to one's responsibilities
or to the work that is in tune with one's inherent nature.

When one abandons work
out of delusion –
that *tyaga* is of the nature of *tamas*.

Tamas is the state of deluded lethargy.
It is an extreme form of laziness and stubbornness.

8When one abandons work
because it is inconvenient,
merely to avoid physical exertion –
that *tyaga* is of the nature of *rajas*.
It does not lead to liberation.

Rajas is the state of relentless activity.
It is an excessive indulgance in luxury.

9When one engages in work
considering it as a responsibility,
abandoning attachments and desires –
that *tyaga* is of the nature of *sattva*.

Sattva is the state of saintly goodness.
It is a mindful and balanced mode of existence.

10Established in *sattva*
and with doubts dispelled,
the wise one renounces.

He doesn't crave for work that is pleasant;
he doesn't avoid work that is unpleasant.

11As a matter of fact, one can't give up all actions;
one has to act, at least to take care of his body.

See 3:5 (page 82).

But one who gives up desire
for the Fruits of action
is said to have relinquished.

'Fruits' of action are the rewards or results of our work.
One should ideally focus on work and not on the Fruits.

12For those who are attached to Fruits of action,
three kinds of rewards –
good, bad, or mixed –
will follow them even upon their death.

'...will follow them even upon their death' refers to
the *vasanas* (residual impact of actions) that we carry to the next life.
See 15:8 (page 228).

There is no such baggage
for those unattached to Fruits of action.

13The scriptures proclaim that
five factors govern the outcome of all actions:
14the situation,
the individual,
the tools he has,
how he uses the tools,
and unknown forces.

'Tools' can refer to knowledge, skills, or resources.

15 Whatever one does
with his body, speech, or mind,
with good or bad intention,
the same five factors
determine the outcome.

16 That being the case,
when one sees himself as the sole cause,
he is truly of limited understanding.
He fails to see the truth.

17 One who is free from ego
and has complete understanding,
even if he kills, he does not kill;
he is not bound.

He is not bound because neither actions nor outcomes affect him.

18 Factors that inspire action are:
the knowable, the knowledge,
and the knower.

Action comprises
the individual, the tools,
and the act.

19 Knowledge, Action, and Individual
are also of three types,
in accordance with the three *gunas*.
This is explained in
the principles of the *gunas*.

Gunas are the inherent tendencies of a human being.

20 The knowledge that helps one to see
the sole imperishable reality in all beings,
undivided in the divided,
that Knowledge is of the nature of *sattva*.

21 The knowledge that makes one to see
only division everywhere and
to perceive each individual
as different from all the others,
that Knowledge is of the nature of *rajas*.

22 The knowledge that drives one
to cling on to an insignificant pursuit
as though it were the only important thing,
without rhyme or reason and
without foundation in the truth,
that Knowledge is of the nature of *tamas*.

23 Action that is performed as prescribed,
free from attachment, and
without obsession or aversion,
by one who is not affected by the outcome
is of the nature of *sattva*.

24 Action that is performed merely for selfish reasons,
with the thought: "I am doing this"
and moreover with undue excitement,
is of the nature of *rajas*.

25 Action that is undertaken blindly,
not considering one's own ability,
without regard for the consequences,
and leading to loss or injury,
is of the nature of *tamas*.

The loss or injury could be to oneself or to others.

26 The Individual who is
without any attachments,
endowed with firmness and enthusiasm,
unperturbed by success or failure, and
never indulging in self-praise
is of the nature of *sattva*.

27 The Individual who is
impure, greedy, overly aggressive,
excessively passionate, and
desires for the rewards of his actions
and is easily affected by their outcomes
is of the nature of *rajas*.

28 The Individual who is
lazy, fickle, wicked, crude,
dishonest, depressed, stubborn,
and forever postponing work
is of the nature of *tamas*.

29 Arjuna, let me now describe
the three kinds of distinctions that prevail
in Intellect and Resolve
as governed by the three *guna*s.

30 The Intellect that knows
when to act and when to let go,
what to do and what to give up,
what to fear and what not to fear, and
what is bondage and what is liberation,
is of the nature of *sattva*.

31 The Intellect that has a wrong notion
of the difference between
what is right and what is wrong, and
what to do and what to abandon,
is of the nature of *rajas*.

32 The Intellect that is engulfed in darkness,
imagines wrong to be right, and
sees all things contrary to what they truly are,
is of the nature of *tamas*.

33 The serenity with which one unites
the *prana*, the senses, and the mind
by pursuing the path of *yoga*,
that Resolve is of the nature of *sattva*.

Prana is the vital force of an organism; it is the life energy.
It can also be called the vital breath,
for without breathing, how can we get energy?

34 The tenacity with which
one vehemently hangs on to the pursuits of
dharma, *artha*, and *kama*,
out of selfish desire for the Fruits of action,
that Resolve is of the nature of *rajas*.

Dharma (good deeds), *artha* (wealth), and *kama* (pleasures) are
three of the four goals of life, the fourth being *moksha* (liberation).

[35]The rigidity with which
one is foolishly preoccupied with
sleep, fear, grief, despair, and arrogance,
that Resolve is of the nature of *tamas*.

[36]The pleasure that people seek
to put an end to their pain
is also of three kinds.
Now hear from me what they are.

[37]The right course of action
as conceived by a clear mind
at first seems like poison but often ends up sweet;
such Pleasure is of the nature of *sattva*.

[38]The Pleasure that arises from
the contact between senses and sensates
is sweet at first but ends up bitter;
it is of the nature of *rajas*.

[39]The Pleasure that comes
from being lazy and careless
is only a delusion from start to end;
it is of the nature of *tamas*.

40 There is no creature either on earth or elsewhere that is free from the influence of the *gunas*, which are born of *prakriti*.

Prakriti refers to nature or environment.
See 14:5 (page 218).

41 Pursuits of *brahmins*, *kshatriyas*,
vaishyas, and *shudras* are prescribed
in accordance with their own basic nature.

Each of us has certain inherent talents and interests,
which make us naturally suited to fulfill certain roles.

The classification of individuals into four groups:
brahmins, *kshatriyas*, *vaishyas*, and *shudras*
is based on their basic aptitudes.

This doesn't mean they totally lack other attributes.

42 Serenity, self-discipline, austerity,
honesty, purity, forgiveness, knowledge,
wisdom, and faith in the almighty
are the basic traits of *brahmins*.

Any individual with natural aptitude for learning,
analyzing, researching, teaching, and
probing into nature's mysteries is called a *brahmin*.

43 Valor, majesty, firmness, skill, courage,
generosity, and lordly disposition
are the basic traits of *kshatriyas*.

Anyone with natural aptitude for warfare,
governance, politics, administration,
and management is called a *kshatriya*.

44 Farming, raising cattle, and trade are
the natural activities of *vaishyas* as per their nature.

Any individual with natural aptitude for managing money,
trading, farming, and skilled labor is called a *vaishya*.

Serving others is the basic trait of *shudras*.

Anyone with natural aptitude for service and physical work is called a *shudra*.

We are defined by our innate talents and interests;
later on, our nurturing environment and mentors shape us.
Who we are has little to do with who we are born to,
because every child is an experiment in life.

Medieval societies of India misunderstood the system of classification
of individuals based on natural aptitudes and casted a rigid social structure
where one's birth determined what profession one was allowed to take up.
Some were even excluded from this misguided social setup and labeled as outcastes.

45 One attains perfection
when he is committed to his work.

I will tell you how one can find fulfillment
by pursuing one's own profession.

46 One finds fulfillment
by working in harmony with his natural abilities
and making that as an offering to the One,
who pervades this universe and
from whom all creatures have arisen.

47 Try to excel in your own *dharma*,
even if it is less glamorous.
It is better than following
the *dharma* of others.

You will never feel guilty
if you follow your inherent nature.

Here, '*dharma*' is a reference to the essence of one's personality
including his attitude, talent, and nurturing environment.

48 It is only natural that
all pursuits have some defect,
just as fire is often obscured by smoke.

But one should not
abandon work suited to one's own nature,
simply because it is less glamorous.

No pursuit is perfect or ideal – there are always hurdles in the way.
When our work is suited to our aptitude and interest,
the hurdles seem insignificant, however big they might be.
When we work against our own nature,
even small hurdles seem big.

49 One who masters himself and
is free from desires and attachments
attains supreme perfection
through renunciation and
transcends all bondages of action.

50 Listen now, as I explain how
one who has attained perfection
also attains *brahman*.

51 Endowed with clear reasoning and firm self-restraint,
he relinquishes sound and all other sensations
while remaining impartial and selfless.
52 Living in solitude, he eats lightly and
regulates his body, mind, and speech
through meditation.
53 Free from ego, greed, desire, arrogance,
anger, aggression, and possession;
he is at peace with himself and others,
and is fit to become one with *brahman*.
54 In that serenity of oneness,
unmoved by sadness or anxiety,
treating everyone in the same manner,
he gains utmost devotion to the supreme.
55 He realizes the essential nature of the supreme
through that ultimate devotion.
After knowing the fundamental truth,
he is instantly united with the supreme.

56 Even while constantly engaged
in worldly activities,
by taking refuge in the supreme
he will reach that eternal, imperishable state.
Such is the divine grace!

[57,58]With firm understanding,
regard me as the supreme,
think of me always, and
consciously dedicate your actions to me.
You shall overcome every hurdle by my grace.

But, out of arrogance
if you refuse to listen to me,
you will perish.

[59,60]Even if you say,
"I will not fight"
out of ego or ignorance,
you can't abide by your decision
because you will be forced
by your own nature
to do so against your will.

We are all obliged to act in accordance with
our own inherent nature.

[61]Arjuna, the lord resides equally
in the hearts of all beings and
by *maya* causes them to move about
as though driven by a machine.

Maya refers to the divine power of illusion.

62 Take refuge in him alone
with your whole being and
by his grace you will attain
that state of eternal peace.

63 Thus, I have taught you the wisdom
that is the greatest of all secrets.

Reflect deeply on these teachings
and then do as you please.

64 Listen again to my final words,
the greatest secret of all.

I shall repeat what is good for you
because you are dear to me.

65 Fix your mind on me,
be devoted to me,
make every act an offering to me,
bow down to me, and
you shall certainly come to me;
this I promise,
for you are dear to me.

66 Giving up all forms of *dharma*
take refuge in me alone.
I will liberate you from all sins,
do not grieve!

Here, *dharma* is used in the widest sense of the word – law, virtue, support, religion, duty, path, etc.

After explaining all the various paths, Krishna finally gives a simple path to liberation: the path of surrender to the Supreme.

This path is readily accessible to everyone, without the need for an organized religion or a mediator; it is free from rules and distinctions.

Giving up *dharma* refers to moving beyond them. Compared to the divine presence in the universe (the highest *dharma*) and its assurance for ready liberation, all other *dharma*s invariably become insignificant.

67 Don't share this sacred truth with
one who lacks discipline and diligence,
one who doesn't care to listen, or
one who speaks ill of me.

The message is ready for all, but not everyone may be ready or interested; and even if they are ready, they may not have faith in the message. Advice is best given when sought; else it might not be taken seriously.

68 But whoever teaches this great secret
with sincerity and devotion
to those who wish to learn it,
he will surely come to me.

69 Further, none can render more pleasing service to me
than the one who teaches this secret to my devotees,
and no one else on earth is dearer to me.

70 Whoever earnestly studies this sacred dialogue –
I consider that person to have honored me
through *jnana yajña*.

Jnana yajña is pursuit of knowledge. In other words, making an effort to understand what was taught. This is the respect that one can show to the wise.

71 Full of reverence and free from malice,
one who merely hears these words
attains liberation and
goes to the happy worlds
of the righteous.

72 Have you heard this teaching with full attention, Arjuna?
Has your confusion caused by ignorance been clarified?

ARJUNA

73 Yes! My doubts are cleared.
I am not confused any more.
I am enlightened by your grace, Krishna.
I stand firm.
I will follow your advice.

Sanjaya

74This wonderful dialogue
between the two great souls
is so thrilling that
it makes my hair stand.

75By the gift of Vyasa,
I saw this supreme yogic mystery
being revealed right in front of my eyes
by the master of *yoga* himself.

Before the war began, sage Vyasa offered divine vision to Dhritarashtra.
But the blind king refused to see this terrible war between brothers.

So, Vyasa gave the ability of remote viewing to Sanjaya,
who could witness the events on the battlefield
without leaving the palace and narrate it to Dhritarashtra.

76As I recall again and again
the splendid and sacred dialogue
between Krishna and Arjuna,
I rejoice over and over again.

77I am spellbound, O King,
as I recollect Krishna's fabulous form.
I rejoice over and over again.

[78]I firmly believe that there will be
prosperity, victory, splendor, and justice
with Krishna, the lord of yoga
and Arjuna, the wielder of the bow
coming together!

Action guided by wisdom leads us to success.
The ideal for life is a combination of spiritual insight and mastery of work.

Epilogue

Just reading the text of Bhagavad-Gita or intellectually understanding its content is not enough if we aim to reap the full benefit of its wisdom. Sometimes, those who have never read a line of the Gita lead a life that epitomizes it and scholars who give hours of explanation for each verse of the Gita lead a life removed from it. Practicing the message is vital if we want to attain the wisdom. In other words, we can go through the Gita several times, but it is very important that we let the Gita go through us at least once.

Of course, we can enjoy the Gita merely as poetry or as an intellectual or academic exercise, but if we want to hear the larger voice of a universal consciousness, indeed we have to go beyond reading a book or attending a lecture. We have to verify our understanding in our daily life, see what works and what doesn't, and constantly review our personal philosophy and world view.

We often tend to make our personal view of the world rather static, but when everything is changing how can we remain still? And if we want to indeed achieve Stillness, then we have to transcend the notion of change once and for all. Krishna calls this the supreme state or the state of *brahman* – a state beyond creation and destruction, growth and decay.

Having read the Bhagavad-Gita and finding it to be a fountain of wisdom, we are interested in how the wisdom can help change our own life. For this reason, the peripheral issues around Gita (Did Krishna really exist? Did the war really take place? Did it take place 5,000 years ago? Was the Gita written by a single author? Was the Gita originally a part of the text of Mahabharata?) go into the background. While these are interesting topics of discussion, since our immediate purpose is to understand the message, we have to take the text at face value and examine it.

A good way to approach the Gita is by trying to understand the mind of Krishna. This is easier said than done. The reason is that Krishna is a mysterious character. He is an eternal paradox, as famed playwright and poet T. P. Kailasam captures in his lovely sonnet on Krishna:

> A woman's witching face, her ways, her eyes;
> A panther's frame, its grace, mayhap its heart;
> An eerie mastery of ev'ry art;
> A honey-tongue that steep'd all truth in lies
> And yet could strip all lies in light of **Truth**
> A smile that mock'd at plight of friend in Woe;
> A breast that bled at sight of fallen foe;
> Ador'd and yet afear'd of all, in sooth:
>
> Thou tangl'd mass of man and god and brute,
> What mortal mind may con thy rainbow-life
> That blazed undimm'd mid storms of human strife,
> And glean the wisdom of thy madd'ning flute,
> Thy love-lit crimes, thy kindly cruelties,
> Thou paradox for all eternities!

Krishna, as a person, is extremely happy and playful, but pragmatic. His religion consists of embracing life in totality and enjoying it as a game. He easily manages good and evil since he knows how to live in the world, by looking at things from an overall perspective.

We humans are rather biased in our tastes – we want the cake and eat it too. We want pleasure but no pain, joy but no sorrow, roses but no thorns, peace but no war. Krishna points out that these are merely two sides of the same coin. Non-violence has relevance only in the face of violence and Comfort takes on meaning only in the face of discomfort. Worldly life is full of dualities and going beyond the opposites leads us to endless peace. Embracing the world with a sense of connectedness is true spirituality.

There can be no single rule for all of human life; one can merely try to act appropriately in all situations. While brokering for peace, Krishna tells Duryodhana that he is about to commit a great sin by insisting on war. The same Krishna tells Arjuna on the battlefield that he is committing a great sin by running away from war. Krishna's life and message is filled with such apparent contradictions, but seen in perspective, the opposing ideas make sense. It takes a while to reconcile with the idea that truths can be contradictory because they are at different levels.

Typically religion divides things into 'sacred' and 'profane'. But Krishna focuses on a more useful division of what is appropriate and what is not. Thus Krishna is able to make statements that are supremely practical and at the same time perfectly spiritual. We have to know this if we want to joyfully participate in the game of life. A knowledge of both the material and the spiritual elements helps us sustain our application of wisdom to daily life.

In many ways, the Bhagavad-Gita is a unifying text. Krishna cuts across class distinctions, mocks at social prejudices, abhors dated traditional practices, and finds convergence for divergent thoughts and beliefs. Krishna declares that the religion of the Vedas is inclusive and talks of egalitarianism, but with focus on the inherent strength of an individual. He challenges Arjuna to think differently and not to buy into traditional baggage, by showing him how external factors mean little when greater heights are reached spiritually.

The journey from ignorance to knowledge consists of opening our minds and learning how to entertain an idea without accepting or rejecting it. To blindly accept or reject anything is ignorance. Objective examination of the evidence, experimentation in daily life, carefully listening to the voice of intuition that comes with years of experience – these are some of the ingredients to forming an all-round view of the world around us and attaining supreme bliss.

Om, salutations!
May the spirit of *yajña* flourish!
May the one with the spirit of *yajña* flourish!
May divine grace be upon us!
May divine grace be upon humankind!
May plants be bountiful!
Auspiciousness to the two-footed!
Auspiciousness to the four-footed!
Om, peace, peace, peace!

(from the Krishna Yajur Veda)

APPENDIX 1 Transliteration Guide

For centuries, the scriptures were learnt in the oral tradition from the *guru* and commited to memory; it was only much later that they were written down. Before 18th century CE, Sanskrit was written in the local vernacular writing system in different regions of India. But with the advent of printing technology in India and the widespread distribution of works in Sanskrit, the *nāgarī* script (often called *devanāgarī*) became predominant. By 19th century it had become the standard writing system for Sanskrit. The *nāgarī* script is written from left to right.

Sanskrit has been transliterated using the Latin alphabet for about three hundred years. A commonly used system is the IAST (International Alphabet of Sanskrit Transliteration) which allows for a lossless romanization of Indic scripts. It evolved from earlier schemes, particularly the one developed by the Tenth International Congress of Orientalists in 1894.

We have used the IAST scheme to transliterate the original text of the Bhagavad-Gītā.

The nāgarī alphabets are:

a ā i ī u ū ṛ ṝ ḷ ḹ
e ai o au aṃ aḥ
k kh g gh ṅ
c ch j jh ñ
ṭ ṭh ḍ ḍh ṇ
t th d dh n
p ph b bh m
y r l v ś ṣ s h

Pronunciation of the vowels:

a as in **away**	i as in **in**	u as in **good**
ā as in **car**	ī as in **free**	ū as in **mood**

ṛ as in **rhythm**	ḷ is **lri** (rolled)
ṝ is **rri** (rolled)	ḹ is **lrri** (rolled)

e as in **say**	o as in **old**	aṁ as in **hum**
ai as in **sky**	au as in **owl**	aḥ is **a-huh**

Pronunciation of the consonants:

k as in **kid**	c as in **ch**at	ṭ as in **ten**
g as in **got**	j as in **joy**	ḍ as in **den**
ṅ as in so**ng**	ñ as in **inch**	ṇ as in e**nd**

t as in **thin**	p as in **pat**
d as is **then**	b as in **bat**
n as in **now**	m as in **mat**

y as in **yes**	l as in **less**	ś as in **shin**	h as in **her**
r as in **ran**	v as in **van**	s as in **sin**	

The consonants kh, gh, ch, jh, ṭh, ḍh, th, dh, ph, bh, and ṣ are the aspirated versions of the consonants k, g, c, j, ṭ, ḍ, t, d, p, b, and ś respectively.

kṣa and jña are popular conjuncts. While kṣa follows the standard rule of pronunciation, jña presents an exception and is pronounced as *gña* (**g-nya**).

For the convenience of the readers, we have retained the popular transliterations of most Sanskrit words in the text. Therefore, we have prefered *avatara* instead of avatāra, Krishna instead of kṛṣṇa, *rishi* instead of ṛṣi and so on. We have included the IAST transliterations of Sanskrit words in the glossary.

In some places in the original text of the Gita, one will find apostrophes, like in the last line of 1:21, *rathaṃ sthāpaya me 'cyuta.*

According to a rule of forming compound words in Sanskrit, when a word ends in 'e' or in 'o' and is followed by a word that begins with an 'a', the 'a' is removed and replaced by a silent 'a', which is denoted by the apostrophe. So in the example, *me + acyuta* becomes *me 'cyuta.*

APPENDIX 2 The Bhagavad-Gita

1

dhṛtarāṣṭra uvāca ||
dharmakṣetre kurukṣetre
samavetā yuyutsavaḥ |
māmakāḥ pāṇḍavāścaiva
kimakurvata sañjaya |1|

sañjaya uvāca ||
dṛṣṭvā tu pāṇḍavānīkaṃ
vyūḍhaṃ duryodhanastadā |
ācāryamupasaṅgamya
rājā vacanamabravīt |2|

paśyaitāṃ pāṇḍuputrāṇāṃ
ācārya mahatīṃ camūm |
vyūḍhāṃ drupadaputreṇa
tava śiṣyeṇa dhīmatā |3|

atra śūrā maheṣvāsāḥ
bhīmārjunasamā yudhi |
yuyudhāno virāṭaśca
drupadaśca mahārathaḥ |4|

dhṛṣṭaketuścekitānaḥ
kāśirājaśca vīryavān |
purujit kuntibhojaśca
śaibyaśca narapuṅgavaḥ |5|

yudhāmanyuśca vikrāntaḥ
uttamaujāśca vīryavān |
saubhadro draupadeyāśca
sarva eva mahārathāḥ |6|

asmākaṃ tu viśiṣṭā ye
tānnibodha dvijottama |
nāyakā mama sainyasya
saṃjñārthaṃ tān bravīmi te |7|

bhavānbhīṣmaśca karṇaśca
kṛpaśca samitiñjayaḥ |
aśvatthāmā vikarṇaśca
saumadattistathaiva ca |8|

anye ca bahavaḥ śūrāḥ
madarthe tyaktajīvitāḥ |
nānāśastrapraharaṇāḥ
sarve yuddhaviśāradāḥ |9|

aparyāptaṃ tadasmākaṃ
balaṃ bhīṣmābhirakṣitam |
paryāptaṃ tvidameteṣāṃ
balaṃ bhīmābhirakṣitam |10|

ayaneṣu ca sarveṣu
yathābhāgamavasthitāḥ |
bhīṣmamevābhirakṣantu
bhavantaḥ sarva eva hi |11|

tasya sañjanayanharṣaṃ
kuruvṛddhaḥ pitāmahaḥ |
siṃhanādaṃ vinadyoccaiḥ
śaṅkhaṃ dadhmau pratāpavān |12|

tataḥ śaṅkhāśca bheryaśca
paṇavānakagomukhāḥ |
sahasaivābhyahanyanta
sa śabdastumulo'bhavat |13|

tataḥ śvetairhayairyukte
mahati syandane sthitau |
mādhavaḥ pāṇḍavaścaiva
divyau śaṅkhau pradadhmatuḥ |14|

pāñcajanyaṃ hṛṣīkeśo
devadattaṃ dhanañjayaḥ |
pauṇḍraṃ dadhmau mahāśaṅkhaṃ
bhīmakarmā vṛkodaraḥ |15|

anantavijayaṃ rājā
kuntīputro yudhiṣṭhiraḥ |
nakulaḥ sahadevaśca
sughoṣamaṇipuṣpakau |16|

kāśyaśca parameṣvāsaḥ
śikhaṇḍī ca mahārathaḥ |
dhṛṣṭadyumno virāṭaśca
sātyakiścāparājitaḥ |17|

drupado draupadeyāśca
sarvaśaḥ pṛthivīpate |
saubhadraśca mahābāhuḥ
śaṅkhāndadhmuḥ pṛthakpṛthak |18|

sa ghoṣo dhārtarāṣṭrāṇāṃ
hṛdayāni vyadārayat |
nabhaśca pṛthivīṃ caiva
tumulo vyanunādayan |19|

atha vyavasthitān dṛṣṭvā
dhārtarāṣṭrānkapidhvajaḥ |
pravṛtte śastrasaṃpāte
dhanurudyamya pāṇḍavaḥ |20|

hṛṣīkeśaṃ tadā vākyaṃ
idamāha mahīpate |

arjuna uvāca ||
senayorubhayormadhye
rathaṃ sthāpaya me'cyuta |21|

yāvadetānnirīkṣe'haṃ
yoddhukāmānavasthitān |
kairmayā saha yoddhavyaṃ
asmin raṇasamudyame |22|

yotsyamānānavekṣe'haṃ
ya ete'tra samāgatāḥ |
dhārtarāṣṭrasya durbuddheḥ
yuddhe priyacikīrṣavaḥ |23|

sañjaya uvāca ||
evamukto hṛṣīkeśo
guḍākeśena bhārata |
senayorubhayormadhye
sthāpayitvā rathottamam |24|

bhīṣmadroṇapramukhataḥ
sarveṣāṃ ca mahīkṣitām |
uvāca pārtha paśyaitān
samavetān kurūniti |25|

tatrāpaśyatsthitānpārthaḥ
pitṝnatha pitāmahān |
ācāryānmātulānbhrātṝn
putrānpautrānsakhīṃstathā |26|

śvaśurān suhṛdaścaiva
senayorubhayorapi |
tānsamīkṣya sa kaunteyaḥ
sarvānbandhūnavasthitān |27|

kṛpayā parayāviṣṭo
viṣīdannidamabravīt |

arjuna uvāca ||
dṛṣṭvemaṃ svajanaṃ kṛṣṇa
yuyutsuṃ samupasthitam |28|

sīdanti mama gātrāṇi
mukhaṃ ca pariśuṣyati |
vepathuśca śarīre me
romaharṣaśca jāyate |29|

gāṇḍīvaṃ sraṃsate hastāt
tvakcaiva paridahyate |
na ca śaknomyavasthātuṃ
bhramatīva ca me manaḥ |30|

nimittāni ca paśyāmi
viparītāni keśava |
na ca śreyo'nupaśyāmi
hatvā svajanamāhave |31|

na kāṅkṣe vijayaṃ kṛṣṇa
na ca rājyaṃ sukhāni ca |
kiṃ no rājyena govinda
kiṃ bhogairjīvitena vā |32|

yeṣāmarthe kāṅkṣitaṃ no
rājyaṃ bhogāḥ sukhāni ca |
ta ime'vasthitā yuddhe
prāṇāṃstyaktvā dhanāni ca |33|

ācāryāḥ pitaraḥ putrāḥ
tathaiva ca pitāmahāḥ |
mātulāḥ śvaśurāḥ pautrāḥ
śyālāḥ saṃbandhinastathā |34|

etānna hantumicchāmi
ghnato'pi madhusūdana |
api trailokyarājyasya
hetoḥ kiṃ nu mahīkṛte |35|

nihatya dhārtarāṣṭrānnaḥ
kā prītiḥ syājjanārdana |
pāpamevāśrayedasmān
hatvaitānātatāyinaḥ |36|

tasmānnārhā vayaṃ hantuṃ
dhārtarāṣṭrānsvabāndhavān
svajanaṃ hi kathaṃ hatvā
sukhinaḥ syāma mādhava |37|

yadyapyete na paśyanti
lobhopahatacetasaḥ |
kulakṣayakṛtaṃ doṣaṃ
mitradrohe ca pātakam |38|

kathaṃ na jñeyamasmābhiḥ
pāpādasmānnivartitum |
kulakṣayakṛtaṃ doṣaṃ
prapaśyadbhirjanārdana |39|

kulakṣaye praṇaśyanti
kuladharmāḥ sanātanāḥ |
dharme naṣṭe kulaṃ kṛtsnaṃ
adharmo'bhibhavatyuta |40|

adharmābhibhavāt kṛṣṇa
praduṣyanti kulastriyaḥ |
strīṣu duṣṭāsu vārṣṇeya
jāyate varṇasaṅkaraḥ |41|

saṅkaro narakāyaiva
kulaghnānāṃ kulasya ca |
patanti pitaro hyeṣāṃ
luptapiṇḍodakakriyāḥ |42|

doṣairetaiḥ kulaghnānāṃ
varṇasaṅkarakārakaiḥ |
utsādyante jātidharmāḥ
kuladharmāśca śāśvatāḥ |43|

utsannakuladharmāṇāṃ
manuṣyāṇāṃ janārdana |
narakeniyataṃ vāso
bhavatītyanuśuśruma |44|

aho bata mahatpāpaṃ
kartuṃ vyavasitā vayam |
yadrājyasukhalobhena
hantuṃ svajanamudyatāḥ |45|

yadi māmapratīkāraṃ
aśastraṃ śastrapāṇayaḥ |
dhārtarāṣṭrā raṇe hanyuḥ
tanme kṣemataraṃ bhavet |46|

***sañjaya uvāca** ||*
evamuktvārjunaḥ saṅkhye
rathopastha upāviśat |
visṛjya saśaraṃ cāpaṃ
śokasaṃvignamānasaḥ |47|

oṃtatsaditi ||
śrīmadbhagavadgītāsūpaniṣatsu
brahmavidyāyāṃ yogaśāstre
śrīkṛṣṇārjunasaṃvāde
arjunaviṣādayogonāma
prathamo'dhyāyaḥ ||

2

***sañjaya uvāca** ||*
taṃ tathā kṛpayāviṣṭaṃ
aśrupūrṇākulekṣaṇam |
viṣīdantamidaṃ vākyaṃ
uvāca madhusūdanaḥ |1|

***śrībhagavānuvāca** ||*
kutastvā kaśmalamidaṃ
viṣame samupasthitam |
anāryajuṣṭamasvargyaṃ
akīrtikaramarjuna |2|

klaibyaṃ mā sma gamaḥ pārtha
naitattvayyupapadyate |
kṣudraṃ hṛdayadaurbalyaṃ
tyaktvottiṣṭha parantapa |3|

***arjuna uvāca** ||*
kathaṃ bhīṣmamahaṃ saṅkhye
droṇaṃ ca madhusūdana |
iṣubhiḥ pratiyotsyāmi
pūjārhāvarisūdana |4|

gurūnahatvā hi mahānubhāvān
śreyo bhoktuṃ bhaikṣyamapīha loke |
hatvārthakāmāṃstu gurūnihaiva
bhuñjīya bhogānrudhirapradigdhān |5|

na caitadvidmaḥ kataranno garīyo
yadvā jayema yadi vā no jayeyuḥ |
yāneva hatvā na jijīviṣāmaḥ
te'vasthitāḥ pramukhe dhārtarāṣṭrāḥ |6|

kārpaṇyadoṣopahatasvabhāvaḥ
pṛcchāmi tvāṃ dharmasaṃmūḍhacetāḥ |
yacchreyaḥ syānniścitaṃ brūhi tanme
śiṣyaste'haṃ śādhi māṃ tvāṃ prapannam |7|

na hi prapaśyāmi mamāpanudyāt
yacchokamucchoṣaṇamindriyāṇām |
avāpya bhūmāvasapatnamṛddhaṃ
rājyaṃ surāṇāmapi cādhipatyam |8|

***sañjaya uvāca** ||*
evamuktvā hṛṣīkeśaṃ
guḍākeśaḥ parantapaḥ |
na yotsya iti govindaṃ
uktvā tūṣṇīṃ babhūva ha |9|

tamuvāca hṛṣīkeśaḥ
prahasanniva bhārata |
senayorubhayormadhye
viṣīdantamidaṃ vacaḥ |10|

***śrībhagavānuvāca** ||*
aśocyānanvaśocastvaṃ
prajñāvādāṃśca bhāṣase |
gatāsūnagatāsūṃśca
nānuśocanti paṇḍitāḥ |11|

na tvevāhaṃ jātu nāsaṃ
na tvaṃ neme janādhipāḥ |
na caiva na bhaviṣyāmaḥ
sarve vayamataḥ param |12|

dehino'sminyathā dehe
kaumāraṃ yauvanaṃ jarā |
tathā dehāntaraprāptih
dhīrastatra na muhyati |13|

mātrāsparśāstu kaunteya
śītoṣṇasukhaduḥkhadāḥ |
āgamāpāyino'nityāḥ
tāṃstitikṣasva bhārata |14|

yaṃ hi na vyathayantyete
puruṣaṃ puruṣarṣabha |
samaduḥkhasukhaṃ dhīraṃ
so'mṛtatvāya kalpate |15|

nāsato vidyate bhāvo
nābhāvo vidyate sataḥ |
ubhayorapi dṛṣṭo'ntaḥ
tvanayostattvadarśibhiḥ |16|

avināśi tu tadviddhi
yena sarvamidaṃ tatam |
vināśamavyayasyāsya
na kaścit kartumarhati |17|

antavanta ime dehāḥ
nityasyoktāḥ śarīriṇaḥ |
anāśino'prameyasya
tasmādyudhyasva bhārata |18|

ya enaṃ vetti hantāraṃ
yaścainaṃ manyate hatam |
ubhau tau na vijānīto
nāyaṃ hanti na hanyate |19|

na jāyate mriyate vā kadācit
nāyaṃ bhūtvā bhavitā vā na bhūyaḥ |
ajo nityaḥ śāśvato'yaṃ purāṇo
na hanyate hanyamāne śarīre |20|

vedāvināśinaṃ nityaṃ
ya enamajamavyayam |
kathaṃ sa puruṣaḥ pārtha
kaṃ ghātayati hanti kam |21|

vāsāṃsi jīrṇāni yathā vihāya
navāni gṛhṇāti naro'parāṇi |
tathā śarīrāṇi vihāya jīrṇāni
anyāni saṃyāti navāni dehī |22|

nainaṃ chindanti śastrāṇi
nainaṃ dahati pāvakaḥ |
na cainaṃ kledayantyāpo
na śoṣayati mārutaḥ |23|

acchedyo'yamadāhyo'yaṃ
akledyo'śoṣya eva ca |
nityaḥ sarvagataḥ sthāṇuḥ
acalo'yaṃ sanātanaḥ |24|

avyakto'yamacintyo'yaṃ
avikāryo'yamucyate |
tasmādevaṃ viditvainaṃ
nānuśocitumarhasi |25|

atha cainaṃ nityajātaṃ
nityaṃ vā manyase mṛtam |
tathāpi tvaṃ mahābāho
naivaṃ śocitumarhasi |26|

jātasya hi dhruvo mṛtyuh
dhruvaṃ janma mṛtasya ca |
tasmādaparihārye'rthe
na tvaṃ śocitumarhasi |27|

avyaktādīni bhūtāni
vyaktamadhyāni bhārata |
avyaktanidhanānyeva
tatra kā paridevanā |28|

āścaryavatpaśyati kaścidenaṃ
āścaryavadvadati tathaiva cānyaḥ |
āścaryavaccainamanyaḥ śṛṇoti
śrutvāpyenaṃ veda na caiva kaścit |29|

dehī nityamavadhyo'yaṃ
dehe sarvasya bhārata |
tasmātsarvāṇi bhūtāni
na tvaṃ śocitumarhasi |30|

svadharmamapi cāvekṣya
na vikampitumarhasi |
dharmyāddhi yuddhācchreyo'nyat
kṣatriyasya na vidyate |31|

yadṛcchayā copapannaṃ
svargadvāramapāvṛtam |
sukhinaḥ kṣatriyāḥ pārtha
labhante yuddhamīdṛśam |32|

atha cettvamimaṃ dharmyaṃ
saṅgrāmaṃ na kariṣyasi |
tataḥ svadharmaṃ kīrtiṃ ca
hitvā pāpamavāpsyasi |33|

akīrtiṃ cāpi bhūtāni
kathayiṣyanti te'vyayām |
saṃbhāvitasya cākīrtiḥ
maraṇādatiricyate |34|

bhayādraṇāduparataṃ
maṃsyante tvāṃ mahārathāḥ
yeṣāṃ ca tvaṃ bahumato
bhūtvā yāsyasi lāghavam |35|

avācyavādāṃśca bahūn
vadiṣyanti tavāhitāḥ |
nindantastava sāmarthyaṃ
tato duḥkhataraṃ nu kim |36|

hato vā prāpsyasi svargaṃ
jitvā vā bhokṣyase mahīm |
tasmāduttiṣṭha kaunteya
yuddhāya kṛtaniścayaḥ |37|

sukhaduḥkhe same kṛtvā
lābhālābhau jayājayau |
tato yuddhāya yujyasva
naivaṃ pāpamavāpsyasi |38|

eṣā te'bhihitā sāṅkhye
buddhiryoge tvimāṃ śṛṇu |
buddhyā yukto yayā pārtha
karmabandhaṃ prahāsyasi |39|

nehābhikramanāśo'sti
pratyavāyo na vidyate |
svalpamapyasya dharmasya
trāyate mahato bhayāt |40|

vyavasāyātmikā buddhih
ekeha kurunandana |
bahuśākhā hyanantāśca
buddhayo'vyavasāyinām |41|

yāmimāṃ puṣpitāṃ vācaṃ
pravadantyavipaścitaḥ |
vedavādaratāḥ pārtha
nānyadastīti vādinaḥ |42|

kāmātmānaḥ svargaparāḥ
janmakarmaphalapradām |
kriyāviśeṣabahulāṃ
bhogaiśvaryagatiṃ prati |43|

bhogaiśvaryaprasaktānāṃ
tayāpahṛtacetasām |
vyavasāyātmikā buddhiḥ
samādhau na vidhīyate |44|

traiguṇyaviṣayā vedāḥ
nistraiguṇyo bhavārjuna
nirdvandvo nityasattvastho
niryogakṣema ātmavān |45|

yāvānartha udapāne
sarvataḥ saṃplutodake |
tāvānsarveṣu vedeṣu
brāhmaṇasya vijānataḥ |46|

karmaṇyevādhikāraste
mā phaleṣu kadācana |
mā karmaphalaheturbhūḥ
mā te saṅgo'stvakarmaṇi |47|

yogasthaḥ kuru karmāṇi
saṅgaṃ tyaktvā dhanañjaya |
siddhyasiddhyoḥ samo bhūtvā
samatvaṃ yoga ucyate |48|

dūreṇa hyavaraṃ karma
buddhiyogāddhanañjaya |
buddhau śaraṇamanviccha
kṛpaṇāḥ phalahetavaḥ |49|

buddhiyukto jahātīha
ubhe sukṛtaduṣkṛte |
tasmādyogāya yujyasva
yogaḥ karmasu kauśalam |50|

karmajaṃ buddhiyuktā hi
phalaṃ tyaktvā manīṣiṇaḥ |
janmabandhavinirmuktāḥ
padaṃ gacchantyanāmayam |51|

yadā te mohakalilaṃ
buddhirvyatitariṣyati |
tadā gantāsi nirvedaṃ
śrotavyasya śrutasya ca |52|

śrutivipratipannā te
yadā sthāsyati niścalā |
samādhāvacalā buddhiḥ
tadā yogamavāpsyasi |53|

arjuna uvāca ||
sthitaprajñasya kā bhāṣā
samādhisthasya keśava |
sthitadhīḥ kiṃ prabhāṣeta
kimāsīta vrajeta kim |54|

śrībhagavānuvāca ||
prajahāti yadā kāmān
sarvānpārtha manogatān |
ātmanyevātmanā tuṣṭaḥ
sthitaprajñastadocyate |55|

duḥkheṣvanudvignamanāḥ
sukheṣu vigataspṛhaḥ |
vītarāgabhayakrodhaḥ
sthitadhīrmunirucyate |56|

yaḥ sarvatrānabhisnehaḥ
tattatprāpya śubhāśubham |
nābhinandati na dveṣṭi
tasya prajñā pratiṣṭhitā |57|

yadā saṃharate cāyaṃ
kūrmo'ṅgānīva sarvaśaḥ |
indriyāṇīndriyārthebhyaḥ
tasya prajñā pratiṣṭhitā |58|

viṣayā vinivartante
nirāhārasya dehinaḥ |
rasavarjaṃ raso'pyasya
paraṃ dṛṣṭvā nivartate |59|

yatato hyapi kaunteya
puruṣasya vipaścitaḥ |
indriyāṇi pramāthīni
haranti prasabhaṃ manaḥ |60|

tāni sarvāṇi saṃyamya
yukta āsīta matparaḥ |
vaśe hi yasyendriyāṇi
tasya prajñā pratiṣṭhitā |61|

dhyāyato viṣayānpuṃsaḥ
saṅgasteṣūpajāyate |
saṅgātsañjāyate kāmaḥ
kāmātkrodho'bhijāyate |62|

krodhādbhavati saṃmohaḥ
saṃmohātsmṛtivibhramaḥ |
smṛtibhraṃśādbuddhināśo
buddhināśāt praṇaśyati |63|

rāgadveṣaviyuktaistu
viṣayānindriyaiścaran |
ātmavaśyairvidheyātmā
prasādamadhigacchati |64|

prasāde sarvaduḥkhānāṃ
hānirasyopajāyate |
prasannacetaso hyāśu
buddhiḥ paryavatiṣṭhate |65|

nāsti buddhirayuktasya
na cāyuktasya bhāvanā |
na cābhāvayataḥ śāntiḥ
aśāntasya kutaḥ sukham |66|

indriyāṇāṃ hi caratāṃ
yanmano'nuvidhīyate |
tadasya harati prajñāṃ
vāyurnāvamivāmbhasi |67|

tasmādyasya mahābāho
nigṛhītāni sarvaśaḥ |
indriyāṇīndriyārthebhyaḥ
tasya prajñā pratiṣṭhitā |68|

yā niśā sarvabhūtānāṃ
tasyāṃ jāgarti saṃyamī |
yasyāṃ jāgrati bhūtāni
sā niśā paśyato muneḥ |69|

āpūryamāṇamacalapratiṣṭhaṃ
samudramāpaḥ praviśanti yadvat |
tadvatkāmāyaṃ praviśanti sarve
sa śāntimāpnoti na kāmakāmī |70|

vihāya kāmānyaḥ sarvān
pumāṃścarati niḥspṛhaḥ |
nirmamo nirahaṅkāraḥ
sa śāntimadhigacchati |71|

eṣā brāhmī sthitiḥ pārtha
naināṃ prāpya vimuhyati |
sthitvāsyāmantakāle'pi
brahmanirvāṇamṛcchati |72|

oṃtatsaditi ||
śrīmadbhagavadgītāsūpaniṣatsu
brahmavidyāyāṃ yogaśāstre
śrīkṛṣṇārjunasaṃvāde
sāṅkhyayogonāma
dvitiyo'dhyāyaḥ ||

3

arjuna uvāca ||
jyāyasī cetkarmaṇaste
matā buddhirjanārdana|
tatkiṃ karmaṇi ghore māṃ
niyojayasi keśava |1|

vyāmiśreṇeva vākyena
buddhiṃ mohayasīva me |
tadekaṃ vada niścitya
yena śreyo'hamāpnuyām |2|

śrībhagavānuvāca ||
loke'smindvividhā niṣṭhā
purā proktā mayānagha |
jñānayogena sāṅkhyānāṃ
karmayogena yogināṃ |3|

na karmaṇāmanārambhāt
naiṣkarmyaṃ puruṣo'śnute |
na ca saṃnyasanādeva
siddhiṃ samadhigacchati |4|

na hi kaścitkṣaṇamapi
jātu tiṣṭhatyakarmakṛt |
kāryate hyavaśaḥ karma
sarvaḥ prakṛtijairguṇaiḥ |5|

karmendriyāṇi saṃyamya
ya āste manasāsmaran |
indriyārthānvimūḍhātmā
mithyācāraḥ sa ucyate |6|

yastvindriyāṇi manasā
niyamyārabhate'rjuna|
karmendriyaiḥ karmayogaṃ
asaktaḥ sa viśiṣyate |7|

niyataṃ kuru karma tvaṃ
karma jyāyo hyakarmaṇaḥ |
śarīrayātrāpi ca te
na prasidhyedakarmaṇaḥ |8|

yajñārthātkarmaṇo'nyatra
loko'yaṃ karmabandhanaḥ |
tadarthaṃ karma kaunteya
muktasaṅgaḥ samācara |9|

sahayajñāḥ prajāḥ sṛṣṭvā
purovāca prajāpatiḥ |
anena prasaviṣyadhvaṃ
eṣa vo'stviṣṭakāmadhuk |10|

devānbhāvayatānena
te devā bhāvayantu vaḥ |
parasparaṃ bhāvayantaḥ
śreyaḥ paramavāpsyatha |11|

iṣṭānbhogān hi vo devāḥ
dāsyante yajñabhāvitāḥ |
tairdattānapradāyaibhyo
yo bhuṅkte stena eva saḥ |12|

yajñaśiṣṭāśinaḥ santo
mucyante sarvakilbiṣaiḥ |
bhuñjate te tvaghaṃ pāpāḥ
ye pacantyātmakāraṇāt |13|

annādbhavanti bhūtāni
parjanyādannasaṃbhavaḥ |
yajñādbhavati parjanyo
yajñaḥ karmasamudbhavaḥ |14|

karma brahmodbhavaṃ viddhi
brahmākṣarasamudbhavam |
tasmātsarvagataṃ brahma
nityaṃ yajñe pratiṣṭhitam |15|

evaṃ pravartitaṃ cakraṃ
nānuvartayatīha yaḥ |
aghāyurindriyārāmo
moghaṃ pārtha sa jīvati |16|

yastvātmaratireva syāt
ātmatṛptaśca mānavaḥ |
ātmanyeva ca saṃtuṣṭaḥ
tasya kāryaṃ na vidyate |17|

naiva tasya kṛtenārtho
nākṛteneha kaścana |
na cāsya sarvabhūteṣu
kaścidarthavyapāśrayaḥ |18|

tasmādasaktaḥ satataṃ
kāryaṃ karma samācara |
asakto hyācarankarma
paramāpnoti pūruṣaḥ |19|

karmaṇaiva hi saṃsiddhiṃ
āsthitā janakādayaḥ |
lokasaṅgrahamevāpi
saṃpaśyankartum arhasi |20|

yadyadācarati śreṣṭhaḥ
tattadevetaro janaḥ |
sa yatpramāṇaṃ kurute
lokastadanuvartate |21|

na me pārthāsti kartavyaṃ
triṣu lokeṣu kiñcana |
nānavāptamavāptavyaṃ
varta eva ca karmaṇi |22|

yadi hyahaṃ na varteyaṃ
jātu karmaṇyatandritaḥ |
mama vartmānuvartante
manuṣyāḥ pārtha sarvaśaḥ |23|

utsīdeyurime lokāḥ
na kuryāṃ karma cedaham |
saṅkarasya ca kartā syāṃ
upahanyāmimāḥ prajāḥ |24|

saktāḥ karmaṇyavidvāṃso
yathā kurvanti bhārata |
kuryādvidvāṃstathāsaktaḥ
cikīrṣurlokasaṅgraham |25|

na buddhibhedaṃ janayet
ajñānāṃ karmasaṅginām |
joṣayetsarvakarmāṇi
vidvānyuktaḥ samācaran |26|

prakṛteḥ kriyamāṇāni
guṇaiḥ karmāṇi sarvaśaḥ |
ahaṅkāravimūḍhātmā
kartāhamiti manyate |27|

tattvavittu mahābāho
guṇakarmavibhāgayoḥ |
guṇā guṇeṣu vartanta
iti matvā na sajjate |28|

prakṛterguṇasaṃmūḍhāḥ
sajjante guṇakarmasu |
tānakṛtsnavido mandān
kṛtsnavinna vicālayet |29|

mayi sarvāṇi karmāṇi
saṃnyasyādhyātmacetasā |
nirāśīrnirmamo bhūtvā
yudhyasva vigatajvaraḥ |30|

ye me matamidaṃ nityaṃ
anutiṣṭhanti mānavāḥ |
śraddhāvanto'nasūyanto
mucyante te'pi karmabhiḥ |31|

ye tvetadabhyasūyanto
nānutiṣṭhanti me matam |
sarvajñānavimūḍhāṃstān
viddhi naṣṭānacetasaḥ |32|

sadṛśaṃ ceṣṭate svasyāḥ
prakṛterjñānavānapi |
prakṛtiṃ yānti bhūtāni
nigrahaḥ kiṃ kariṣyati |33|

indriyasyendriyasyārthe
rāgadveṣau vyavasthitau |
tayorna vaśamāgacchet
tau hyasya paripanthinau |34|

śreyānsvadharmo viguṇaḥ
paradharmātsvanuṣṭhitāt |
svadharme nidhanaṃ śreyaḥ
paradharmo bhayāvahaḥ |35|

***arjuna uvāca** ||*
atha kena prayukto'yaṃ
pāpaṃ carati pūruṣaḥ |
anicchannapi vārṣṇeya
balādiva niyojitaḥ |36|

***śrībhagavānuvāca** ||*
kāma eṣakrodha eṣaḥ
rajoguṇasamudbhavaḥ |
mahāśano mahāpāpmā
viddhyenamiha vairiṇam |37|

dhūmenāvriyate vahniḥ
yathādarśo malena ca |
yatholbenāvṛto garbhaḥ
tathā tenedamāvṛtam |38|

āvṛtaṃ jñānametena
jñānino nityavairiṇā |
kāmarūpeṇa kaunteya
duṣpūreṇānalena ca |39|

indriyāṇi mano buddhiḥ
asyādhiṣṭhānamucyate |
etairvimohayatyeṣa
jñānamāvṛtya dehinam |40|

tasmāttvamindriyāṇyādau
niyamya bharatarṣabha |
pāpmānaṃ prajahi hyenaṃ
jñānavijñānanāśanam |41|

indriyāṇi parāṇyāhuḥ
indriyebhyaḥ paraṃ manaḥ |
manasastu parā buddhiḥ
yo buddheḥ paratastu saḥ |42|

evaṃ buddheḥ paraṃ buddhvā
saṃstabhyātmānamātmanā |
jahi śatruṃ mahābāho
kāmarūpaṃ durāsadam |43|

oṃtatsaditi ||
śrīmadbhagavadgītāsūpaniṣatsu
brahmavidyāyāṃ yogaśāstre
śrīkṛṣṇārjunasaṃvāde
karmayogo nāma
tṛtīyo'dhyāyaḥ ||

4

***śrībhagavānuvāca** ||*
imaṃ vivasvate yogaṃ
proktavānahamavyayam |
vivasvānmanave prāha
manurikṣvākave'bravīt |1|

evaṃ paramparāprāptaṃ
imaṃ rājarṣayo viduḥ |
sa kāleneha mahatā
yogo naṣṭaḥ paraṃtapa |2|

sa evāyaṃ mayā te'dya
yogaḥ proktaḥ purātanaḥ |
bhakto'si me sakhā ceti
rahasyaṃ hyetaduttamam |3|

arjuna uvāca ||
aparaṃ bhavato janma
paraṃ janma vivasvataḥ |
kathametadvijānīyāṃ
tvamādau proktavāniti |4|

śrībhagavānuvāca ||
bahūni me vyatītāni
janmāni tava cārjuna
tānyahaṃ veda sarvāṇi
na tvaṃ vettha parantapa |5|

ajo'pi sannavyayātmā
bhūtānāmīśvaro'pi san |
prakṛtiṃ svāmadhiṣṭhāya
saṃbhavāmyātmamāyayā |6|

yadā yadā hi dharmasya
glānirbhavati bhārata |
abhyutthānamadharmasya
tadātmānaṃ sṛjāmyaham |7|

paritrāṇāya sādhūnāṃ
vināśāya ca duṣkṛtām |
dharmasaṃsthāpanārthāya
saṃbhavāmi yuge yuge |8|

janma karma ca me divyaṃ
evaṃ yo vetti tattvataḥ |
tyaktvā dehaṃ punarjanma
naiti māmeti so'rjuna |9|

vītarāgabhayakrodhāḥ
manmayā māmupāśritāḥ |
bahavo jñānatapasā
pūtā madbhāvamāgatāḥ |10|

ye yathā māṃ prapadyante
tāṃstathaiva bhajāmyaham |
mama vartmānuvartante
manuṣyāḥ pārtha sarvaśaḥ |11|

kāṅkṣantaḥ karmaṇāṃ siddhiṃ
yajanta iha devatāḥ |
kṣipraṃ hi mānuṣe loke
siddhirbhavati karmajā |12|

cāturvarṇyaṃ mayā sṛṣṭaṃ
guṇakarmavibhāgaśaḥ |
tasya kartāramapi māṃ
viddhyakartāramavyayam |13|

na māṃ karmāṇi limpanti
na me karmaphale spṛhā |
iti māṃ yo'bhijānāti
karmabhirna sa badhyate |14|

evaṃ jñātvā kṛtaṃ karma
pūrvairapi mumukṣubhiḥ |
kuru karmaiva tasmāttvaṃ
pūrvaiḥ pūrvataraṃ kṛtam |15|

kiṃ karma kimakarmeti
kavayo'pyatra mohitāḥ |
tatte karma pravakṣyāmi
yajjñātvā mokṣyase'śubhāt |16|

karmaṇohyapi boddhavyaṃ
boddhavyaṃ ca vikarmaṇaḥ |
akarmaṇaśca boddhavyaṃ
gahanā karmaṇo gatiḥ |17|

karmaṇyakarma yaḥ paśyet
akarmaṇi ca karma yaḥ |
sa buddhimānmanuṣyeṣu
sa yuktaḥ kṛtsnakarmakṛt |18|

yasya sarve samārambhāḥ
kāmasaṅkalpavarjitāḥ |
jñānāgnidagdhakarmāṇaṃ
tamāhuḥ paṇḍitaṃ budhāḥ |19|

tyaktvā karmaphalāsaṅgaṃ
nityatṛpto nirāśrayaḥ |
karmaṇyabhipravṛtto'pi
naiva kiñcitkaroti saḥ |20|

nirāśīryatacittātmā
tyaktasarvaparigrahaḥ |
śārīraṃ kevalaṃ karma
kurvannāpnoti kilbiṣam |21|

yadṛcchālābhasantuṣṭo
dvandvātīto vimatsaraḥ |
samaḥ siddhāvasiddhau ca
kṛtvāpi na nibadhyate |22|

gatasaṅgasya muktasya
jñānāvasthitacetasaḥ |
yajñāyācarataḥ karma
samagraṃ pravilīyate |23|

brahmārpaṇaṃ brahma haviḥ
brahmāgnau brahmaṇā hutam |
brahmaiva tena gantavyaṃ
brahmakarmasamādhinā |24|

daivamevāpare yajñaṃ
yoginaḥ paryupāsate |
brahmāgnāvapare yajñaṃ
yajñenaivopajuhvati |25|

śrotrādīnīndriyāṇyanye
saṃyamāgniṣu juhvati |
śabdādīnviṣayānanya
indriyāgniṣu juhvati |26|

sarvāṇīndriyakarmāṇi
prāṇakarmāṇi cāpare |
ātmasaṃyamayogāgnau
juhvati jñānadīpite |27|

dravyayajñāstapoyajñāḥ
yogayajñāstathāpare |
svādhyāyajñānayajñāśca
yatayaḥ saṃśitavratāḥ |28|

apāne juhvati prāṇaṃ
prāṇe'pānaṃ tathāpare |
prāṇāpānagatī ruddhvā
prāṇāyāmaparāyaṇāḥ |29|

apare niyatāhārāḥ
prāṇānprāṇeṣu juhvati |
sarve'pyete yajñavido
yajñakṣapitakalmaṣāḥ |30|

yajñaśiṣṭāmṛtabhujo
yānti brahma sanātanam |
nāyaṃ loko'styayajñasya
kuto'nyaḥ kurusattama |31|

evaṃ bahuvidhā yajñāḥ
vitatā brahmaṇo mukhe |
karmajānviddhi tānsarvān
evaṃ jñātvā vimokṣyase |32|

śreyāndravyamayādyajñāt
jñānayajñaḥ parantapa |
sarvaṃ karmākhilaṃ pārtha
jñāne parisamāpyate |33|

tadviddhi praṇipātena
paripraśnena sevayā |
upadekṣyanti te jñānaṃ
jñāninastattvadarśinaḥ |34|

yajjñātvā na punarmohaṃ
evaṃ yāsyasi pāṇḍava |
yena bhūtānyaśeṣeṇa
drakṣyasyātmanyatho mayi |35|

api cedasi pāpebhyaḥ
sarvebhyaḥ pāpakṛttamaḥ |
sarvaṃ jñānaplavenaiva
vṛjinaṃ santariṣyasi |36|

yathaidhāṃsi samiddho'gniḥ
bhasmasātkurute'rjuna |
jñānāgniḥ sarvakarmāṇi
bhasmasātkurute tathā |37|

na hi jñānena sadṛśaṃ
pavitramiha vidyate |
tatsvayaṃ yogasaṃsiddhaḥ
kālenātmani vindati |38|

śraddhāvān labhate jñānaṃ
tatparaḥ saṃyatendriyaḥ |
jñānaṃ labdhvā parāṃ śāntiṃ
acireṇādhigacchati |39|

ajñaścāśraddadhānaśca
saṃśayātmā vinaśyati |
nāyaṃ loko'sti na paro
na sukhaṃ saṃśayātmanaḥ |40|

yogasaṃnyastakarmāṇaṃ
jñānasañchinnasaṃśayam |
ātmavantaṃ na karmāṇi
nibadhnanti dhanañjaya |41|

tasmādajñānasaṃbhūtaṃ
hṛtsthaṃ jñānāsinātmanaḥ |
chittvainaṃ saṃśayaṃ yogam
ātiṣṭhottiṣṭha bhārata |42|

oṃtatsaditi ||
śrīmadbhagavadgītāsūpaniṣatsu
brahmavidyāyāṃ yogaśāstre
śrīkṛṣṇārjunasaṃvāde
jñānakarmasaṃnyāsayogo nāma
caturtho'dhyāyaḥ ||

5

arjuna uvāca ||
saṃnyāsaṃ karmaṇāṃ kṛṣṇa
punaryogaṃ ca śaṃsasi |
yacchreya etayorekaṃ
tanme brūhi suniścitam |1|

śrībhagavānuvāca ||
saṃnyāsaḥ karmayogaśca
niḥśreyasakarāvubhau |
tayostu karmasaṃnyāsāt
karmayogo viśiṣyate |2|

jñeyaḥ sa nityasaṃnyāsī
yo na dveṣṭi na kāṅkṣati |
nirdvandvo hi mahābāho
sukhaṃ bandhātpramucyate |3|

sāṅkhyayogau pṛthagbālāḥ
pravadanti na paṇḍitāḥ |
ekamapyāsthitaḥ samyak
ubhayorvindate phalam |4|

yatsāṅkhyaiḥ prāpyate sthānaṃ
tadyogairapi gamyate |
ekaṃ sāṅkhyaṃ ca yogaṃ ca
yaḥ paśyati sa paśyati |5|

saṃnyāsastu mahābāho
duḥkhamāptumayogataḥ |
yogayukto munirbrahma
nacireṇādhigacchati |6|

yogayukto viśuddhātmā
vijitātmā jitendriyaḥ |
sarvabhūtātmabhūtātmā
kurvannapi na lipyate |7|

naiva kiṃcitkaromīti
yukto manyeta tattvavit |
paśyañśṛṇvanspṛśañjighran
aśnangacchansvapañśvasan |8|

pralapanvisṛjangṛhṇan
unmiṣannimiṣannapi |
indriyāṇīndriyārtheṣu
vartanta iti dhārayan |9|

brahmaṇyādhāya karmāṇi
saṅgaṃ tyaktvā karoti yaḥ |
lipyate na sa pāpena
padmapatramivāmbhasā |10|

kāyena manasā buddhyā
kevalairindriyairapi |
yoginaḥ karma kurvanti
saṅgaṃ tyaktvātmaśuddhaye |11|

yuktaḥ karmaphalaṃ tyaktvā
śāntimāpnoti naiṣṭhikīm |
ayuktaḥ kāmakāreṇa
phale sakto nibadhyate |12|

sarvakarmāṇi manasā
saṃnyasyāste sukhaṃ vaśī |
navadvāre pure dehī
naiva kurvan na kārayan |13|

na kartṛtvaṃ na karmāṇi
lokasya sṛjati prabhuḥ |
na karmaphalasaṃyogaṃ
svabhāvastu pravartate |14|

nādatte kasyacitpāpaṃ
na caiva sukṛtaṃ vibhuḥ |
ajñānenāvṛtaṃ jñānaṃ
tena muhyanti jantavaḥ |15|

jñānena tu tadajñānaṃ
yeṣāṃ nāśitamātmanaḥ |
teṣāmādityavajjñānaṃ
prakāśayati tatparam |16|

tadbuddhayas tadātmānaḥ
tanniṣṭhāstatparāyaṇāḥ |
gacchantyapunarāvṛttiṃ
jñānanirdhūtakalmaṣāḥ |17|

vidyāvinayasaṃpanne
brāhmaṇe gavi hastini |
śuni caiva śvapāke ca
paṇḍitāḥ samadarśinaḥ |18|

ihaiva tairjitaḥ sargo
yeṣāṃ sāmye sthitaṃ manaḥ |
nirdoṣaṃ hi samaṃ brahma
tasmādbrahmaṇi te sthitāḥ |19|

na prahṛṣyetpriyaṃ prāpya
nodvijetprāpya cāpriyam |
sthirabuddhirasaṃmūḍho
brahmavidbrahmaṇi sthitaḥ |20|

bāhyasparśeṣvasaktātmā
vindatyātmani yatsukham |
sa brahmayogayuktātmā
sukhamakṣayamaśnute |21|

ye hi saṃsparśajā bhogāḥ
duḥkhayonaya eva te |
ādyantavantaḥ kaunteya
na teṣu ramate budhaḥ |22|

śaknotīhaiva yaḥ soḍhuṃ
prākśarīravimokṣaṇāt |
kāmakrodhodbhavaṃ vegaṃ
sa yuktaḥ sa sukhī naraḥ |23|

yo'ntaḥsukho'ntarārāmaḥ
tathāntarjyotireva yaḥ |
sa yogī brahmanirvāṇaṃ
brahmabhūto'dhigacchati |24|

labhante brahmanirvāṇam
ṛṣayaḥ kṣīṇakalmaṣāḥ |
chinnadvaidhā yatātmānaḥ
sarvabhūtahite ratāḥ |25|

kāmakrodhaviyuktānāṃ
yatīnāṃ yatacetasām |
abhito brahmanirvāṇaṃ
vartate viditātmanām |26|

sparśānkṛtvā bahirbāhyān
cakṣuścaivāntare bhruvoḥ |
prāṇāpānau samau kṛtvā
nāsābhyantaracāriṇau |27|

yatendriyamanobuddhiḥ
munirmokṣaparāyaṇaḥ |
vigatecchābhayakrodho
yaḥ sadā mukta eva saḥ |28|

bhoktāraṃ yajñatapasāṃ
sarvalokamaheśvaram |
suhṛdaṃ sarvabhūtānāṃ
jñātvā māṃ śāntimṛcchati |29|

oṃtatsaditi ||
śrīmadbhagavadgītāsūpaniṣatsu
brahmavidyāyāṃ yogaśāstre
śrīkṛṣṇārjunasaṃvāde
saṃnyāsayogo nāma
pañcamo'dhyāyaḥ ||

6

śrībhagavānuvāca *||*
anāśritaḥ karmaphalaṃ
kāryaṃ karma karoti yaḥ |
sa saṃnyāsī ca yogī ca
na niragnirnacākriyaḥ |1|

yaṃ saṃnyāsamiti prāhuḥ
yogaṃ taṃ viddhi pāṇḍava |
na hyasaṃnyastasaṅkalpo
yogī bhavati kaścana |2|

ārurukṣormuneryogaṃ
karma kāraṇamucyate|
yogārūḍhasya tasyaiva
śamaḥ kāraṇamucyate |3|

yadā hi nendriyārtheṣu
na karmasvanuṣajjate |
sarvasaṅkalpasaṃnyāsī
yogārūḍhastadocyate |4|

uddharedātmanātmānaṃ
nātmānamavasādayet |
ātmaiva hyātmano bandhuḥ
ātmaiva ripurātmanaḥ |5|

bandhurātmātmanastasya
yenātmaivātmanā jitaḥ |
anātmanastu śatrutve
vartetātmaiva śatruvat |6|

jitātmanaḥ praśāntasya
paramātmā samāhitaḥ |
śītoṣṇasukhaduḥkheṣu
tathā mānāpamānayoḥ |7|

jñānavijñānatṛptātmā
kūṭastho vijitendriyaḥ |
yukta ityucyate yogī
samaloṣṭāśmakāñcanaḥ |8|

suhṛnmitrāryudāsīna
madhyasthadveṣyabandhuṣu |
sādhuṣvapi ca pāpeṣu
samabuddhirviśiṣyate |9|

yogī yuñjīta satataṃ
ātmānaṃ rahasi sthitaḥ |
ekākī yatacittātmā
nirāśīraparigrahaḥ |10|

śucau deśe pratiṣṭhāpya
sthiramāsanamātmanaḥ |
nātyucchritaṃ nātinīcaṃ
cailājinakuśottaram |11|

tatraikāgraṃ manaḥ kṛtvā
yatacittendriyakriyaḥ |
upaviśyāsane yuñjyāt
yogamātmaviśuddhaye |12|

samaṃ kāyaśirogrīvaṃ
dhārayannacalaṃ sthiraḥ |
saṃprekṣya nāsikāgraṃ svaṃ
diśaścānavalokayan |13|

praśāntātmā vigatabhīḥ
brahmacārivrate sthitaḥ |
manaḥ saṃyamya maccitto
yukta āsīta matparaḥ |14|

yuñjannevaṃ sadātmānaṃ
yogī niyatamānasaḥ |
śāntiṃ nirvāṇaparamāṃ
matsaṃsthāmadhigacchati |15|

nātyaśnatastu yogo'sti
na caikāntamanaśnataḥ |
na cātisvapnaśīlasya
jāgrato naiva cārjuna |16|

yuktāhāravihārasya
yuktaceṣṭasya karmasu |
yuktasvapnāvabodhasya
yogo bhavati duḥkhahā |17|

yadā viniyataṃ cittaṃ
ātmanyevāvatiṣṭhate |
niḥspṛhaḥ sarvakāmebhyo
yukta ityucyate tadā |18|

yathā dīpo nivātastho
neṅgate sopamā smṛtā |
yogino yatacittasya
yuñjato yogamātmanaḥ |19|

yatroparamate cittaṃ
niruddhaṃ yogasevayā |
yatra caivātmanātmānaṃ
paśyannātmani tuṣyati |20|

sukham ātyantikaṃ yattat
buddhigrāhyamatīndriyam |
vetti yatra na caivāyaṃ
sthitaścalati tattvataḥ |21|

yaṃ labdhvā cāparaṃ lābhaṃ
manyate nādhikaṃ tataḥ |
yasmin sthito na duḥkhena
guruṇāpi vicālyate |22|

taṃ vidyād duḥkhasaṃyoga-
viyogaṃ yogasaṃjñitam |
sa niścayena yoktavyo
yogo'nirviṇṇacetasā |23|

saṅkalpaprabhavānkāmān
tyaktvā sarvānaśeṣataḥ |
manasaivendriyagrāmaṃ
viniyamya samantataḥ |24|

śanaiḥ śanairuparamet
buddhyā dhṛtigṛhītayā |
ātmasaṃsthaṃ manaḥ kṛtvā
na kiñcidapi cintayet |25|

yato yato niścarati
manaścañcalamasthiram |
tatastato niyamyaitat
ātmanyeva vaśaṃ nayet |26|

praśāntamanasaṃ hyenaṃ
yoginaṃ sukhamuttamam |
upaiti śāntarajasaṃ
brahmabhūtamakalmaṣam |27|

yuñjannevaṃ sadātmānaṃ
yogī vigatakalmaṣaḥ |
sukhena brahmasaṃsparśaṃ
atyantaṃ sukhamaśnute |28|

sarvabhūtasthamātmānaṃ
sarvabhūtāni cātmani |
īkṣate yogayuktātmā
sarvatra samadarśanaḥ |29|

yo māṃ paśyati sarvatra
sarvaṃ ca mayi paśyati |
tasyāhaṃ na praṇaśyāmi
sa ca me na praṇaśyati |30|

sarvabhūtasthitaṃ yo māṃ
bhajatyekatvamāsthitaḥ |
sarvathā vartamāno'pi
sa yogī mayi vartate |31|

ātmaupamyena sarvatra
samaṃ paśyati yo'rjuna |
sukhaṃ vā yadi vā duḥkhaṃ
sa yogī paramo mataḥ |32|

arjuna uvāca ||
yo'yaṃ yogastvayā proktaḥ
sāmyena madhusūdana |
etasyāhaṃ na paśyāmi
cañcalatvātsthitiṃ sthirām |33|

cañcalaṃ hi manaḥ kṛṣṇa
pramāthi balavaddṛḍham |
tasyāhaṃ nigrahaṃ manye
vāyoriva suduṣkaram |34|

śrībhagavānuvāca ||
asaṃśayaṃ mahābāho
mano durṇigrahaṃ calam |
abhyāsena tu kaunteya
vairāgyeṇa ca gṛhyate |35|

asaṃyatātmanā yogo
duṣprāpa iti me matiḥ |
vaśyātmanā tu yatatā
śakyo'vāptumupāyataḥ |36|

arjuna uvāca ||
ayatiḥ śraddhayopeto
yogāccalitamānasaḥ|
aprāpya yogasaṃsiddhiṃ
kāṃ gatiṃ kṛṣṇa gacchati |37|

kaccinnobhayavibhraṣṭo
chinnābhramiva naśyati |
apratiṣṭho mahābāho
vimūḍho brahmaṇaḥ pathi |38|

etanme saṃśayaṃ kṛṣṇa
chettumarhasyaśeṣataḥ |
tvadanyaḥ saṃśayasyāsya
chettā na hyupapadyate |39|

śrībhagavānuvāca ||
pārtha naiveha nāmutra
vināśastasya vidyate |
na hi kalyāṇakṛtkaścit
durgatiṃ tāta gacchati |40|

prāpya puṇyakṛtāṃ lokān
uṣitvā śāśvatīḥ samāḥ |
śucīnāṃ śrīmatāṃ gehe
yogabhraṣṭo'bhijāyate |41|

atha vā yogināmeva
kule bhavati dhīmatām |
etaddhi durlabhataraṃ
loke janma yadīdṛśam |42|

tatra taṃ buddhisaṃyogaṃ
labhate paurvadehikam |
yatate ca tato bhūyaḥ
saṃsiddhau kurunandana |43|

pūrvābhyāsena tenaiva
hriyate hyavaśo'pi saḥ |
jijñāsurapi yogasya
śabdabrahmātivartate |44|

prayatnādyatamānastu
yogī saṃśuddhakilbiṣaḥ |
anekajanmasaṃsiddhaḥ
tato yāti parāṃ gatim |45|

tapasvibhyo'dhiko yogī
jñānibhyo'pi mato'dhikaḥ |
karmibhyaścādhiko yogī
tasmādyogī bhavārjuna |46|

yogināmapi sarveṣāṃ
madgatenāntarātmanā |
śraddhāvān bhajate yo māṃ
sa me yuktatamo mataḥ |47|

oṃtatsaditi ||
śrīmadbhagavadgītāsūpaniṣatsu
brahmavidyāyāṃ yogaśāstre
śrīkṛṣṇārjunasaṃvāde
dhyānayogo nāma
ṣaṣṭo'dhyāyaḥ ||

7

śrībhagavānuvāca ||
mayyāsaktamanāḥ pārtha
yogaṃ yuñjanmadāśrayaḥ |
asaṃśayaṃ samagraṃ māṃ
yathā jñāsyasi tacchṛṇu |1|

jñānaṃ te'haṃ savijñānaṃ
idaṃ vakṣyāmyaśeṣataḥ |
yajjñātvā neha bhūyo'nyat
jñātavyamavaśiṣyate |2|

manuṣyāṇāṃ sahasreṣu
kaścidyatati siddhaye |
yatatāmapi siddhānāṃ
kaścinmāṃ vetti tattvataḥ |3|

bhūmirāpo'nalo vāyuḥ
khaṃ mano buddhireva ca |
ahaṅkāra itīyaṃme
bhinnā prakṛtiraṣṭadhā |4|

apareyamitastvanyāṃ
prakṛtiṃ viddhi me parām |
jīvabhūtāṃ mahābāho
yayedaṃ dhāryate jagat |5|

etadyonīni bhūtāni
sarvāṇītyupadhāraya |
ahaṃ kṛtsnasya jagataḥ
prabhavaḥ pralayastathā |6|

mattaḥ parataraṃ nānyat
kiñcidasti dhanañjaya |
mayi sarvamidaṃ protaṃ
sūtre maṇigaṇā iva |7|

raso'hamapsu kaunteya
prabhāsmi śaśisūryayoḥ |
praṇavaḥ sarvavedeṣu
śabdaḥ khe pauruṣaṃ nṛṣu |8|

puṇyo gandhaḥ pṛthivyāṃ ca
tejaścāsmi vibhāvasau |
jīvanaṃ sarvabhūteṣu
tapaścāsmi tapasviṣu |9|

bījaṃ māṃ sarvabhūtānāṃ
viddhi pārtha sanātanam |
buddhirbuddhimatāmasmi
tejastejasvināmaham |10|

balaṃbalavatāṃ cāhaṃ
kāmarāgavivarjitam |
dharmāviruddho bhūteṣu
kāmo'smi bharatarṣabha |11|

ye caiva sāttvikā bhāvā
rājasāstāmasāśca ye |
matta eveti tānviddhi
na tvahaṃ teṣu te mayi |12|

tribhirguṇamayairbhāvaiḥ
ebhiḥ sarvamidaṃ jagat |
mohitaṃ nābhijānāti
māmebhyaḥ paramavyayam |13|

daivī hyeṣā guṇamayī
mama māyā duratyayā |
māmeva ye prapadyante
māyāmetāṃ taranti te |14|

na māṃ duṣkṛtino mūḍhāḥ
prapadyante narādhamāḥ |
māyayāpahṛtajñānāḥ
āsuraṃ bhāvamāśritāḥ |15|

caturvidhā bhajante māṃ
janāḥ sukṛtino'rjuna |
ārto jijñāsurarthārthī
jñānī ca bharatarṣabha |16|

teṣāṃ jñānī nityayuktaḥ
ekabhaktirviśiṣyate |
priyo hi jñānino'tyarthaṃ
ahaṃ sa ca mama priyaḥ |17|

udārāḥ sarva evaite
jñānī tvātmaiva me matam |
āsthitaḥ sa hi yuktātmā
mām evānuttamāṃ gatim |18|

bahūnāṃ janmanāmante
jñānavānmāṃ prapadyate |
vāsudevaḥ sarvamiti
sa mahātmā sudurlabhaḥ |19|

kāmaistaistairhṛtajñānāḥ
prapadyante'nyadevatāḥ |
taṃ taṃ niyamamāsthāya
prakṛtyā niyatāḥ svayā |20|

yo yo yāṃ yāṃ tanuṃ bhaktaḥ
śraddhayārcitumicchati |
tasya tasyācalāṃ śraddhāṃ
tāmeva vidadhāmyaham |21|

sa tayā śraddhayā yuktaḥ
tasyārādhanamīhate |
labhate ca tataḥ kāmān
mayaiva vihitānhitān |22|

antavattu phalaṃ teṣāṃ
tadbhavatyalpamedhasām |
devāndevayajo yānti
madbhaktā yānti māmapi |23|

avyaktaṃ vyaktimāpannaṃ
manyante māmabuddhayaḥ|
paraṃ bhāvamajānanto
mamāvyayamanuttamam |24|

nāhaṃ prakāśaḥ sarvasya
yogamāyāsamāvṛtaḥ |
mūḍho'yaṃ nābhijānāti
loko māmajamavyayam |25|

vedāhaṃ samatītāni
vartamānāni cārjuna |
bhaviṣyāṇi ca bhūtāni
māṃ tu veda na kaścana |26|

icchādveṣasamutthena
dvandvamohena bhārata |
sarvabhūtāni saṃmohaṃ
sarge yānti parantapa |27|

yeṣāṃ tvantagataṃ pāpaṃ
janānāṃ puṇyakarmaṇām |
te dvandvamohanirmuktāḥ
bhajante māṃ dṛḍhavratāḥ |28|

jarāmaraṇamokṣāya
māmāśritya yatanti ye |
te brahma tadviduḥ kṛtsnaṃ
adhyātmaṃ karma cākhilam |29|

sādhibhūtādhidaivaṃ māṃ
sādhiyajñaṃ ca ye viduḥ |
prayāṇakāle'pi ca māṃ
te viduryuktacetasaḥ |30|

oṃtatsaditi ||
śrīmadbhagavadgītāsūpaniṣatsu
brahmavidyāyāṃ yogaśāstre
śrīkṛṣṇārjunasaṃvāde
jñānavijñānayogo nāma
saptamo'dhyāyaḥ ||

8

arjuna uvāca ||
kiṃ tadbrahma kimadhyātmaṃ
kiṃ karma puruṣottama |
adhibhūtaṃ ca kiṃ proktaṃ
adhidaivaṃ kimucyate |1|

adhiyajñaḥ kathaṃ ko'tra
dehe'sminmadhusūdana |
prayāṇakāle ca kathaṃ
jñeyo'si niyatātmabhiḥ |2|

śrībhagavānuvāca ||
akṣaraṃ brahma paramaṃ
svabhāvo'dhyātmamucyate |
bhūtabhāvodbhavakaro
visargaḥ karmasaṃjñitaḥ |3|

adhibhūtaṃ kṣaro bhāvaḥ
puruṣaścādhidaivatam |
adhiyajño'hamevātra
dehe dehabhṛtāṃ vara |4|

antakāle ca māmeva
smaranmuktvā kalevaram |
yaḥ prayāti sa madbhāvaṃ
yāti nāstyatra saṃśayaḥ |5|

yaṃ yaṃ vāpi smaranbhāvaṃ
tyajatyante kalevaram |
taṃ tamevaiti kaunteya
sadā tadbhāvabhāvitaḥ |6|

tasmātsarveṣu kāleṣu
māmanusmara yudhya ca |
mayyarpitamanobuddhiḥ
māmevaiṣyasyasaṃśayaḥ |7|

abhyāsayogayuktena
cetasā nānyagāminā |
paramaṃ puruṣaṃ divyaṃ
yāti pārthānucintayan |8|

kaviṃ purāṇamanuśāsitāraṃ
aṇoraṇīyāṃsamanusmaredyaḥ |
sarvasya dhātāramacintyarūpaṃ
ādityavarṇaṃ tamasaḥ parastāt |9|

prayāṇakāle manasācalena
bhaktyā yukto yogabalena caiva |
bhruvormadhye prāṇamāveśya samyak
sa taṃ paraṃ puruṣamupaiti divyam |10|

yadakṣaraṃ vedavido vadanti
viśanti yadyatayo vītarāgāḥ |
yadicchanto brahmacaryaṃ caranti
tatte padaṃ saṅgraheṇa pravakṣye |11|

sarvadvārāṇi saṃyamya
mano hṛdi nirudhya ca |
mūrdhnyādhāyātmanaḥ prāṇaṃ
āsthito yogadhāraṇām |12|

omityekākṣaraṃ brahma
vyāharanmāmanusmaran |
yaḥ prayāti tyajandehaṃ
sa yāti paramāṃ gatim |13|

ananyacetāḥ satataṃ
yo māṃ smarati nityaśaḥ |
tasyāhaṃ sulabhaḥ pārtha
nityayuktasya yoginaḥ |14|

māmupetya punarjanma
duḥkhālayamaśāśvatam |
nāpnuvanti mahātmānaḥ
saṃsiddhiṃ paramāṃ gatāḥ |15|

ābrahmabhuvanāllokāḥ
punarāvartino'rjuna |
māmupetya tu kaunteya
punarjanma na vidyate |16|

sahasrayugaparyantaṃ
aharyadbrahmaṇo viduḥ |
rātriṃ yugasahasrāntāṃ
te'horātravido janāḥ |17|

avyaktādvyaktayaḥ sarvāḥ
prabhavantyaharāgame |
rātryāgame pralīyante
tatraivāvyaktasaṃjñake |18|

bhūtagrāmaḥ sa evāyaṃ
bhūtvā bhūtvā pralīyate |
rātryāgame'vaśaḥ pārtha
prabhavatyaharāgame |19|

parastasmāttu bhāvo'nyo-
'vyakto'vyaktātsanātanaḥ |
yaḥ sa sarveṣu bhūteṣu
naśyatsu na vinaśyati |20|

avyakto'kṣara ityuktaḥ
tamāhuḥ paramāṃ gatim |
yaṃ prāpya na nivartante
taddhāma paramaṃ mama |21|

puruṣaḥ sa paraḥ pārtha
bhaktyā labhyastvananyayā |
yasyāntaḥsthāni bhūtāni
yena sarvamidaṃ tatam |22|

yatra kāle tvanāvṛttiṃ
āvṛttiṃ caiva yoginaḥ |
prayātā yānti taṃ kālaṃ
vakṣyāmi bharatarṣabha |23|

agnirjyotirahaḥ śuklaḥ
ṣaṇmāsā uttarāyaṇam |
tatra prayātā gacchanti
brahma brahmavido janāḥ |24|

dhūmo rātristathākṛṣṇaḥ
ṣaṇmāsā dakṣiṇāyanam |
tatra cāndramasaṃ jyotiḥ
yogī prāpya nivartate |25|

śuklakṛṣṇe gatī hyete
jagataḥ śāśvate mate |
ekayā yātyanāvṛttiṃ
anyayāvartate punaḥ |26|

naite sṛtī pārtha jānan
yogī muhyati kaścana |
tasmātsarveṣu kāleṣu
yogayukto bhavārjuna |27|

vedeṣu yajñeṣu tapaḥsu caiva
dāneṣu yatpuṇyaphalaṃ pradiṣṭam |
atyeti tatsarvamidaṃ viditvā
yogī paraṃ sthānamupaiti cādyam |28|

oṃtatsaditi ||
śrīmadbhagavadgītāsūpaniṣatsu
brahmavidyāyāṃ yogaśāstre
śrīkṛṣṇārjunasaṃvāde
akṣarabrahmayogo nāma
aṣṭamo'dhyāyaḥ ||

9

śrībhagavānuvāca ||
idaṃ tu te guhyatamaṃ
pravakṣyāmyanasūyave |
jñānaṃ vijñānasahitaṃ
yajjñātvā mokṣyase'śubhāt |1|

rājavidyā rājaguhyaṃ
pavitramidamuttamam |
pratyakṣāvagamaṃ dharmyaṃ
susukhaṃ kartumavyayam |2|

aśraddadhānāḥ puruṣāḥ
dharmasyāsya parantapa |
aprāpya māṃ nivartante
mṛtyusaṃsāravartmani |3|

mayā tatamidaṃ sarvaṃ
jagadavyaktamūrtinā |
matsthāni sarvabhūtāni
na cāhaṃ teṣvavasthitaḥ |4|

na ca matsthāni bhūtāni
paśya me yogamaiśvaram |
bhūtabhṛn na ca bhūtastho
mamātmā bhūtabhāvanaḥ |5|

yathākāśasthito nityaṃ
vāyuḥ sarvatrago mahān |
tathā sarvāṇi bhūtāni
matsthānītyupadhāraya |6|

sarvabhūtāni kaunteya
prakṛtiṃ yānti māmikām |
kalpakṣaye punastāni
kalpādau visṛjāmyaham |7|

prakṛtiṃ svāmavaṣṭabhya
visṛjāmi punaḥ punaḥ |
bhūtagrāmamimaṃ kṛtsnaṃ
avaśaṃ prakṛtervaśāt |8|

na ca māṃ tāni karmāṇi
nibadhnanti dhanañjaya |
udāsīnavadāsīnam
asaktaṃ teṣu karmasu |9|

mayādhyakṣeṇa prakṛtiḥ
sūyate sacarācaram |
hetunānena kaunteya
jagadviparivartate |10|

avajānanti māṃ mūḍhāḥ
mānuṣīṃ tanumāśritam |
paraṃ bhāvamajānanto
mama bhūtamaheśvaram |11|

moghāśā moghakarmāṇo
moghajñānā vicetasaḥ |
rākṣasīṃ āsurīṃ caiva
prakṛtiṃ mohinīṃ śritāḥ |12|

mahātmānas tu māṃ pārtha
daivīṃ prakṛtimāśritāḥ |
bhajantyananyamanaso
jñātvā bhūtādimavyayam |13|

satataṃ kīrtayanto māṃ
yatantaśca dṛḍhavratāḥ |
namasyantaśca māṃ bhaktyā
nityayuktā upāsate |14|

jñānayajñena cāpyanye
yajanto māmupāsate |
ekatvena pṛthaktvena
bahudhā viśvatomukham |15|

ahaṃ kraturahaṃ yajñaḥ
svadhāhamahamauṣadham |
mantro'hamahamevājyaṃ
ahamagnirahaṃ hutam |16|

pitāhamasya jagato
mātā dhātā pitāmahaḥ |
vedyaṃ pavitramoṃkāraḥ
ṛksāma yajureva ca |17|

gatirbhartā prabhuḥ sākṣī
nivāsaḥ śaraṇaṃ suhṛt |
prabhavaḥ pralayaḥ sthānaṃ
nidhānaṃ bījamavyayam |18|

tapāmyahamahaṃ varṣaṃ
nigṛhṇāmyutsṛjāmi ca |
amṛtaṃ caiva mṛtyuśca
sadasaccāhamarjuna |19|

traividyā māṃ somapāḥ pūtapāpāḥ
yajñairiṣṭvā svargatiṃ prārthayante |
te puṇyamāsādya surendralokaṃ
aśnanti divyāndivi devabhogān |20|

te taṃ bhuktvā svargalokaṃ viśālaṃ
kṣīṇe puṇye martyalokaṃ viśanti |
evaṃ trayīdharmamanuprapannāḥ
gatāgataṃ kāmakāmā labhante |21|

ananyāścintayanto māṃ
ye janāḥ paryupāsate |
teṣāṃ nityābhiyuktānāṃ
yogakṣemaṃ vahāmyaham |22|

ye'pyanyadevatābhaktāḥ
yajante śraddhayānvitāḥ |
te'pi māmeva kaunteya
yajanty avidhipūrvakam |23|

ahaṃ hi sarvayajñānāṃ
bhoktā ca prabhureva ca |
na tu māmabhijānanti
tattvenātaścyavanti te |24|

yānti devavratā devān
pitṝnyānti pitṛvratāḥ |
bhūtāni yānti bhūtejyāḥ
yānti madyājino'pi mām |25|

patraṃ puṣpaṃ phalaṃ toyaṃ
yo me bhaktyā prayacchati |
tadahaṃ bhaktyupahṛtam
aśnāmi prayatātmanaḥ |26|

yatkaroṣi yadaśnāsi
yajjuhoṣi dadāsi yat |
yattapasyasi kaunteya
tatkuruṣva madarpaṇam |27|

śubhāśubhaphalairevaṃ
mokṣyase karmabandhanaiḥ |
saṃnyāsayogayuktātmā
vimukto māmupaiṣyasi |28|

samo'haṃ sarvabhūteṣu
na me dveṣyo'sti na priyaḥ |
ye bhajanti tu māṃ bhaktyā
mayi te teṣu cāpyaham |29|

api cetsudurācāro
bhajate māmananyabhāk |
sādhureva sa mantavyaḥ
samyagvyavasito hi saḥ |30|

kṣipraṃ bhavati dharmātmā
śaśvacchāntiṃ nigacchati |
kaunteya pratijānīhi
na me bhaktaḥ praṇaśyati |31|

māṃ hi pārtha vyapāśritya
ye'pi syuḥ pāpayonayaḥ |
striyo vaiśyāstathā śūdrāḥ
te'pi yānti parāṃ gatim |32|

kiṃ punarbrāhmaṇāḥ puṇyāḥ
bhaktā rājarṣayastathā |
anityamasukhaṃ lokaṃ
imaṃ prāpya bhajasva mām |33|

manmanā bhava madbhakto
madyājī māṃ namaskuru|
māmevaiṣyasi yuktvaivaṃ
ātmānaṃ matparāyaṇaḥ |34|

oṃtatsaditi ||
śrīmadbhagavadgītāsūpaniṣatsu
brahmavidyāyāṃ yogaśāstre
śrīkṛṣṇārjunasaṃvāde
rājavidyārājaguhayayogo nāma
navamo'dhyāyaḥ ||

10

śrībhagavānuvāca ||
bhūya eva mahābāho
śṛṇu me paramaṃ vacaḥ |
yatte'haṃ prīyamāṇāya
vakṣyāmi hitakāmyayā |1|

na me viduḥ suragaṇāḥ
prabhavaṃ na maharṣayaḥ |
ahamādirhi devānāṃ
maharṣīṇāṃ ca sarvaśaḥ |2|

yo māmajamanādiṃ ca
vetti lokamaheśvaram |
asaṃmūḍhaḥ sa martyeṣu
sarvapāpaiḥ pramucyate |3|

buddhirjñānamasaṃmohaḥ
kṣamā satyaṃ damaḥ śamaḥ |
sukhaṃ duḥkhaṃ bhavo'bhāvo
bhayaṃ cābhayameva ca |4|

ahiṃsā samatā tuṣṭiḥ
tapo dānaṃ yaśo'yaśaḥ |
bhavanti bhāvā bhūtānāṃ
matta eva pṛthagvidhāḥ |5|

maharṣayaḥ sapta pūrve
catvāro manavastathā|
madbhāvā mānasā jātāḥ
yeṣāṃ loka imāḥ prajāḥ |6|

etāṃ vibhūtiṃ yogaṃ ca
mama yo vetti tattvataḥ |
so'vikampena yogena
yujyate nātra saṃśayaḥ |7|

ahaṃ sarvasya prabhavo
mattaḥ sarvaṃ pravartate |
iti matvā bhajante māṃ
budhā bhāvasamanvitāḥ |8|

maccittā madgataprāṇāḥ
bodhayantaḥ parasparam |
kathayantaśca māṃ nityaṃ
tuṣyanti ca ramanti ca |9|

teṣāṃ satatayuktānāṃ
bhajatāṃ prītipūrvakam |
dadāmi buddhiyogaṃ taṃ
yena māmupayānti te |10|

teṣāmevānukampārthaṃ
ahamajñānajaṃ tamaḥ |
nāśayāmyātmabhāvastho
jñānadīpena bhāsvatā |11|

arjuna uvāca ||
paraṃ brahma paraṃdhāma
pavitraṃ paramaṃ bhavān |
puruṣaṃ śāśvataṃ divyaṃ
ādidevamajaṃ vibhum |12|

āhustvāmṛṣayaḥ sarve
devarṣirnāradastathā |
asito devalo vyāsaḥ
svayaṃ caiva bravīṣi me |13|

sarvametadṛtaṃ manye
yanmāṃ vadasi keśava |
na hi te bhagavan vyaktiṃ
vidurdevā na dānavāḥ |14|

svayamevātmanātmānaṃ
vettha tvaṃ puruṣottama |
bhūtabhāvana bhūteśa
devadeva jagatpate |15|

vaktumarhasyaśeṣeṇa
divyā hyātmavibhūtayaḥ |
yābhirvibhūtibhirlokān
imāṃstvaṃ vyāpyatiṣṭhasi |16|

kathaṃ vidyāmahaṃ yogin
tvāṃ sadā paricintayan |
keṣu keṣu ca bhāveṣu
cintyo'si bhagavanmayā |17|

vistareṇātmano yogaṃ
vibhūtiṃ ca janārdana |
bhūyaḥ kathaya tṛptirhi
śṛṇvato nāsti me'mṛtam |18|

śrībhagavānuvāca ||
hanta te kathayiṣyāmi
divyā hyātmavibhūtayaḥ |
prādhānyataḥ kuruśreṣṭha
nāstyanto vistarasya me |19|

ahamātmā guḍākeśa
sarvabhūtāśayasthitaḥ |
ahamādiśca madhyaṃ ca
bhūtānāmanta eva ca |20|

ādityānāmahaṃ viṣṇuḥ
jyotiṣāṃ raviraṃśumān |
marīcirmarutāmasmi
nakṣatrāṇāmahaṃ śaśī |21|

vedānāṃ sāmavedo'smi
devānāmasmi vāsavaḥ |
indriyāṇāṃ manaścāsmi
bhūtānāmasmi cetanā |22|

rudrāṇāṃ śaṅkaraścāsmi
vitteśo yakṣarakṣasām |
vasūnāṃ pāvakaścāsmi
meruḥ śikhariṇāmaham |23|

purodhasāṃ ca mukhyaṃ māṃ
viddhi pārtha bṛhaspatim |
senānīnāmahaṃ skandaḥ
sarasāmasmi sāgaraḥ |24|

maharṣīṇāṃ bhṛguraham
girāmasmyekamakṣaram |
yajñānāṃ japayajño'smi
sthāvarāṇāṃ himālayaḥ |25|

aśvatthaḥ sarvavṛkṣāṇāṃ
devarṣīṇāṃ ca nāradaḥ |
gandharvāṇāṃ citrarathaḥ
siddhānāṃ kapilo muniḥ |26|

uccaiḥśravasamaśvānāṃ
viddhi māmamṛtodbhavam |
airāvataṃ gajendrāṇāṃ
narāṇāṃ ca narādhipam |27|

āyudhānāmahaṃ vajraṃ
dhenūnāmasmi kāmadhuk |
prajanaścāsmi kandarpaḥ
sarpāṇāmasmi vāsukiḥ |28|

anantaścāsmi nāgānāṃ
varuṇo yādasāmaham |
pitṝṇāmaryamā cāsmi
yamaḥ saṃyamatāmaham |29|

prahlādaścāsmi daityānāṃ
kālaḥ kalayatāmaham |
mṛgāṇāṃ ca mṛgendro'haṃ
vainateyaśca pakṣiṇām |30|

pavanaḥ pavatāmasmi
rāmaḥ śastrabhṛtāmaham |
jhaṣāṇāṃ makaraścāsmi
srotasāmasmi jāhnavī |31|

sargāṇāmādirantaśca
madhyaṃ caivāhamarjuna |
adhyātmavidyā vidyānāṃ
vādaḥ pravadatāmaham |32|

akṣarāṇāmakāro'smi
dvandvaḥ sāmāsikasya ca |
ahamevākṣayaḥ kālo
dhātāhaṃ viśvatomukhaḥ |33|

mṛtyuḥ sarvaharaścāhaṃ
udbhavaśca bhaviṣyatām |
kīrtiḥ śrīrvākca nārīṇāṃ
smṛtirmedhā dhṛtiḥ kṣamā |34|

bṛhatsāma tathā sāmnāṃ
gāyatrī chandasāmaham |
māsānāṃ mārgaśīrṣo'haṃ
ṛtūnāṃ kusumākaraḥ |35|

dyūtaṃ chalayatāmasmi
tejas tejasvināmaham |
jayo'smi vyavasāyo'smi
sattvaṃ sattvavatāmaham |36|

vṛṣṇīnāṃ vāsudevo'smi
pāṇḍavānāṃ dhanañjayaḥ |
munīnāmapyahaṃ vyāsaḥ
kavīnāmuśanā kaviḥ |37|

daṇḍo damayatāmasmi
nītirasmi jigīṣatām |
maunaṃ caivāsmi guhyānāṃ
jñānaṃ jñānavatāmaham |38|

yaccāpi sarvabhūtānāṃ
bījaṃ tadahamarjuna |
na tadasti vinā yatsyāt
mayā bhūtaṃ carācaram |39|

nānto'sti mama divyānāṃ
vibhūtīnāṃ parantapa |
eṣa tūddeśataḥ prokto
vibhūtervistaro mayā |40|

yadyadvibhūtimatsattvaṃ
śrīmadūrjitamevavā |
tattadevāvagacchatvaṃ
mama tejo'ṃśasaṃbhavam |41|

athavā bahunaitena
kiṃ jñātena tavārjuna |
viṣṭabhyāhamidaṃ kṛtsnam
ekāṃśena sthito jagat |42|

oṃtatsaditi ||
śrīmadbhagavadgītāsūpaniṣatsu
brahmavidyāyāṃ yogaśāstre
śrīkṛṣṇārjunasaṃvāde
vibhūtiyogo nāma
daśamo'dhyāyaḥ ||

11

arjuna uvāca ||
madanugrahāya param
guhyamadhyātmasaṃjñitam |
yattvayoktaṃ vacastena
moho'yaṃvigato mama |1|

bhavāpyayau hi bhūtānāṃ
śrutau vistaraśo mayā |
tvattaḥ kamalapatrākṣa
māhātmyamapi cāvyayam |2|

evametadyathātthatvaṃ
ātmānaṃ parameśvara |
draṣṭumicchāmi te rūpaṃ
aiśvaraṃ puruṣottama |3|

manyase yadi tacchakyaṃ
mayā draṣṭumiti prabho |
yogeśvara tato me tvaṃ
darśayātmānamavyayam |4|

śrībhagavānuvāca ||
paśya me pārtha rūpāṇi
śataśo'tha sahasraśaḥ |
nānāvidhāni divyāni
nānāvarṇākṛtīni ca |5|

paśyādityān vasūnrudrān
aśvinau marutastathā |
bahūnyadṛṣṭapūrvāṇi
paśyāścaryāṇi bhārata |6|

ihaikasthaṃ jagatkṛtsnaṃ
paśyādya sacarācaram |
mama dehe guḍākeśa
yaccānyaddraṣṭumicchasi |7|

na tu māṃ śakyase draṣṭum
anenaiva svacakṣuṣā |
divyaṃ dadāmi te cakṣuḥ
paśya me yogamaiśvaram |8|

sañjaya uvāca ||
evamuktvā tato rājan
mahāyogeśvaro hariḥ |
darśayāmāsa pārthāya
paramaṃ rūpamaiśvaram |9|

anekavaktranayanaṃ
anekādbhutadarśanam |
anekadivyābharaṇaṃ
divyānekodyatāyudham |10|

divyamālyāmbaradharaṃ
divyagandhānulepanam |
sarvāścaryamayaṃ devaṃ
anantaṃ viśvatomukham |11|

divi sūryasahasrasya
bhavedyugapadutthitā |
yadi bhāḥ sadṛśī sā syāt
bhāsastasya mahātmanaḥ |12|

tatraikasthaṃ jagatkṛtsnaṃ
pravibhaktamanekadhā |
apaśyaddevadevasya
śarīre pāṇḍavastadā |13|

tataḥ sa vismayāviṣṭo
hṛṣṭaromā dhanañjayaḥ |
praṇamya śirasā devaṃ
kṛtāñjalirabhāṣata |14|

arjuna uvāca ||
paśyāmi devāṃstava deva dehe
sarvāṃstathā bhūtaviśeṣasaṅghān |
brahmāṇamīśaṃ kamalāsanasthaṃ
ṛṣīṃśca sarvānuragāṃśca divyān |15|

anekabāhūdaravaktranetraṃ
paśyāmi tvāṃ sarvato'nantarūpam |
nāntaṃ na madhyaṃ na punastavādiṃ
paśyāmi viśveśvara viśvarūpa |16|

kirīṭinaṃ gadinaṃ cakriṇaṃ ca
tejorāśiṃ sarvato dīptimantam |
paśyāmi tvāṃ durnirīkṣyaṃ samantāt
dīptānalārkadyutimaprameyam |17|

tvamakṣaraṃ paramaṃ veditavyaṃ
tvamasya viśvasya paraṃ nidhānam |
tvamavyayaḥ śāśvatadharmagoptā
sanātanastvaṃ puruṣo mato me |18|

anādimadhyāntamanantavīryaṃ
anantabāhuṃ śaśisūryanetram |
paśyāmi tvāṃ dīptahutāśavaktraṃ
svatejasā viśvamidaṃ tapantam |19|

dyāvāpṛthivyoridamantaraṃ hi
vyāptaṃ tvayaikena diśaścasarvāḥ|
dṛṣṭvādbhutaṃ rūpamugram tavedaṃ
lokatrayaṃ pravyathitaṃ mahātman |20|

amī hi tvāṃ surasaṅghā viśanti
kecidbhītāḥ prāñjalayo gṛṇanti |
svastītyuktvā maharṣisiddhasaṅghāḥ
stuvanti tvāṃ stutibhiḥ puṣkalābhiḥ |21|

rudrādityā vasavo ye ca sādhyāḥ
viśve'śvinau marutaścoṣma pāśca |
gandharvayakṣāsurasiddhasaṅghāḥ
vīkṣante tvāṃ vismitāścaiva sarve |22|

rūpaṃ mahatte bahuvaktranetraṃ
mahābāhobahubāhūrupādam |
bahūdaraṃ bahudaṃṣṭrākarālaṃ
dṛṣṭvālokāḥ pravyathitāstathāham |23|

nabhaḥspṛśaṃ dīptamanekavarṇaṃ
vyāttānanaṃ dīptaviśāla netram |
dṛṣṭvā hi tvāṃ pravyathitāntarātmā
dhṛtiṃ na vindāmi śamaṃ ca viṣṇo |24|

daṃṣṭrākarālāni ca te mukhāni
dṛṣṭvaiva kālānalasannibhāni |
diśo na jāne na labhe ca śarma
prasīdadeveśa jagannivāsa |25|

amī ca tvāṃ dhṛtarāṣṭrasya putrāḥ
sarve sahaivāvanipālasaṅghaiḥ |
bhīṣmodroṇaḥ sūtaputrastathāsau
sahāsmadīyairapi yodhamukhyaiḥ |26|

vaktrāṇi te tvaramāṇā viśanti
daṃṣṭrākarālāni bhayānakāni |
kecidvilagnā daśanāntareṣu
saṃdṛśyante cūrṇitairuttamāṅgaiḥ |27|

yathā nadīnāṃ bahavo'mbuvegāḥ
samudramevābhimukhā dravanti |
tathā tavāmī naraloka vīrāḥ
viśanti vaktrāṇyabhivijvalanti |28|

yathā pradīptaṃ jvalanaṃ pataṅgāḥ
viśanti nāśāya samṛddhavegāḥ |
tathaiva nāśāya viśanti lokāḥ
tavāpi vaktrāṇi samṛddhavegāḥ |29|

lelihyase grasamānaḥ samantāt
lokān samagrān vadanairjvaladbhiḥ |
tejobhirāpūrya jagatsamagraṃ
bhāsastavogrāḥ pratapanti viṣṇo |30|

ākhyāhi me ko bhavānugra rūpo
namo'stu te devavara prasīda |
vijñātumicchāmi bhavantamādyaṃ
na hi prajānāmi tava pravṛttim |31|

śrībhagavānuvāca ||
kālo'smi lokakṣayakṛtpravṛddho
lokānsamāhartumiha pravṛttaḥ |
ṛte'pi tvām na bhaviṣyanti sarve
ye'vasthitāḥ pratyanīkeṣu yodhāḥ |32|

tasmāttvamuttiṣṭha yaśo labhasva
jitvā śatrūnbhuṅkṣva rājyaṃ samṛddham |
mayaivaite nihatāḥ pūrvameva
nimittamātraṃ bhava savyasācin |33|

droṇaṃ ca bhīṣmaṃ ca jayadrathaṃ ca
karṇaṃ tathānyānapi yodhavīrān |
mayā hatāṃstvaṃ jahi mā vyathiṣṭhāḥ
yudhyasva jetāsi raṇe sapatnān |34|

sañjaya uvāca ||
etacchrutvā vacanaṃ keśavasya
kṛtāñjalirvepamānaḥ kirīṭī |
namaskṛtvā bhūya evāha kṛṣṇaṃ
sagadgadaṃ bhītabhītaḥ praṇamya |35|

arjuna uvāca ||
sthāne hṛṣīkeśa tava prakīrtyā
jagatprahṛṣyatyanurajyate ca |
rakṣāṃsi bhītāni diśodravanti
sarve namasyanti ca siddhasaṅghāḥ |36|

kasmācca te na nameranmahātman
garīyase brahmaṇo'pyādikartre |
ananta deveśa jagannivāsa
tvamakṣaraṃ sadasattatparaṃ yat |37|

tvamādidevaḥ puruṣaḥ purāṇaḥ
tvamasya viśvasya paraṃ nidhānam |
vettāsi vedyaṃ ca paraṃ ca dhāma
tvayā tataṃ viśvamanantarūpa |38|

vāyuryamo'gnirvaruṇaḥ śaśāṅkaḥ
prajāpatistvaṃ prapitāmahaśca |
namo namaste'stu sahasrakṛtvaḥ
punaśca bhūyo'pi namo namaste |39|

namaḥ purastādatha pṛṣṭhataste
namo'stu te sarvata eva sarva |
anantavīryāmitavikramastvaṃ
sarvaṃ samāpnoṣi tato'si sarvaḥ |40|

sakheti matvā prasabhaṃ yaduktaṃ
he kṛṣṇa he yādava he sakheti |
ajānatā mahimānaṃ tavedaṃ
mayā pramādātpraṇayenavāpi |41|

yaccāvahāsārthamasatkṛto'si
vihāraśayyāsanabhojaneṣu |
eko'thavāpyacyuta tatsamakṣaṃ
tatkṣāmayetvāmahamaprameyam |42|

pitāsi lokasya carācarasya
tvamasya pūjyaśca gururgarīyān |
na tvatsamo'styabhyadhikaḥ kuto'nyo
lokatraye'pyapratimaprabhāva |43|

tasmātpraṇamya praṇidhāya kāyaṃ
prasādayetvām ahamīśamīḍyam |
piteva putrasya sakheva sakhyuḥ
priyaḥ priyāyārhasi deva soḍhum |44|

adṛṣṭapūrvaṃ hṛṣito'smi dṛṣṭvā
bhayena ca pravyathitaṃ manome|
tadeva me darśaya deva rūpaṃ
prasīda deveśa jagannivāsa |45|

kirīṭinaṃ gadinaṃ cakrahastaṃ
icchāmi tvāṃ draṣṭumahaṃ tathaiva |
tenaiva rūpeṇa caturbhujena
sahasrabāho bhava viśvamūrte |46|

***śrībhagavānuvāca** ||*
mayā prasannena tavārjunedaṃ
rūpaṃ paraṃ darśitamātmayogāt |
tejomayaṃ viśvamanantamādyaṃ
yanme tvadanyena na dṛṣṭapūrvam |47|

na vedayajñādhyayanairnadānaiḥ
na ca kriyābhirnatapobhirugraiḥ |
evaṃrūpaḥ śakyamahaṃ nṛloke
draṣṭuṃ tvadanyena kurupravīra |48|

mā te vyathā mā ca vimūḍhabhāvo
dṛṣṭvā rūpaṃ ghoramīdṛṅmamedam |
vyapetabhīḥ prītamanāḥ punastvaṃ
tadeva me rūpamidaṃ prapaśya |49|

***sañjaya uvāca** ||*
ityarjunaṃ vāsudevastathoktvā
svakaṃ rūpaṃ darśayāmāsa bhūyaḥ |
āśvāsayāmāsa ca bhītamenaṃ
bhūtvā punaḥ saumyavapurmahātmā |50|

***arjuna uvāca** ||*
dṛṣṭvedaṃ mānuṣaṃ rūpaṃ
tava saumyaṃ janārdana |
idānīmasmi saṃvṛttaḥ
sacetāḥ prakṛtiṃ gataḥ |51|

***śrībhagavānuvāca** ||*
sudurdarśamidaṃ rūpaṃ
dṛṣṭavānasi yanmama |
devā apyasya rūpasya
nityaṃ darśanakāṅkṣiṇaḥ |52|

nāhaṃ vedairna tapasā
na dānena na cejyayā |
śakya evaṃ vidho draṣṭuṃ
dṛṣṭavānasi māṃ yathā |53|

bhaktyā tvananyayā śakyaḥ
ahamevaṃvidho'rjuna |
jñātuṃ draṣṭuṃ ca tattvena
praveṣṭuṃ ca paraṃtapa |54|

matkarmakṛnmatparamo
madbhaktaḥ saṅgavarjitaḥ |
nirvairaḥ sarvabhūteṣu
yaḥ sa māmeti pāṇḍava |55|

oṃtatsaditi ||
śrīmadbhagavadgītāsūpaniṣatsu
brahmavidyāyāṃ yogaśāstre
śrīkṛṣṇārjunasaṃvāde
viśvarūpadarśanayogo nāma
ekādaśo'dhyāyaḥ ||

12

***arjuna uvāca** ||*
evaṃ satatayuktā ye
bhaktāstvāṃ paryupāsate |
ye cāpyakṣaramavyaktaṃ
teṣāṃ ke yogavittamāḥ |1|

***śrībhagavānuvāca** ||*
mayyāveśya mano ye māṃ
nityayuktā upāsate |
śraddhayā parayopetāḥ
te me yuktatamā matāḥ |2|

ye tvakṣaramanirdeśyaṃ
avyaktaṃ paryupāsate |
sarvatragamacintyaṃ ca
kūṭasthamacalaṃ dhruvam |3|

saṃniyamyendriyagrāmaṃ
sarvatra samabuddhayaḥ |
te prāpnuvanti māmeva
sarvabhūtahite ratāḥ |4|

kleśo'dhikatarasteṣāṃ
avyaktāsaktacetasām |
avyaktā hi gatirduḥkhaṃ
dehavadbhiravāpyate |5|

ye tu sarvāṇi karmāṇi
mayi saṃnyasya matparāḥ |
ananyenaiva yogena
māṃ dhyāyanta upāsate |6|

teṣāmahaṃ samuddhartā
mṛtyusaṃsārasāgarāt |
bhavāmi nacirātpārtha
mayyāveśitacetasām |7|

mayyeva mana ādhatsva
mayi buddhiṃ niveśaya |
nivasiṣyasi mayyeva
ata ūrdhvaṃ na saṃśayaḥ |8|

atha cittaṃ samādhātuṃ
na śaknoṣi mayisthiram |
abhyāsayogena tato
māmicchāptuṃ dhanañjaya |9|

abhyāse'pyasamartho'si
matkarmaparamo bhava |
madarthamapi karmāṇi
kurvansiddhimavāpsyasi |10|

athaitadapyaśakto'si
kartuṃ madyogamāśritaḥ |
sarvakarmaphalatyāgaṃ
tataḥ kuru yatātmavān |11|

śreyo hi jñānamabhyāsāt
jñānāddhyānaṃ viśiṣyate |
dhyānātkarmaphalatyāgaḥ
tyāgācchāntiranantaram |12|

adveṣṭā sarvabhūtānāṃ
maitraḥ karuṇa eva ca |
nirmamo nirahaṅkāraḥ
samaduḥkhasukhaḥ kṣamī |13|

saṃtuṣṭaḥ satataṃ yogī
yatātmā dṛḍhaniścayaḥ |
mayyarpitamanobuddhiḥ
yo madbhaktaḥ sa me priyaḥ |14|

yasmānnodvijate loko
lokānnodvijate ca yaḥ |
harṣāmarṣabhayodvegaiḥ
mukto yaḥ sa ca me priyaḥ |15|

anapekṣaḥ śucirdakṣa
udāsīno gatavyathaḥ |
sarvārambhaparityāgī
yo madbhaktaḥ sa me priyaḥ |16|

yo na hṛṣyati na dveṣṭi
na śocati na kāṅkṣati |
śubhāśubhaparityāgī
bhaktimānyaḥ sa me priyaḥ |17|

samaḥ śatrau ca mitre ca
tathā mānāpamānayoḥ |
śītoṣṇasukhaduḥkheṣu
samaḥ saṅgavivarjitaḥ |18|

tulyanindāstutirmaunī
santuṣṭo yena kenacit |
aniketaḥ sthiramatiḥ
bhaktimān me priyo naraḥ |19|

ye tu dharmyāmṛtamidaṃ
yathoktaṃ paryupāsate |
śraddadhānā matparamāḥ
bhaktāste'tīva me priyāḥ |20|

oṃtatsaditi ||
śrīmadbhagavadgītāsūpaniṣatsu
brahmavidyāyāṃ yogaśāstre
śrīkṛṣṇārjunasaṃvāde
bhaktiyogo nāma
dvādaśo'dhyāyaḥ ||

13

***arjuna uvāca** ||*
prakṛtiṃ puruṣaṃ caiva
kṣetram kṣetrajñameva ca |
etadveditumicchāmi
jñānaṃ jñeyaṃ ca keśava |0|

***śrībhagavānuvāca** ||*
idaṃ śarīraṃ kaunteya
kṣetramityabhidhīyate |
etadyo vetti taṃprāhuḥ
kṣetrajña iti tadvidaḥ |1|

kṣetrajñaṃ cāpi māṃ viddhi
sarvakṣetreṣu bhārata |
kṣetrakṣetrajñayorjñānaṃ
yat tajjñānaṃ mataṃ mama |2|

tat kṣetraṃ yacca yādṛkca
yadvikāri yataśca yat |
sa ca yo yatprabhāvaśca
tat samāsena me śṛṇu |3|

ṛṣibhirbahudhā gītaṃ
chandobhirvividhaiḥ pṛthak |
brahmasūtrapadaiścaiva
hetumadbhirviniścitaiḥ |4|

mahābhūtānyahaṅkāro
buddhiravyaktameva ca |
indriyāṇi daśaikaṃ ca
pañcacendriyagocarāḥ |5|

icchādveṣaḥ sukhaṃ duḥkhaṃ
saṅghātaścetanā dhṛtiḥ |
etatkṣetraṃ samāsena
savikāramudāhṛtam |6|

amānitvamadambhitvaṃ
ahiṃsā kṣāntirārjavam |
ācāryopāsanaṃ śaucaṃ
sthairyamātmavinigrahaḥ |7|

indriyārtheṣu vairāgyaṃ
anahaṅkāra eva ca |
janmamṛtyujarāvyādhi
duḥkhadoṣānudarśanam |8|

asaktiranabhiṣvaṅgaḥ
putradāragṛhādiṣu |
nityaṃ ca samacittatvaṃ
iṣṭāniṣṭopapattiṣu |9|

mayi cānanyayogena
bhaktiravyabhicāriṇī |
viviktadeśasevitvaṃ
aratirjanasaṃsadi |10|

adhyātmajñānanityatvaṃ
tattvajñānārthadarśanam |
etajjñānam iti proktaṃ
ajñānaṃ yadato'nyathā |11|

jñeyaṃ yattat pravakṣyāmi
yajjñātvāmṛtamaśnute |
anādimatparaṃ brahma
na sattannāsaducyate |12|

sarvataḥ pāṇipādaṃ tat
sarvato'kṣiśiromukham |
sarvataḥ śrutimalloke
sarvamāvṛtya tiṣṭhati |13|

sarvendriyaguṇābhāsaṃ
sarvendriyavivarjitam |
asaktaṃ sarvabhṛccaiva
nirguṇaṃ guṇabhoktṛ ca |14|

bahirantaśca bhūtānāṃ
acaraṃ carameva ca |
sūkṣmatvāt tadavijñeyaṃ
dūrasthaṃ cāntike ca tat |15|

avibhaktaṃ ca bhūteṣu
vibhaktamiva ca sthitam |
bhūtabhartṛ ca tajjñeyaṃ
grasiṣṇu prabhaviṣṇu ca |16|

jyotiṣāmapi tajjyotiḥ
tamasaḥ paramucyate |
jñānaṃ jñeyaṃ jñāna gamyaṃ
hṛdi sarvasya viṣṭhitam |17|

iti kṣetraṃ tathā jñānaṃ
jñeyaṃ coktaṃ samāsataḥ |
madbhakta etadvijñāya
madbhāvāyopapadyate |18|

prakṛtiṃ puruṣaṃ caiva
viddhyanādī ubhāvapi |
vikārāṃśca guṇāṃścaiva
viddhi prakṛtisaṃbhavān |19|

kāryakāraṇakartṛtve
hetuḥ prakṛtirucyate |
puruṣaḥ sukhaduḥkhānāṃ
bhoktṛtve heturucyate |20|

puruṣaḥ prakṛtistho hi
bhuṅkte prakṛtijānguṇān |
kāraṇaṃ guṇasaṅgo'sya
sadasadyonijanmasu |21|

upadraṣṭānumantā ca
bhartā bhoktā maheśvaraḥ |
paramātmeti cāpyukto
dehe'smin puruṣaḥ paraḥ |22|

ya evaṃ vetti puruṣaṃ
prakṛtiṃ ca guṇaiḥ saha |
sarvathā vartamāno'pi
na sa bhūyo'bhijāyate |23|

dhyānenātmani paśyanti
kecidātmānamātmanā |
anye sāṅkhyena yogena
karmayogena cāpare |24|

anye tvevamajānantaḥ
śrutvānyebhya upāsate |
te'pi cātitarantyeva
mṛtyuṃ śrutiparāyaṇāḥ |25|

yāvatsañjāyate kincit
sattvaṃ sthāvarajaṅgamam |
kṣetrakṣetrajñasaṃyogāt
tadviddhi bharatarṣabha |26|

samaṃ sarveṣu bhūteṣu
tiṣṭhantaṃ parameśvaram |
vinaśyatsvavinaśyantaṃ
yaḥ paśyati sa paśyati |27|

samaṃ paśyan hi sarvatra
samavasthitamīśvaram |
na hinastyātmanātmānaṃ
tato yāti parāṃ gatim |28|

prakṛtyaiva ca karmāṇi
kriyamāṇāni sarvaśaḥ |
yaḥ paśyati tathātmānaṃ
akartāraṃ sa paśyati |29|

yadā bhūtapṛthagbhāvaṃ
ekastham anupaśyati |
tata eva ca vistāraṃ
brahma saṃpadyate tadā |30|

anāditvān nirguṇatvāt
paramātmāyamavyayaḥ |
śarīrastho'pi kaunteya
na karoti na lipyate |31|

yathā sarvagataṃ saukṣmyāt
ākāśaṃ nopalipyate |
sarvatrāvasthito dehe
tathātmā nopalipyate |32|

yathā prakāśayatyekaḥ
kṛtsnaṃ lokamimaṃ raviḥ |
kṣetraṃ kṣetrī tathā kṛtsnaṃ
prakāśayati bhārata |33|

kṣetrakṣetrajñayorevaṃ
antaraṃ jñānacakṣuṣā |
bhūtaprakṛtimokṣaṃ ca
ye viduryānti te param |34|

oṃtatsaditi ||
śrīmadbhagavadgītāsūpaniṣatsu
brahmavidyāyāṃ yogaśāstre
śrīkṛṣṇārjunasaṃvāde
kṣetrakṣetrajñavibhāgayogo nāma
trayodaśo'dhyāyaḥ ||

14

śrībhagavānuvāca *||*
paraṃ bhūyaḥ pravakṣyāmi
jñānānāṃ jñānamuttamam |
yajjñātvā munayaḥ sarve
parāṃ siddhimitogatāḥ |1|

idaṃ jñānamupāśritya
mama sādharmyamāgatāḥ |
sarge'pi nopajāyante
pralaye na vyathanti ca |2|

mama yonirmahadbrahma
tasmingarbhaṃ dadhāmyaham |
saṃbhavaḥ sarvabhūtānāṃ
tatobhavati bhārata |3|

sarvayoniṣu kaunteya
mūrtayaḥ saṃbhavanti yāḥ |
tāsāṃ brahma mahadyoniḥ
ahaṃ bījapradaḥ pitā |4|

sattvaṃ rajastama iti
guṇāḥ prakṛtisaṃbhavāḥ |
nibadhnanti mahābāho
dehe dehinamavyayam |5|

tatra sattvaṃ nirmalatvāt
prakāśakamanāmayam |
sukhasaṅgena badhnāti
jñānasaṅgena cānagha |6|

rajo rāgātmakaṃ viddhi
tṛṣṇāsaṅgasamudbhavam |
tannibadhnāti kaunteya
karmasaṅgena dehinam |7|

tamastvajñānajaṃ viddhi
mohanaṃ sarvadehinām |
pramādālasyanidrābhiḥ
tannibadhnāti bhārata |8|

sattvaṃ sukhe sañjayati
rajaḥ karmaṇi bhārata |
jñānamāvṛtya tu tamaḥ
pramāde sañjayatyuta |9|

rajastamaścābhibhūya
sattvaṃ bhavati bhārata |
rajaḥ sattvaṃ tamaścaiva
tamaḥ sattvaṃ rajastathā |10|

sarvadvāreṣu dehe'smin
prakāśa upajāyate |
jñānaṃ yadā tadā vidyāt
vivṛddhaṃ sattvamityuta |11|

lobhaḥ pravṛttirārambhaḥ
karmaṇām aśamaḥ spṛhā |
rajasyetāni jāyante
vivṛddhe bharatarṣabha |12|

aprakāśo'pravṛttiśca
pramādo moha eva ca |
tamasyetāni jāyante
vivṛddhe kurunandana |13|

yadā sattve pravṛddhe tu
pralayaṃ yāti dehabhṛt |
tadottamavidāṃ lokān
amalān pratipadyate |14|

rajasi pralayaṃ gatvā
karmasaṅgiṣu jāyate |
tathā pralīnastamasi
mūḍhayoniṣu jāyate |15|

karmaṇaḥ sukṛtasyāhuḥ
sāttvikaṃ nirmalaṃ phalam |
rajasastu phalaṃ duḥkhaṃ
ajñānaṃ tamasaḥ phalam |16|

sattvātsañjāyate jñānaṃ
rajaso lobha eva ca |
pramādamohau tamaso
bhavato'jñānameva ca |17|

ūrdhvaṃ gacchanti sattvasthāḥ
madhye tiṣṭhanti rājasāḥ |
jaghanyaguṇavṛttasthāḥ
adho gacchanti tāmasāḥ |18|

nānyaṃ guṇebhyaḥ kartāraṃ
yadā draṣṭānupaśyati |
guṇebhyaśca paraṃ vetti
madbhāvaṃ so'dhigacchati |19|

guṇānetānatītya trīn
dehī dehasamudbhavān |
janmamṛtyujarāduḥkhaiḥ
vimukto'mṛtamaśnute |20|

***arjuna uvāca** ||*
kair liṅgaistrīnguṇānetān
atīto bhavati prabho |
kimācāraḥ kathaṃ caitān
trīnguṇānativartate |21|

***śrībhagavānuvāca** ||*
prakāśaṃ ca pravṛttiṃ ca
mohameva ca pāṇḍava|
na dveṣṭi saṃpravṛttāni
na nivṛttāni kāṅkṣati |22|

udāsīnavadāsīno
guṇairyo na vicālyate |
guṇā vartanta ityeva
yo'vatiṣṭhati neṅgate |23|

samaduḥkhasukhaḥ svasthaḥ
samaloṣṭāśmakāñcanaḥ |
tulyapriyāpriyo dhīraḥ
tulyanindātmasaṃstutiḥ |24|

mānāpamānayos tulyaḥ
tulyo mitrāripakṣayoḥ |
sarvārambhaparityāgī
guṇātītaḥ sa ucyate |25|

māṃ ca yo'vyabhicāreṇa
bhaktiyogena sevate |
sa guṇān samatītyaitān
brahmabhūyāya kalpate |26|

brahmaṇo hi pratiṣṭhāhaṃ
amṛtasyāvyayasya ca |
śāśvatasya ca dharmasya
sukhasyaikāntikasya ca |27|

oṃtatsaditi ||
śrīmadbhagavadgītāsūpaniṣatsu
brahmavidyāyāṃ yogaśāstre
śrīkṛṣṇārjunasaṃvāde
guṇatrayavibhāgayogo nāma
caturdaśo'dhyāyaḥ ||

15

***śrībhagavānuvāca** ||*
ūrdhvamūlamadhaḥśākhaṃ
aśvatthaṃ prāhuravyayam |
chandāṃsi yasya parṇāni
yastaṃ veda sa vedavit |1|

adhaścordhvaṃ prasṛtās tasya śākhāḥ
guṇapravṛddhā viṣayapravālāḥ |
adhaśca mūlānyanusaṃtatāni
karmānubandhīni manuṣyaloke |2|

na rūpamasyeha tathopalabhyate
nānto na cādirna ca saṃpratiṣṭhā |
aśvatthamenaṃ suvirūḍhamūlaṃ
asaṅgaśastreṇa dṛḍhena chittvā |3|

tataḥ padaṃ tatparimārgitavyaṃ
yasmingatā na nivartanti bhūyaḥ |
tameva cādyaṃ puruṣaṃ prapadye
yataḥ pravṛttiḥ prasṛtā purāṇī |4|

nirmānamohā jitasaṅgadoṣāḥ
adhyātmanityā vinivṛttakāmāḥ |
dvandvairvimuktāḥ sukhaduḥkhasaṃjñaiḥ
gacchantyamūḍhāḥ padamavyayaṃ tat |5|

na tadbhāsayate sūryo
na śaśāṅko na pāvakaḥ |
yadgatvā na nivartante
taddhāma paramaṃ mama |6|

mamaivāṃśo jīvaloke
jīvabhūtaḥ sanātanaḥ |
manaḥṣaṣṭhānīndriyāṇi
prakṛtisthāni karṣati |7|

śarīraṃ yadavāpnoti
yaccāpyutkrāmatīśvaraḥ |
gṛhītvaitāni saṃyāti
vāyurgandhānivāśayāt |8|

śrotraṃ cakṣuḥ sparśanaṃ ca
rasanaṃ ghrāṇameva ca |
adhiṣṭhāya manaścāyaṃ
viṣayānupasevate |9|

utkrāmantaṃ sthitaṃ vāpi
bhuñjānaṃ vā guṇānvitam |
vimūḍhā nānupaśyanti
paśyanti jñānacakṣuṣaḥ |10|

yatanto yoginaścainaṃ
paśyantyātmanyavasthitam |
yatanto'pyakṛtātmāno
nainaṃ paśyantyacetasaḥ |11|

yadādityagataṃ tejo
jagadbhāsayate'khilam |
yaccandramasi yaccāgnau
tattejo viddhi māmakam |12|

gāmāviśya ca bhūtāni
dhārayāmyahamojasā |
puṣṇāmi cauṣadhīḥ sarvāḥ
somo bhūtvā rasātmakaḥ |13|

ahaṃ vaiśvānaro bhūtvā
prāṇināṃ dehamāśritaḥ |
prāṇāpānasamāyuktaḥ
pacāmyannaṃ caturvidham |14|

sarvasya cāhaṃ hṛdi saṃniviṣṭo
mattaḥ smṛtirjñānamapohanaṃ ca |
vedaiśca sarvairaham eva vedyo
vedāntakṛdvedavideva cāham |15|

dvāvimau puruṣau loke
kṣaraścākṣara eva ca |
kṣaraḥ sarvāṇi bhūtāni
kūṭastho'kṣara ucyate |16|

uttamaḥ puruṣastvanyaḥ
paramātmetyudāhṛtaḥ |
yo lokatrayamāviśya
bibhartyavyaya īśvaraḥ |17|

yasmāt kṣaramatīto'haṃ
akṣarādapi cottamaḥ |
ato'smi loke vede ca
prathitaḥ puruṣottamaḥ |18|

yo māmevamasaṃmūḍho
jānāti puruṣottamam |
sa sarvavidbhajati māṃ
sarvabhāvena bhārata |19|

iti guhyatamaṃ śāstraṃ
idamuktaṃ mayānagha |
etadbuddhvā buddhimān syāt
kṛtakṛtyaśca bhārata |20|

oṃtatsaditi ||
śrīmadbhagavadgītāsūpaniṣatsu
brahmavidyāyāṃ yogaśāstre
śrīkṛṣṇārjunasaṃvāde
puruṣottamayogo nāma
pañcadaśo'dhyāyaḥ ||

16

śrībhagavānuvāca ||
abhayaṃ sattvasaṃśuddhiḥ
jñānayogavyavasthitiḥ |
dānaṃ damaśca yajñaśca
svādhyāyas tapa ārjavam |1|

ahiṃsā satyamakrodhaḥ
tyāgaḥ śāntirapaiśunam |
dayā bhūteṣvaloluptvaṃ
mārdavaṃ hrīracāpalam |2|

tejaḥ kṣamā dhṛtiḥ śaucaṃ
adroho nātimānitā |
bhavanti saṃpadaṃ daivīm
abhijātasya bhārata |3|

dambho darpo'timānaśca
krodhaḥ pāruṣyameva ca |
ajñānaṃ cābhijātasya
pārtha saṃpadamāsurīm |4|

daivī saṃpadvimokṣāya
nibandhāyāsurī matā |
mā śucaḥ saṃpadaṃ daivīṃ
abhijāto'si pāṇḍava |5|

dvau bhūtasargau loke'smin
daiva āsura eva ca |
daivo vistaraśaḥ proktaḥ
āsuraṃ pārtha me śṛṇu |6|

pravṛttiṃ ca nivṛttiṃ ca
janā na vidurāsurāḥ |
na śaucaṃ nāpi cācāro
na satyaṃ teṣu vidyate |7|

asatyam apratiṣṭhaṃ te
jagadāhuranīśvaram |
aparasparasaṃbhūtaṃ
kimanyat kāmahaitukam |8|

etāṃ dṛṣṭimavaṣṭabhya
naṣṭātmāno'lpabuddhayaḥ |
prabhavantyugrakarmāṇaḥ
kṣayāya jagato'hitāḥ |9|

kāmamāśritya duṣpūraṃ
dambhamānamadānvitāḥ |
mohādgṛhītvāsadgrāhān
pravartante'śucivratāḥ |10|

cintāmaparimeyāṃ ca
pralayāntāmupāśritāḥ |
kāmopabhogaparamā
etāvaditi niścitāḥ |11|

āśāpāśaśatairbaddhāḥ
kāmakrodhaparāyaṇāḥ |
īhante kāmabhogārthaṃ
anyāyenārthasañcayān |12|

idamadya mayā labdham
idaṃ prāpsye manoratham |
idamastīdamapi me
bhaviṣyati punardhanam |13|

asau mayā hataḥ śatruḥ
haniṣye cāparānapi |
īśvaro'hamahaṃ bhogī
siddho'haṃ balavān sukhī |14|

āḍhyo'bhijanavānasmi
ko'nyo'sti sadṛśo mayā |
yakṣye dāsyāmi modiṣya
ityajñānavimohitāḥ |15|

anekacittavibhrāntā
mohajālasamāvṛtāḥ |
prasaktāḥ kāmabhogeṣu
patanti narake'śucau |16|

ātmasaṃbhāvitāḥ stabdhā
dhanamānamadānvitāḥ |
yajante nāmayajñaiste
dambhenāvidhipūrvakam |17|

ahaṅkāraṃ balaṃ darpaṃ
kāmaṃ krodhaṃ ca saṃśritāḥ |
māmātmaparadeheṣu
pradviṣanto'bhyasūyakāḥ |18|

tānahaṃ dviṣataḥ krūrān
saṃsāreṣu narādhamān |
kṣipāmyajasram aśubhān
āsurīṣveva yoniṣu |19|

āsurīṃ yonimāpannā
mūḍhā janmani janmani |
māmaprāpyaiva kaunteya
tato yāntyadhamāṃ gatim |20|

trividhaṃ narakasyedaṃ
dvāraṃ nāśanamātmanaḥ |
kāmaḥ krodhastathā lobhaḥ
tasmādetattrayaṃ tyajet |21|

etairvimuktaḥ kaunteya
tamodvāraistribhirnaraḥ |
ācaratyātmanaḥ śreyaḥ
tato yāti parāṃ gatim |22|

yaḥ śāstravidhimutsṛjya
vartate kāmakārataḥ |
na sa siddhimavāpnoti
na sukhaṃ na parāṃ gatim |23|

tasmācchāstraṃ pramāṇaṃ te
kāryākāryavyavasthitau |
jñātvā śāstravidhānoktaṃ
karma kartumihārhasi |24|

oṃtatsaditi ||
śrīmadbhagavadgītāsūpaniṣatsu
brahmavidyāyāṃ yogaśāstre
śrīkṛṣṇārjunasaṃvāde
daivāsurasampadvibhāgayogo nāma
ṣoḍaśo'dhyāyaḥ ||

17

arjuna uvāca ||
ye śāstravidhimutsṛjya
yajante śraddhayānvitāḥ |
teṣāṃ niṣṭhā tu kā kṛṣṇa
sattvamāho rajastamaḥ |1|

śrībhagavānuvāca ||
trividhā bhavati śraddhā
dehināṃ sā svabhāvajā |
sāttvikī rājasī caiva
tāmasī ceti tāṃ śṛṇu |2|

sattvānurūpā sarvasya
śraddhā bhavati bhārata |
śraddhāmayo'yaṃ puruṣo
yo yacchraddhaḥ sa eva saḥ |3|

yajante sāttvikā devān
yakṣarakṣāṃsi rājasāḥ |
pretān bhūtagaṇāṃścānye
yajante tāmasā janāḥ |4|

aśāstravihitaṃ ghoraṃ
tapyante ye tapo janāḥ |
dambhāhaṅkārasaṃyuktāḥ
kāmarāgabalānvitāḥ |5|

karśayantaḥ śarīrasthaṃ
bhūtagrāmamacetasaḥ |
māṃ caivāntaḥśarīrasthaṃ
tānviddhyāsuraniścayān |6|

āhārastvapi sarvasya
trividho bhavati priyaḥ |
yajñastapastathā dānaṃ
teṣāṃ bhedamimaṃ śṛṇu |7|

āyuḥsattvabalārogya
sukhaprītivivardhanāḥ |
rasyāḥ snigdhāḥ sthirā hṛdyā
āhārāḥ sāttvikapriyāḥ |8|

kaṭvamlalavaṇātyuṣṇa
tīkṣṇarūkṣavidāhinaḥ |
āhārā rājasasyeṣṭā
duḥkhaśokāmayapradāḥ |9|

yātayāmaṃ gatarasaṃ
pūti paryuṣitaṃ ca yat |
ucchiṣṭamapi cāmedhyaṃ
bhojanaṃ tāmasapriyam |10|

aphalākāṅkṣibhiryajño
vidhidṛṣṭo ya ijyate |
yaṣṭavyameveti manaḥ
samādhāya sa sāttvikaḥ |11|

abhisaṃdhāya tu phalaṃ
dambhārthamapi caiva yat |
ijyate bharataśreṣṭha
taṃ yajñaṃ viddhi rājasam |12|

vidhihīnamasṛṣṭānnaṃ
mantrahīnamadakṣiṇam |
śraddhāvirahitaṃ yajñaṃ
tāmasaṃ paricakṣate |13|

devadvijaguruprājña
pūjanaṃ śaucamārjavam |
brahmacaryam ahiṃsā ca
śārīraṃ tapa ucyate |14|

anudvegakaraṃ vākyaṃ
satyaṃ priyahitaṃ ca yat |
svādhyāyābhyasanaṃ caiva
vāṅmayaṃ tapa ucyate |15|

manaḥprasādaḥ saumyatvaṃ
maunamātmavinigrahaḥ |
bhāvasaṃśuddhirityetat
tapo mānasam ucyate |16|

śraddhayā parayā taptaṃ
tapastattrividhaṃ naraiḥ |
aphalākāṅkṣibhiryuktaiḥ
sāttvikaṃ paricakṣate |17|

satkāramānapūjārthaṃ
tapo dambhena caiva yat |
kriyate tadiha proktaṃ
rājasaṃ calamadhruvam |18|

mūḍhagrāheṇātmano yat
pīḍayā kriyate tapaḥ |
parasyotsādanārthaṃ vā
tattāmasamudāhṛtam |19|

dātavyamiti yaddānaṃ
dīyate'nupakāriṇe |
deśe kāle ca pātre ca
taddānaṃ sāttvikaṃ smṛtam |20|

yattu pratyupakārārthaṃ
phalamuddiśya vā punaḥ |
dīyate ca parikliṣṭaṃ
taddānaṃ rājasaṃ smṛtam |21|

adeśakāle yaddānaṃ
apātrebhyaśca dīyate |
asatkṛtamavajñātaṃ
tattāmasamudāhṛtam |22|

oṃ tatsaditi nirdeśo
brahmaṇastrividhaḥ smṛtaḥ |
brāhmaṇāstena vedāśca
yajñāśca vihitāḥ purā |23|

tasmādomityudāhṛtya
yajñadānatapaḥkriyāḥ |
pravartante vidhānoktāḥ
satataṃ brahmavādinām |24|

tadityanabhisaṃdhāya
phalaṃ yajñatapaḥkriyāḥ |
dānakriyāśca vividhāḥ
kriyante mokṣakāṅkṣibhiḥ |25|

sadbhāve sādhubhāve ca
sadityetatprayujyate |
praśaste karmaṇi tathā
sacchabdaḥ pārtha yujyate |26|

yajñe tapasi dāne ca
sthitiḥ saditi cocyate |
karma caiva tadarthīyaṃ
sadityevābhidhīyate |27|

aśraddhayā hutaṃ dattaṃ
tapastaptaṃ kṛtaṃ ca yat |
asadityucyate pārtha
na ca tatpretya no iha |28|

oṃtatsaditi ||
śrīmadbhagavadgītāsūpaniṣatsu
brahmavidyāyāṃ yogaśāstre
śrīkṛṣṇārjunasaṃvāde
śraddhātrayavibhāgayogo nāma
saptadaśo'dhyāyaḥ ||

18

***arjuna uvāca** ||*
saṃnyāsasya mahābāho
tattvamicchāmi veditum |
tyāgasya ca hṛṣīkeśa
pṛthakkeśiniṣūdana |1|

***śrībhagavānuvāca** ||*
kāmyānāṃ karmaṇāṃ nyāsaṃ
saṃnyāsaṃ kavayo viduḥ |
sarvakarmaphalatyāgaṃ
prāhustyāgaṃ vicakṣaṇāḥ |2|

tyājyaṃ doṣavadityeke
karma prāhurmanīṣiṇaḥ |
yajñadānatapaḥkarma
na tyājyam iti cāpare |3|

niścayaṃ śṛṇu me tatra
tyāge bharatasattama |
tyāgo hi puruṣavyāghra
trividhaḥ saṃprakīrtitaḥ |4|

yajñadānatapaḥkarma
na tyājyaṃ kāryameva tat |
yajño dānaṃ tapaścaiva
pāvanāni manīṣiṇām |5|

etānyapi tu karmāṇi
saṅgaṃ tyaktvā phalāni ca |
kartavyānīti me pārtha
niścitaṃ matamuttamam |6|

niyatasya tu saṃnyāsaḥ
karmaṇonopapadyate |
mohāttasya parityāgaḥ
tāmasaḥ parikīrtitaḥ |7|

duḥkhamityeva yatkarma
kāyakleśabhayāt tyajet |
sa kṛtvā rājasaṃ tyāgaṃ
naiva tyāgaphalaṃ labhet |8|

kāryamityeva yatkarma
niyataṃ kriyate'rjuna |
saṅgaṃ tyaktvā phalaṃ caiva
sa tyāgaḥ sāttviko mataḥ |9|

na dveṣṭyakuśalaṃ karma
kuśale nānuṣajjate |
tyāgī sattvasamāviṣṭo
medhāvī chinnasaṃśayaḥ |10|

na hi dehabhṛtā śakyaṃ
tyaktuṃ karmāṇyaśeṣataḥ |
yastu karmaphalatyāgī
sa tyāgītyabhidhīyate |11|

aniṣṭamiṣṭaṃ miśraṃ ca
trividhaṃ karmaṇaḥ phalam |
bhavatyatyāgināṃ pretya
na tu saṃnyāsināṃ kvacit |12|

pañcaitāni mahābāho
kāraṇāni nibodha me |
sāṅkhye kṛtānte proktāni
siddhaye sarvakarmaṇām |13|

adhiṣṭhānaṃ tathā kartā
karaṇaṃ ca pṛthagvidham |
vividhāśca pṛthakceṣṭā
daivaṃ caivātra pañcamam |14|

śarīravāṅmanobhiryat
karma prārabhate naraḥ |
nyāyyaṃ vā viparītaṃ vā
pañcaite tasya hetavaḥ |15|

tatraivaṃ sati kartāram
ātmānaṃ kevalaṃ tu yaḥ |
paśyatyakṛtabuddhitvāt
na sa paśyati durmatiḥ |16|

yasya nāhaṅkṛto bhāvo
buddhiryasya na lipyate |
hatvāpi sa imāṁllokān
na hanti na nibadhyate |17|

jñānaṃ jñeyaṃ parijñātā
trividhā karmacodanā |
karaṇaṃ karma karteti
trividhaḥ karmasaṅgrahaḥ |18|

jñānaṃ karma ca kartā ca
tridhaiva guṇabhedataḥ |
procyate guṇasaṅkhyāne
yathāvacchṛṇu tānyapi |19|

sarvabhūteṣu yenaikaṃ
bhāvamavyayamīkṣate |
avibhaktaṃ vibhakteṣu
tajjñānaṃ viddhi sāttvikam |20|

pṛthaktvena tu yajjñānaṃ
nānābhāvān pṛthagvidhān |
vetti sarveṣu bhūteṣu
tajjñānaṃ viddhi rājasam |21|

yattu kṛtsnavadekasmin
kārye saktamahaitukam |
atattvārthavadalpaṃ ca
tattāmasamudāhṛtam |22|

niyataṃ saṅgarahitaṃ
arāgadveṣataḥ kṛtam |
aphalaprepsunā karma
yattat sāttvikamucyate |23|

yattu kāmepsunā karma
sāhaṅkāreṇa vā punaḥ |
kriyate bahulāyāsaṃ
tadrājasamudāhṛtam |24|

anubandhaṃ kṣayaṃ hiṃsāṃ
anapekṣya ca pauruṣam |
mohādārabhyate karma
yattattāmasamucyate |25|

muktasaṅgo'nahaṃvādī
dhṛtyutsāhasamanvitaḥ |
siddhyasiddhyornirvikāraḥ
kartā sāttvikaucyate |26|

rāgī karmaphalaprepsuḥ
lubdho hiṃsātmako'śuciḥ |
harṣaśokānvitaḥ kartā
rājasaḥ parikīrtitaḥ |27|

ayuktaḥ prākṛtaḥ stabdhaḥ
śaṭho naikṛtiko'lasaḥ |
viṣādī dīrghasūtrī ca
kartā tāmasamucyate |28|

buddherbhedaṃ dhṛteścaiva
guṇata trividhaṃ śṛṇu |
procyamānamaśeṣeṇa
pṛthaktvena dhanañjaya |29|

pravṛttiṃ ca nivṛttiṃ ca
kāryākārye bhayābhaye |
bandhaṃ mokṣaṃ ca yā vetti
buddhiḥ sā pārtha sāttvikī |30|

yayā dharmamadharmaṃ ca
kāryaṃcākāryameva ca |
ayathāvatprajānāti
buddhiḥ sā pārtha rājasī |31|

adharmaṃdharmamiti yā
manyate tamasāvṛtā |
sarvārthān viparītāṃśca
buddhiḥ sā pārtha tāmasī |32|

dhṛtyā yayā dhārayate
manaḥprāṇendriyakriyāḥ |
yogenāvyabhicāriṇyā
dhṛtiḥ sā pārtha sāttvikī |33|

yayā tu dharmakāmārthān
dhṛtyā dhārayate'rjuna |
prasaṅgena phalākāṅkṣī
dhṛtiḥ sā pārtha rājasī |34|

yayā svapnaṃ bhayaṃ śokaṃ
viṣādaṃ madameva ca |
na vimuñcati durmedhā
dhṛtiḥ sā pārtha tāmasī |35|

sukhaṃ tvidānīṃ trividhaṃ
śṛṇu me bharatarṣabha |
abhyāsādramate yatra
duḥkhāntaṃ ca nigacchati |36|

yattadagre viṣamiva
pariṇāme'mṛtopamam |
tatsukhaṃ sāttvikaṃ proktaṃ
ātmabuddhiprasādajam |37|

viṣayendriyasaṃyogāt
yattadagre'mṛtopamam |
pariṇāme viṣamiva
tatsukhaṃ rājasaṃ smṛtam |38|

yadagre cānubandhe ca
sukhaṃ mohanamātmanaḥ |
nidrālasyapramādotthaṃ
tattāmasamudāhṛtam |39|

na tadasti pṛthivyāṃ vā
divideveṣu vā punaḥ |
sattvaṃ prakṛtijairmuktaṃ
yadebhiḥ syāttribhirguṇaiḥ |40|

brāhmaṇakṣatriyaviśāṃ
śūdrāṇāṃ ca parantapa |
karmāṇi pravibhaktāni
svabhāvaprabhavairguṇaiḥ |41|

śamo damastapaḥ śaucaṃ
kṣāntirārjavameva ca |
jñānaṃ vijñānamāstikyaṃ
brahmakarma svabhāvajam |42|

śauryaṃ tejo dhṛtirdākṣyaṃ
yuddhe cāpyapalāyanam |
dānamīśvarabhāvaśca
kṣātraṃkarma svabhāvajam |43|

kṛṣigorakṣyavāṇijyaṃ
vaiśyakarma svabhāvajam |
paricaryātmakaṃ karma
śūdrasyāpi svabhāvajam |44|

sve sve karmaṇyabhirataḥ
saṃsiddhiṃ labhate naraḥ |
svakarmanirataḥ siddhiṃ
yathā vindati tacchṛṇu |45|

yataḥ pravṛttirbhūtānāṃ
yena sarvamidaṃ tatam |
svakarmaṇā tamabhyarcya
siddhiṃ vindati mānavaḥ |46|

śreyānsvadharmo viguṇaḥ
paradharmāt svanuṣṭhitāt |
svabhāvaniyataṃ karma
kurvannāpnoti kilbiṣam |47|

sahajaṃ karma kaunteya
sadoṣamapi na tyajet |
sarvārambhā hi doṣeṇa
dhūmenāgnirivāvṛtāḥ |48|

asaktabuddhiḥ sarvatra
jitātmā vigataspṛhaḥ |
naiṣkarmyasiddhiṃ paramāṃ
saṃnyāsenādhigacchati |49|

siddhiṃprāpto yathā brahma
tathāpnoti nibodha me |
samāsenaiva kaunteya
niṣṭhājñānasya yā parā |50|

buddhyā viśuddhayā yukto
dhṛtyātmānaṃ niyamya ca |
śabdādīn viṣayāṃstyaktvā
rāgadveṣau vyudasya ca |51|

viviktasevī laghvāśī
yatavākkāyamānasaḥ |
dhyānayogaparo nityaṃ
vairāgyaṃ samupāśritaḥ |52|

ahaṅkāraṃ balaṃ darpaṃ
kāmaṃ krodhaṃ parigraham |
vimucya nirmamaḥ śānto
brahmabhūyāya kalpate |53|

brahmabhūtaḥ prasannātmā
na śocati na kāṅkṣati |
samaḥ sarveṣu bhūteṣu
madbhaktiṃ labhate parām |54|

bhaktyā māmabhijānāti
yāvān yaścāsmi tattvataḥ |
tato māṃ tattvato jñātvā
viśate tadanantaram |55|

sarvakarmāṇyapi sadā
kurvāṇo madvyapāśrayaḥ |
matprasādādavāpnoti
śāśvataṃ padamavyayam |56|

cetasā sarvakarmāṇi
mayi saṃnyasya matparaḥ |
buddhiyogamupāśritya
maccittaḥ satataṃ bhava |57|

maccittaḥ sarvadurgāṇi
matprasādāt tariṣyasi |
atha cettvamahaṅkārāt
na śroṣyasi vinaṅkṣyasi |58|

yadahaṅkāramāśritya
na yotsya iti manyase |
mithyaiṣa vyavasāyaste
prakṛtistvāṃ niyokṣyati |59|

svabhāvajena kaunteya
nibaddhaḥ svena karmaṇā |
kartuṃ necchasi yanmohāt
kariṣyasyavaśo'pi tat |60|

īśvaraḥ sarvabhūtānāṃ
hṛddeśe'rjuna tiṣṭhati |
bhrāmayansarvabhūtāni
yantrārūḍhāni māyayā |61|

tameva śaraṇaṃ gaccha
sarvabhāvena bhārata |
tatprasādātparāṃ śāntiṃ
sthānaṃ prāpsyasi śāśvatam |62|

iti te jñānamākhyātaṃ
guhyādguhyataraṃ mayā |
vimṛśyaitadaśeṣeṇa
yathecchasi tathā kuru |63|

sarvaguhyatamaṃ bhūyaḥ
śṛṇu me paramaṃ vacaḥ |
iṣṭo'si me dṛḍham iti
tato vakṣyāmi te hitam |64|

manmanā bhava madbhakto
madyājī māṃ namaskuru |
māmevaiṣyasi satyaṃ te
pratijāne priyo'si me |65|

sarvadharmānparityajya
māmekaṃ śaraṇaṃ vraja |
ahaṃ tvā sarvapāpebhyo
mokṣayiṣyāmi mā śucaḥ |66|

idaṃ te nātapaskāya
nābhaktāya kadā cana |
na cāśuśrūṣave vācyaṃ
na ca māṃ yo'bhyasūyati |67|

ya idaṃ paramaṃ guhyaṃ
madbhakteṣvabhidhāsyati |
bhaktiṃ mayi parāṃ kṛtvā
māmevaiṣyatyasaṃśayaḥ |68|

na ca tasmān manuṣyeṣu
kaścinme priyakṛttamaḥ |
bhavitā na ca me tasmāt
anyaḥ priyataro bhuvi |69|

adhyeṣyate ca ya imaṃ
dharmyaṃ saṃvādamāvayoḥ |
jñānayajñena tenāhaṃ
iṣṭaḥsyāmiti me matiḥ |70|

śraddhāvān anasūyaśca
śṛṇuyādapi yo naraḥ |
so'pi muktaḥ śubhāṁllokān
prāpnuyātpuṇyakarmaṇām |71|

kaccid etacchrutaṃ pārtha
tvayaikāgreṇa cetasā |
kaccidajñānasaṃmohaḥ
pranaṣṭaste dhanañjaya |72|

***arjuna uvāca** ||*
naṣṭo mohaḥ smṛtirlabdhā
tvatprasādānmayācyuta |
sthito'smi gatasaṃdehaḥ
kariṣye vacanaṃ tava |73|

***sañjaya uvāca** ||*
ityahaṃ vāsudevasya
pārthasya ca mahātmanaḥ |
saṃvādamimamaśrauṣam
adbhutaṃ romaharṣaṇam |74|

vyāsaprasādācchrutavān
etadguhyamahaṃ param |
yogaṃ yogeśvarātkṛṣṇāt
sākṣātkathayataḥ svayam |75|

rājansaṃsmṛtya saṃsmṛtya
saṃvādamimam adbhutam |
keśavārjunayoḥ puṇyaṃ
hṛṣyāmi ca muhurmuhuḥ |76|

tacca saṃsmṛtya saṃsmṛtya
rūpamatyadbhutaṃ hareḥ |
vismayo me mahānrājan
hṛṣyāmi ca punaḥ punaḥ |77|

yatra yogeśvaraḥ kṛṣṇo
yatra pārtho dhanurdharaḥ |
tatra śrīrvijayo bhūtiḥ
dhruvā nītirmatirmama |78|

oṃtatsaditi ||
śrīmadbhagavadgītāsūpaniṣatsu
brahmavidyāyāṃ yogaśāstre
śrīkṛṣṇārjunasaṃvāde
mokṣasaṃnyāsayogo nāma
aṣṭādaśo'dhyāyaḥ ||

APPENDIX 3 Glossary

Some Important Concepts in Hinduism

Harmony • Truth is one, god is one; people call it by different names. Different people have different perspectives and so in a broad sense, there are as many religions as there are people. Hinduism is pluralistic, tolerant, and encompasses diverse paths. It emphasizes on conduct more than creed. And everyone is free to practice it.

Inner Voice • Hinduism encourages introspection and intuitive approach to learning. It considers personal experience more real than knowledge gained by reading or listening. True happiness is within; embark on that inward journey and listen to the inner voice.

Nurture • Life supports life; avoid causing harm. Some Hindu groups stress on vegetarianism but it is not a must for a Hindu. Enjoy all blessings (food, wealth, relationships, fame, etc.) with gratitude and detachment, and don't be greedy after another's share.

Dharma • Support what is right, for the greater good. This is a necessity and is the basis of sustaining harmony. Not supporting *dharma* is akin to chopping branches of a tree under which one is taking shade.

Unity • All living beings and non-living objects are inter-connected; they are essentially manifestations of *brahman*. The world is one family.

Inner Strength • One should neither degrade oneself nor be pretentious. One should elevate oneself by one's own efforts – this is a personal responsibility. A little effort in the right direction goes a long way and also no effort ever goes waste.

Supreme • One becomes sustained if one knows the sustaining power of the Supreme (god, *brahman*). When things get out of control, the Supreme incarnates into an earthly form to set things right. One can worship the Supreme as a god with pretty much any form, or as a formless spirit. On the whole, it is more important to respect the divine presence in the universe. Thus, Hinduism readily appeals to both theists and agnostics.

Moksha • It is the highest goal of life and it refers to 'liberation from cycles of birth and death', 'going beyond the dualities', and 'becoming one with *brahman*'. There are numerous paths and opportunities for attaining *moksha*, including: *karma yoga* (selfless action), *jnana yoga* (path of knowledge), *bhakti yoga* (devotion), *prapatti* (surrender to Supreme), *raja yoga* (control of body, mind, and intellect), *dhyana* (meditation), and *japa* (repetition of a *mantra*, a sacred word or verse used for prayer or meditation). The other goals of life are *dharma* (good deeds), *artha* (wealth), and *kama* (pleasures). To achieve the goals of life, it is best to stay close to one's own attitudes and aptitudes.

Few Important Terms in the Gita

atman (ātman) • The inner, higher self of an individual. It also refers to 'soul' or 'spirit'.

avatara (avatāra) • Incarnation; usually refers to incarnation of the Supreme. History has shown that during a great crisis, someone rises to the occasion, assumes leadership, and brings about change. In the Bhagavad-Gita, Krishna presents the concept of *avatara* without any limitations of space or time.

brahman (brahman) • The imperishable, supreme being. *Brahman* is the source and sustainer of the entire universe; there is nothing beyond *brahman.*

brahmacharya (brahmacarya) • Following the path of *brahman.* It refers to leading a life of purity and not letting the mind wander around trivial things.

dharma (dharma) • That which sustains everything; refers to harmony in the universe that sustains greater good. By definition, *dharma* protects one who protects it. The word '*dharma*' has many different meanings; depending on the context, it can mean one or more of: virtue, moral principle, righteousness, religion, law, duty, path, state, etc.

guna (guṇa) • In general refers to the inherent tendencies or traits of a human being. In the context of *guna-traya*, it represents three types of *guna*: *sattva* (saintly goodness), *rajas* (restless activity), and *tamas* (deluded lethargy). Often these *guna-traya* are simply referred to as *guna.*

guru (guru) • Remover of darkness and ignorance, spiritual guide, or teacher.

karma (karma) • Action; includes all spheres of work. *Karma* is also the work that is suited to *guna.* In general, *karma* refers to all the activities associated with origin, sustenance, and destruction, including the creative impulse that brought all creation into existence and keeps it going. *Karma* also refers to the consequences of our actions (see *vasana*).

karma yoga (karma yoga) • Path of selfless action.

maya (māyā) • The divine power of illusion.

om (om) • The most sacred sound in Hinduism; this single syllable word represents god and the universe. '*Om*' has four parts: 'a', 'u', 'm', and silence. The 'a' represents birth, 'u' represents growth, 'm' represents letting go, and the silence represents immortality.

prakriti (prakṛti) • Material nature or surrounding environment; the source of the five elements and the body, including the five senses, mind, ego, intellect, *guna*, and *prana*.

prana (prāṇa) • The 'vital force' or 'life energy' of an organism. It is also known as the 'vital breath', for without breathing, there is no life. *Prana* is distributed all over the body as it energizes all the cells.

purusha (puruṣa) • It is the supreme spirit; same as *brahman*. It is the basis of one's feeling of being alive and the associated experiences of pleasures and pains.

sankhya (sāṅkhya) • It the path of reasoning (or knowledge). It is also one of the six schools of Indian philosophy.

sanyasa (sanyāsa) • Giving up actions driven by selfish desire. A *sanyasi* is one who follows the path of *sanyasa*, i.e. renouncing the rewards of an action and not the action itself. The idea of a *sanyasi* in the Bhagavad-Gita is different from the typical image of an old man who has given up everything and has fully retired from active life.

varna (varṇa) • Basic traits of individuals that influence the roles they play in a society. The four categories according to the principle of *varna* are *brahmins* (scholars/teachers), *kshatriyas* (warriors/administrators), *vaishyas* (traders/artisans), and *shudras* (workers).

vasana (vāsana) • Residual impact of actions. In other words, the consequences of one's *karma*. The soul carries experiences from previous births, which to some extent influence the present life – for better or for worse, depending on the experiences.

yajña (yajña) • It is a Vedic fire ritual, in which fire is raised in an enclosed altar, typically a square-shaped structure made of bricks, with the top portion open to air. The sacred fire is both a deity as well as the medium to deliver offerings made to other deities. The deities to be worshiped are invoked during the *yajña*. Clarified butter (the fuel for *yajña*), medicinal herbs, twigs of Peepul tree and other offerings are put into the fire, accompanied by chanting specific hymns from the Vedas. Metaphorically, *yajña* can also refer to 'an act of self-dedication' or 'service above self'.

yoga (yoga) • It is a form of physical and mental discipline. In a broader sense, *yoga* can mean 'union with the Supreme', 'contemplation', 'oneness of body and mind', 'path', or 'the path of action'. It is also one of the six schools of Indian philosophy. A *yogi* is one who practices *yoga*.

yuga (yuga) • Age or epoch. There are four *yugas* – Satya *yuga*, Treta *yuga*, Dvapara *yuga*, and Kali *yuga*. Together these four *yugas* make a *mahayuga* (Great Age) that spans 4,320,000 human years.

Some Characters from Mahabharata

Abhimanyu (abhimanyu) • Son of Arjuna and Subhadra (Krishna's sister). He was just sixteen when he was killed in the Mahabharata war. He was married to Uttara (Virata's daughter) and fathered Parikshit, who inherited the throne after the Pandavas retired.

Arjuna (arjuna) • See page 30.

Ashvatthama (aśvatthāma) • Son of Drona and Kripi (Kripa's sister). He was among the few survivors from the Kaurava army. He killed the sons of the Pandavas while they were sleeping and also tried to kill Uttara who was then pregnant with Parikshit.

Bharata (bharatha) • Famous ancestor of the Pandavas and Kauravas. The name of epic (Mahabharata) is derived from king Bharata.

Bhima (bhīma) • Second of the five Pandava brothers. His immense strength (equal to a thousand elephants) and ghastly nature especially scared Duryodhana.

Bhishma (bhīṣma) • See page 27.

Dhrishtadhyumna (dṛṣṭadyumna) • Son of Drupada and a student of Drona. He was the commander-in-chief of the Pandava army on the first day of war.

Dhritarashtra (dhṛtarāṣṭra) • Blind son of Vyasa, born of Ambika after the death of her husband, Vichitravirya. Since he was blind, his younger brother Pandu ascended the throne. However, Dhritarashtra became the caretaker king after Pandu's untimely death. He was the father of the Kauravas.

Draupadi (draupadi) • Daughter of Drupada and wife of the five Pandavas.

Drona (droṇa) • See page 28.

Drupada (drupada) • King of Panchala and a staunch ally of the Pandavas; he was respected as the seniormost king in their side. He was also a sworn enemy of Drona.

Duryodhana (duryodhana) • See page 29.

Gandhari (gāndhāri) • Daughter of the king of Gandhara, wife of Dhritarashtra, and mother of the Kauravas.

Kuru Family Tree

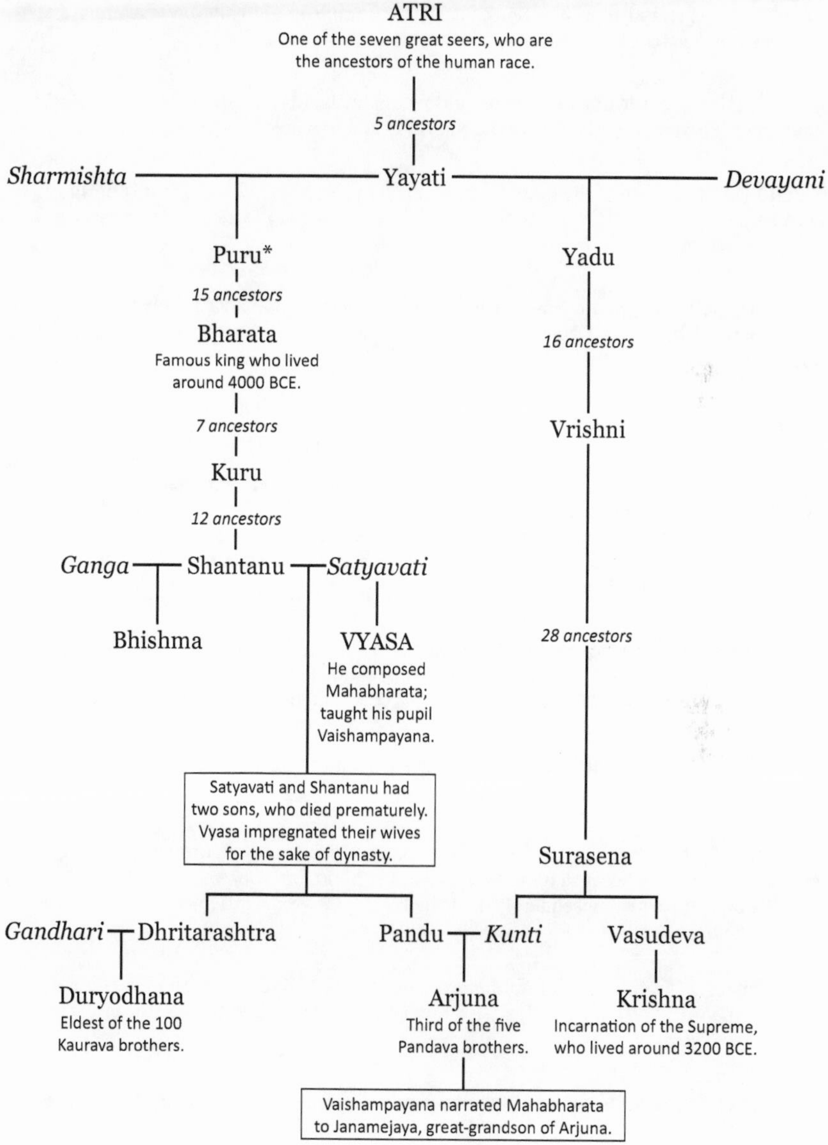

LEGEND

SAGES Men *Women* Notes *Ancestors*

*Not to be confused with Pururava, the grandfather of Yayati.

Janamejaya (janamejaya) • Son of Parikshit (grandson of Arjuna). Vaishampayana (Vyasa's son) recited the Mahabharata to him.

Jayadratha (jayadratha) • King of Sindhu and husband of Dushala (Dhritarashtra's daughter). He fought on the side of the Kauravas and was killed by Arjuna.

Karna (karṇa) • Son of the unmarried Kunti from her union with the Sun god. He became the chief support and best friend of Duryodhana, who made him the king of Anga. He was killed by Arjuna.

Kripa (kṛpa) • Son of sage Sharadvan, raised by king Shantanu. Kripa, along with Drona, taught martial arts to the Kauravas and Pandavas. Kripa survived the war and was later appointed as the preceptor of king Parikshit.

Krishna (kṛṣṇa) • See page 30.

Kunti (kunti) • Daughter of Surasena (grandfather of Krishna) and first wife of Pandu. When she was still a baby, her father gave her away to his close friend king Kuntibhoja, who had no children. She was named Pritha at birth but was called Kunti as she was raised by Kuntibhoja. Yudhistira, Bhima, and Arjuna are her sons from Pandu. She had a son, Karna, before her marriage.

Kuru (kuru) • Famous ancestor of the Pandavas and Kauravas and founder of the Kuru dynasty. He performed many noble deeds in the vast plains of his kingdom, which came to be known as Kurukshetra. It was revered as a sacred land by his descendants.

Nakula (nakula) • Fourth of the five Pandava brothers. Son of Pandu and his second wife Madri.

Pandu (pāṇḍu) • Son of Vyasa, born of Ambalika, Vichitravirya's widow. Pandu ascended the throne because his elder brother was blind, but soon retired to the forest because of a curse and subsequently died. He had two wives: Kunti and Madri. His sons are the Pandavas.

Parikshit (parīkṣit) • Son of Abhimanyu and Uttara. He was born after his father's death in the war. The Pandavas installed him as king when they retired to the forest after ruling for 36 years.

Sahadeva (sahadeva) • Last of the five Pandava brothers. Son of Pandu and his second wife Madri.

Sanjaya (sañjaya) • See page 28.

Map of Ancient India

Satyavati (satyavati) • Mother of Vyasa; later became wife of Shantanu and gave birth to Vichitravirya and Chitrangada.

Shakuni (śakuni) • Brother of Gandhari and advisor to Duryodhana. For the sake of Duryodhana and his brothers, he orchestrated many devious schemes to destroy the Pandavas.

Shantanu (śāntanu) • Famous king of the Kuru dynasty. He was the father of Bhishma from his first marriage to Ganga. Later he married Satyavati.

Shikandhi (śikaṇḍi) • Son of Drupada who was a woman in his previous life and a sworn enemy of Bhishma.

Vasudeva (vasudeva) • Krishna's father and brother of Kunti.

Vaishampayana (vaiśampāyana) • Student of Vyasa, from whom he learned the original version of the Mahabharata. He later narrated it to king Janamejaya, the great grandson of Arjuna. Vaishampayana was also the first teacher of the Krishna Yajur Veda.

Virata (virāṭa) • King of Matsya, where the Pandavas spent their final year in exile. He fought the war on the side of the Pandavas.

Vyasa (vyāsa) • See page 27.

Yudhistira (yudhiṣṭira) • See page 29.

A Few Epithets of Krishna in the Gita

Achutya (acyuta) • Immaculate, changeless, unshaken
Adideva (ādideva) • Foremost god, primal god, god from the beginning
Adikarta (ādikarta) • Original creator
Adyam (ādyam) • One who has existed from the beginning, primal one
Ajam (ajam) • Unborn, without birth, birthless
Aksharam (akṣaram) • Imperishable, unchanging, indestructible
Anadimadhyantam (anādimadhyantam) • Without beginning, middle, or end
Ananta (ananta) • Endless, infinite
Aprameyam (aprameyam) • Immeasurable, boundless
Apratimaprabhava (apratimaprabhāva) • Unmatched valor, of incomparable power
Arisudana (arisūdana) • Destroyer of enemies

Avinashi (avināśi) • Imperishable
Bhagavan (bhagavān) • God, blessed lord, endowed with six attributes (infinite wealth, splendor, strength, knowledge, glory, and renunciation).
Bhutabhavana (bhūtabhāvana) • One who brings welfare to all beings
Bhutesha (bhūteśa) • Lord of beings
Deva (deva) • The shining one, lord, deity
Devavara (devavara) • Best of gods, chosen of gods
Devadeva (devadeva) • Lord of lords
Devesha (deveśa) • King of lords
Dharmagopta (dharmagopta) • Defender of *dharma*
Divyam (divyam) • Divine, heavenly
Gururgariyan (gururgarīyān) • Most venerable teacher
Govinda (govinda) • Friend of cows, chief herdsman, delighter of the senses
Hari (hari) • Lord Vishnu, stealer of hearts
Hrishikesha (hṛṣikeśa) • Lord of the senses, one with bristling hair
Ishamidyam (iśamidyam) • Adorable one
Jagannivasa (jagannivāsa) • Cosmic guardian, abode of the universe
Jagatpati (jagatpati) • Lord of the universe
Janardana (janārdana) • Protector of men
Kamalapatraksha (kamalapatrākṣa) • Lotus-eyed
Keshava (keśava) • Lord of creation, preservation, and dissolution
Keshinisudana (keśinisūdana) • Killer of demon Keshi
Krishna (kṛṣṇa) • Dark, one who attracts
Madhava (mādhava) • Personification of sweetness, god of fortune
Madhusudana (madhusūdana) • Killer of demon Madhu, destroyer of ignorance
Mahabaho (mahābāho) • Mighty-armed
Mahatma (mahātma) • Great soul
Parabrahma (parabrahma) • Supreme *brahman*
Paramam (paramam) • Supreme
Parameshvara (parameśvara) • Supreme lord
Paramdhama (paraṃdhāma) • Supreme abode
Pavitram (pavitram) • Purifier
Prabhu (prabhu) • Lord, master
Purusham (puruṣa) • Spirit, all-encompassing person, supreme lord
Purushotthama (puruṣottama) • Supreme spirit, highest among men
Sahasrabahu (sahasrabāhu) • Thousand-armed
Shashvatam (śāśvatam) • Permanent, eternal
Varshneya (vārṣṇeya) • A descendent of the Vrishni clan

Vasudeva (vāsudeva) • Lord of the world, soul of the universe, son of Vasudeva

Vibhu (vibhu) • All pervading, omnipresent

Vishnu (viśṇu) • All-pervading

Vishvamurte (viśvamūrte) • Embodiment of the universe who has all forms

Vishvarupa (viśvarūpa) • Embodiment of the universe

Vishveshvara (viśveśvara) • Lord of the universe

Yadava (yādava) • A descendent of the Yadava clan

Yogeshvara (yogeśvara) • Master of *yoga*

A Few Epithets of Arjuna in the Gita

Anagha (anagha) • Sinless

Arjuna (arjuna) • Free, plain, having no binding

Bharata (bhārata) • A descendent of king Bharata

Bharatashreshtha (bharataśreṣṭha) • Best of the Bharatas

Bharatarshabha (bharatarṣabha) • Bull (chief) among the Bharatas

Bharatasattama (bharatasattama) • Best of the Bharatas

Dehabhritamvara (dehabhṛtāṃvara) • Supreme among humans

Dhananjaya (dhanañjaya) • Conqueror of wealth

Gudakesa (guḍākeśa) • Conqueror of sleep, one with thick hair

Kaunteya (kaunteya) • Son of Kunti

Kiritin (kirīṭin) • Adorned with a crown

Kurunandana (kurunandana) • The joy of the Kurus, choice son of the Kurus

Kurupravira (kurupravīra) • Great hero of the Kurus

Kurusattama (kurusattama) • Best of the Kurus

Kurushreshtha (kuruśreṣṭha) • Best of the Kurus

Mahabaho (mahābāho) • Mighty-armed

Pandava (pāṇḍava) • Son of Pandu

Parantapa (paraṃtapa) • Scorcher of enemies

Partha (pārtha) • Son of Pritha (Kunti)

Purusharshabha (puruṣarṣabha) • Bull (chief) among men

Purushavyaghra (puruṣavyāghra) • Tiger among men

Savyasachin (savyasācin) • Ambidextrous archer

Tata (tāta) • Son, father; Krishna addresses Arjuna as 'my son' out of affection.

APPENDIX 4 Influence of the Bhagavad-Gita

The influence of the Bhagavad-Gita has not been limited to a single period in history or a single place in the world; it has not been bound to a single school of philosophy or a single sect of people. It transcends all boundaries and distinctions.

"The Gita is a great song to live by. What other scriptures do we require?"
TRADITIONAL

"If all the Upanishads are cows, Krishna, the cowherd boy, milks them. Arjuna is the calf, and the pure ones the partakers of the milk, which is the supreme Gita."
VAISHNAVIYA TANTRASARA (TRADITIONAL)

"Though engaged in the performance of worldly duties, one who is regular in the study of the Gita becomes free. He is the happy man in this world. He is not bound by karma.*"*
VARAHA PURANA (TRADITIONAL)

"From a clear knowledge of the Bhagavad-Gita all the goals of human existence become fulfilled. Bhagavad-Gita is the manifest quintessence of all the teachings of the Vedic scriptures."
SHANKARACHARYA (788-820)
INDIAN SAINT, PHILOSOPHER, AND PERPETUATOR OF ADVAITA PHILOSOPHY

"The Bhagavad-Gita was spoken by Lord Krishna to reveal the science of devotion to God which is the essence of all spiritual knowledge."
RAMANUJACHARYA (1017-1137)
INDIAN PHILOSOPHER, SOCIAL REFORMER, AND PERPETUATOR OF VISHISHTADVAITA PHILOSOPHY

"Mahabharata has all the essential ingredients necessary to evolve and protect humanity and that within it. The Bhagavad-Gita is the epitome of the Mahabharata just as ghee *is the essence of milk and pollen is the essence of flowers."*
MADHVACHARYA (1238-1317)
INDIAN PHILOSOPHER, THEOLOGIAN, AND PERPETUATOR OF DVAITA PHILOSOPHY

"[In the story of the Mahabharata]...there is a discourse, which was given by Lord Krishna to Arjuna, of Vyasa's intelligence, after churning the sea of the Vedas. Men of dispassion seek it, the saints constantly enjoy it, and the adepts rejoice in it... It is heard eagerly by the devotees and is highly esteemed in the three worlds... It is called the Bhagavad-Gita..."
JNANESHWAR (1275-1296)
INDIAN SAINT, POET, PHILOSOPHER, AND YOGI OF THE NATHA TRADITION

"I advise everyone to follow the instructions of the Bhagavad-Gita as spoken by Lord Krishna."
Chaitanya Mahaprabhu (1486-1533)
Indian ascetic, social reformer, and chief proponent of Gaudiya Vaishnavism

"The Bhagavad Gita teaches us that one attains union with God through knowledge, love and action. These three must develop together...this is integral yoga."
Samarth Ramdas (1608-1682)
Indian saint, poet, and spiritual teacher

"I hesitate not to pronounce the Geeta a performance of great originality, of a sublimity of conception, reasoning, and diction almost unequalled; and a single exception, amongst all the known religions of mankind."
Warren Hastings (1754-1826)
British official and first Governor-General of British India

"This episode of the Mahabharata was the most beautiful; perhaps the only true philosophical song existing in any known tongue...the deepest and loftiest thing the world has to show."
Wilhelm von Humboldt (1767-1835)
Prussian minister of education, philosopher, and linguist

"In the Bhagavad Gita Krishna thus raises the mind of his young pupil Arjuna when, seized with compunction at the sight of the arrayed hosts... Krishna leads him to this point of view [the world is the empty delusion of Maya], and the death of thousands can no longer retrain him; he gives the sign for battle."
Arthur Schopenhauer (1788–1860)
German philosopher and author

"I read more of the Bhagavat Geeta and felt how surpassingly fine were the sentiments; these, or selections from this book should be included in a Bible for Mankind."
Amos Bronson Alcott (1799-1888)
US-American author, teacher, and philosopher

"I owed a magnificent day to the Bhagavat Geeta. It was the first of books; it was as if an empire spoke to us, nothing small or unworthy, but large, serene, consistent, the voice of an old intelligence which in another age and climate had pondered and thus disposed of the same questions which exercise us."
Ralph Waldo Emerson (1803-1882)
US-American transcendentalist philosopher and poet

"It is a wonderful book and has greatly excited my curiosity to know more of the religious literature of the East."
John Greenleaf Whittier (1807-1892)
US-American Quaker poet and social activist

"In the morning I bathe my intellect in the stupendous and cosmogonal philosophy of the Bhagvat-Geeta, since whose composition years of the gods have elapsed, and in comparison with which our modern world and its literature seem puny and trivial..."
HENRY DAVID THOREAU (1817-1862)
US-AMERICAN TRANSCENDENTALIST PHILOSOPHER AND AUTHOR

"...probably the most beautiful book which has ever come from the hand of man."
ÉMILE-LOUIS BURNOUF (1821-1907)
FRENCH ORIENTALIST, AUTHOR, AND RACIALIST

"In plain but noble language it unfolds a philosophical system...blending as it does the doctrine of Kapila, Patanjali, and the Vedas."
EDWIN ARNOLD (1832-1904)
ENGLISH POET, JOURNALIST, AND TRANSLATOR

"What is the significance of the Gita? It is what you get by repeating the word ten times. It is reversed into 'tagi', a person who has renounced everything for god."
RAMAKRISHNA PARAMAHAMSA (1836-1886)
INDIAN ASCETIC AND SPIRITUAL TEACHER

"Among the priceless teachings that may be found in the great Hindu poem of the Mahabharata, there is none so rare and priceless as this, 'The Lord's Song'."
ANNIE BESANT (1847-1933)
IRISH THEOSOPHIST AND AUTHOR

*"Bhagavad Gita is one of the most brilliant and pure gems of our ancient sacred books. It would be difficult to find a simpler work in Sanskrit literature or even in all the literature of the world than the Gita, which explains to us in an unambiguous and succinct manner the deep, and sacred principles of the sacred science of the self (*atman*), after imparting to us the knowledge of the human body and the cosmos, and on the authority of those principles acquaints every human being with the most perfect and complete condition of the self..."*
BAL GANGADHAR TILAK (1856-1920)
INDIAN NATIONALIST, SOCIAL REFORMER, AND FREEDOM-FIGHTER

"I believe that in all the living languages of the world, there is no book so full of true knowledge and yet so handy. To my knowledge, there is no book in the whole range of the world's literature as high above as the Bhagavad-Gita, which is the treasure-house of dharma *not only for the Hindus but for all mankind."*
MADAN MOHAN MALAVIYA (1861-1946)
INDIAN FREEDOM-FIGHTER, SOCIAL REFORMER, AND FOUNDER OF BENARAS HINDU UNIVERSITY

"In order to approach a creation as sublime as the Bhagavad-Gita with full understanding, it is necessary to attune our soul to it."
RUDOLF STEINER (1861-1925)
AUSTRIAN PHILOSOPHER, ARTIST, LITERARY SCHOLAR, AND FOUNDER OF ANTHROPOSOPHY

"The Bhagavad Gita represents one of the highest flights of the conditioned spirit to its unconditioned Source ever achieved."
Elizabeth Louisa Moresby a.k.a Lily Adams Beck (1862-1931)
British novelist and fantasy writer

"...a magnificent flower of Hindu mysticism."
Count Maurice Maeterlinck (1862-1949)
Belgian essayist, poet, and playwright

"A great landmark in the history of religion is here...religions of fear and of temptations were gone forever, and in spite of the fear of hell and temptation of enjoyment in heaven, came the grandest of ideals, love for love's sake, duty for duty's sake, work for work's sake... The human race will never again see such a brain as his who wrote the Gita."
Swami Vivekananda (1863-1902)
Indian spiritual leader, social reformer, and founder of the Ramakrishna Mission

"The Bhagavad-Gita and the Upanishads contain such godlike fullness of wisdom on all things that I feel the authors must have looked with calm remembrance back through a thousand passionate lives, full of feverish strife for and with shadows, ere they could have written with such certainty of things which the soul feels to be sure."
Æ George Russell (1867-1935)
Anglo-Irish poet, painter, and author

"The Bhagavad Gita is one of the noblest scriptures of India, one of the deepest scriptures of the world...with many meanings, containing many truths..."
Charles Johnston (1867-1935)
English civil servant and scholar

"...one of the greatest of the religious phenomena of the world...the earliest and still the greatest monument of Hindu religion."
Edward Joseph Thomas (1869-1958)
British author, librarian and Pali scholar

"I find a solace in the Bhagavad-Gita that I miss even in the Sermon on the Mount. When doubts haunt me, when disappointments stare me in the face, and I see not one ray of hope on the horizon, I turn to Bhagavad-Gita and find a verse to comfort me; and I immediately begin to smile in the midst of overwhelming tragedies."
Mohandas Karamchand Gandhi (1869-1948)
Indian politician, freedom-fighter, and leader of civil disobedience movement

"...a true scripture of the human race, a living creation rather than a book, with a new message for every age and a new meaning for every civilization."
Sri Aurobindo (1872-1950)
Indian nationalist, evolutionary philosopher, and spiritual teacher

"The charm of the Bhagavad-Gītā is due to this idea of spiritualised activity which springs only from the highest motives... The Bhagavad-Gītā has a sphinx-like character. It contains such marvellous phrases about inner detachment from the world, about the attitude of mind which knows no hatred and is kind, and about loving self-devotion to God, that we are wont to overlook its non-ethical contents. It is not merely the most read but also the most idealised book in world-literature."
ALBERT SCHWEITZER (1875-1965)
GERMAN-FRENCH PHYSICIAN, PHILOSOPHER, AND MUSICIAN

"...probably the most important single work ever produced in India; this book of eighteen chapters is not, as it has been sometimes called, a 'sectarian' work, but one universally studied and often repeated daily from memory by millions of Indians of all persuasions."
ANAND KENTISH COOMARASWAMY (1877-1947)
INDIAN HISTORIAN, ART PHILOSOPHER, AND METAPHYSICIAN

"The idea that man is like unto an inverted tree seems to have been current in bygone ages. The link with Vedic conceptions is provided by Plato in his Timaeus in which it states: 'behold we are not an earthly but a heavenly plant'. This correlation can be discerned by what Krishna expresses in chapter 15 of Bhagavad-Gita."
CARL GUSTAV JUNG (1875-1961)
SWISS PSYCHIATRIST AND FOUNDER OF ANALYTICAL PSYCHOLOGY

"Uncounted millions have drawn from it comfort and joy. In it they have found an end to perplexity, a clear, if difficult, road to salvation."
ARTHUR WILLIAM RYDER (1877-1938)
US-AMERICAN PROFESSOR, TRANSLATOR, AND AUTHOR

"The marvel of the Bhagavad-Gita is its truly beautiful revelation of life's wisdom which enables philosophy to blossom into religion."
HERMAN HESSE (1877-1962)
GERMAN-SWISS POET, PAINTER, AND AUTHOR

"The Gita *is one of the most authoritative sources of Hindu doctrine and ethics, and is accepted as such by Hindus of all denominations. A study of even selections from it, strengthened by earnest meditation, will enable young men and women to understand the religion of our fathers, which is the background of all the noble philosophy, art, literature and civilization that we have inherited."*
CHAKRAVARTHI RAJAGOPALACHARI (1878-1972)
INDIAN LAWYER, STATESMAN, AUTHOR, AND LAST GOVERNOR-GENERAL OF INDIA

"...Bhagavad-Gita, perhaps the most beautiful work of literature of the world."
COUNT HERMANN KEYSERLING (1880-1946)
GERMAN ARISTROCRAT, PHILOSOPHER, AUTHOR, AND PHILANTHROPIST

"...a work of imperishable significance...gives us profound insights that are valid for all times and for all religious life."
Jakob Wilhelm Hauer (1881-1961)
German indologist, teacher, and author

"Some people think of the Bhagavad-Gita as a scripture for dharma *alone, i.e. its aim is to exhort men to do their work. This is not the right summary. It is primarily a scripture for liberation. The main idea of the Gita is to teach man the ways to work himself out of all his miseries."*
Subramanya Bharati (1882-1921)
Indian poet, social reformer, and freedom fighter

"...the noblest of scriptures and the grandest of sagas..."
Kanhaiyalal Maneklal Munshi (1887-1971)
Indian freedom fighter, lawyer, Politician, and founder of Bharatiya Vidya Bhavan

"The Gita is a gospel for the whole world. It is meant for the generality of mankind."
Swami Sivananda Saraswati (1887-1963)
Indian physician, spiritual teacher, and founder of The Divine Life Society

"The Gita appeals to us not only by its force of thought and majesty of vision, but also by its fervor of devotion and sweetness of spiritual emotion."
Sarvepalli Radhakrishnan (1888-1975)
Indian philosopher, teacher, statesman, and former President

"...very thankful for having had the opportunity to study the Bhagavad Gita and the religious and philosophical beliefs, so different from my own."
Thomas Stearns Eliot (1888-1965)
American-British poet and dramatist

"The Bhagavad-Gita deals essentially with the spiritual foundation of human existence. It is a call of action to meet the obligations and duties of life; yet keeping in view the spiritual nature and grander purpose of the universe."
Jawaharlal Nehru (1889-1964)
Indian freedom-fighter and first Prime Minister of independent India

"...no other didactic poem is in a position, like the Gita, to combine – absolutely free from the hard limitations of a narrow-minded dogmatism – such a variety of views and to offer to the readers of the most different schools and directions poetical pleasure, ethical teaching and religious edification."
Helmuth von Glasenapp (1891-1963)
German Indologist, religious scholar, and author

"...words of spiritual guidance that are timeless in their applicability..."
Paramahansa Yogananda (1893–1952)
Indian yogi, spiritual teacher, and author

"...the most systematic statement of spiritual evolution. It is one of the most clear and comprehensive summaries of perennial philosophy ever revealed; hence its enduring value is subject not only to India but to all of humanity."
Aldous Huxley (1894-1963)
English essayist, author, and philosopher

"In the Bhagavad Gita, there is no long discussion, nothing elaborate... everything stated in the Gita is meant to be tested in the life of every man; it is intended to be verified in practice."
Vinoba Bhave (1895-1982)
Indian spiritual teacher and social reformer

"For almost everyone the Bhagavad-Gita is the book par excellence."
Louis Renou (1896-1966)
French Indologist, professor, and author

"The greatness of the Bhagavad Gita is the greatness of the universe, but even as the wonder of the stars in heaven only reveals itself in the silence of the night, the wonder of this poem only reveals itself in the silence of the soul."
Juan Mascaró (1897-1987)
Spanish author, translator, and professor

"...the mental quintessence and successful synthesis of the various systems of religion and philosophy, it offers a unique epitome of the high culture of prehistoric India."
Paul Brunton (1898-1981)
British philosopher, mystic, traveler, and author

"It is impossible to do justice to the profound insights and philosophical majesty of the Bhagavad Gita as a whole. The Gita shows the way to live a complete and satisfying life."
Horace Alexander (1899-1989)
English Quaker, diplomat, author, and ornithologist

"We knew the world would not be the same. A few people laughed, a few people cried, most people were silent. I remembered the line from the Hindu scripture, the Bhagavad-Gita. Vishnu is trying to persuade the Prince that he should do his duty and to impress him takes on his multi-armed form and says, 'Now I am become Death, the destroyer of worlds.' I suppose we all thought that, one way or another."
J. Robert Oppenheimer (1904-1967)
US-American theoretical physicist and scientific director of the Manhattan Project

"Which other religion has its God say, as Krishna does in the Bhagavad Gita, 'All paths lead to me'?"
Robert Charles Zaehner (1913-1974)
British religious historian and intelligence officer

"The hero of the Bhagavad-Gītā [Krishna] is doubly heroic: he is a warrior and a saint, a man of action and a quietest philosopher."
OCTAVIO PAZ (1914-1998)
MEXICAN AUTHOR, POET, AND DIPLOMAT

"The Gita can be seen as the main literary support for the great religious civilization of India, the oldest surviving culture in the world. It brings to the West a salutary reminder that our highly activistic and one-sided culture is faced with a crisis that may end in self-destruction because it lacks the inner depth of an authentic metaphysical consciousness."
THOMAS MERTON (1915-1968)
US-AMERICAN TRAPPIST MONK, POET, AUTHOR, AND SOCIAL CRITIC

"When such a perfect combination of both science and philosophy is sung to perfection that Krishna was, we have in this piece of work an appeal both to the head and heart."
SWAMI CHINMAYANANDA (1916-1993)
INDIAN JOURNALIST, SOCIAL REFORMER, AND SPIRITUAL TEACHER

"The Bhagavad-Gita is...a complete guide to practical life. It provides all that is needed to raise the consciousness of man to the highest possible level."
MAHARISHI MAHESH YOGI (1917-2008)
INDIAN SPIRITUAL TEACHER AND FOUNDER OF TRANSCENDENTAL MEDITATION

"The Bhagavad Gita is both supremely realistic and extremely idealistic, certainly the most acute, penetrating depiction of human nature and true morality, however remote it may seem from our own."
AMAURY DE RIENCOURT (B. 1918)
FRENCH HISTORIAN AND AUTHOR

"It answers all moral concerns and needs of the world, be it man's quest for inner peace, his need for belonging to the rest of the human and natural community, his concern for the environment, or his attitude towards work and...death."
ATAL BEHARI VAJPAYEE (B. 1924)
INDIAN FREEDOM-FIGHTER, POET, AND FORMER PRIME MINISTER

"I was fortified by the Bhagavad Gita which taught that if one were morally right, one need not hesitate to fight injustice."
BÜLENT ECEVIT (1925-2006)
TURKISH POLITICIAN, JOURNALIST, POET, AND FORMER PRIME MINISTER

"The Gita is the greatest harmonizer of yogas*...once the Gita is made the guiding star of your life, the way you act will be* karma yoga*, the way you feel will be* bhakti yoga*, the way you reason will be* jnana yoga*. What you do will be in line with* dharma*; what you feel will foster* prema*; what you think will reveal* satya*."*
SATYA SAI BABA (B. 1926)
INDIAN SPIRITUAL LEADER AND SOCIAL REFORMER

"...the Gita's popularity and authority have been unrivalled."
Johannes van Buitenen (1928-1979)
American indologist, professor, and author

"...the quest for Truth is the quest for God. This is the core teaching of all religions. The scientist's motivation is to seek the very kind of truth that Krishna speaks about in the Bhagavad Gita."
Harvey Cox (b. 1929)
US-American theologian, author, and professor of divinity

"The first psychological scripture...long before Freud, Adler and Jung."
Osho Rajneesh (1931-1990)
Indian mystic, philosopher, and spiritual teacher

"The Bhagavad Gita is par excellence the book of democracy; that is what gives it its peculiar radiance. It unites all men in the same principle which "resides in all hearts". If Krishna makes no distinction between races, castes, sects, he also shows us how men, nations, can sink in the typhoon of unchained passions. The message of the Gita is a universal call to democracy, liberty for the peoples, liberty for each individual. The great affirmation of the Bhagavad Gita is that every individual, whatever he may be, rich or poor, can and must raise himself on life's path and that he has a right to his emancipation, social, intellectual, and spiritual."
Louis Revel (?)
French author

APPENDIX 5 Bibliography

Books, Articles, and Web-pages

Alexander, Horace. Consider India: An Essay in Values. Asia Publishing House, 1961

Anantharangacharya, N. S. *Srimadgeetaa Bhaashya*. Bangalore: Ramanuja Seva Trust, 1993

Anantharangacharya, N. S. *Geetaamruta*. Bangalore: Deshika Sukti Prakashana, 1978

Antonov, Vladimir. Bhagavad Gita: With Commentaries. Trans. Nikolenko, Mikhail. Ontario: New Atlanteans, 2008

Arnold, Edwin. The Song Celestial or Bhagavad-Gita. New York: Truslove, Hanson & Comba, 1900. 16 Oct. 2008 <http://www.yogamovement.com/texts/gita.html>

Aurobindo, Sri. Essays on the Gita. Pondicherry: Sri Aurobindo Ashram, 1997

Barnett, Lionel D. Bhagavad-gītā or The Lord's Song. London: J. M. Dent & Sons, 1905

Besant, Annie. The Bhagavad Gītā: The Lord's Song. London: Theosophical Publishing House, 1895

Beck, L. Adams. The Story of Oriental Philosophy. New York: Farrar & Rinehard, 1928

Berry, Thomas. Religions of India. New York: Columbia University Press, 1996

Bharathi, Subramanya. *Bhagavad Gitai*. 12 Feb. 2011 <http://www.scribd.com/doc/8051489/Bhagavad-Gita-Tamil-By-Bharathiar>

Bhattacharya, Pradip. The Mahabharata in Arabic and Persian. 24 Feb. 2011 <http://www.boloji.com/history/048.htm>

Bhattacharya, Pradip. The First Bengali Mahabharata. 8 Apr. 2011 <http://mahabharata-resources.org/variations/kabism.html>

Bhave, Vinoba. Talks on the Gita. Sarva Seva Sangh Prakashan, 1970

Brunton, Paul. Indian Philosophy and Modern Culture. E. P. Dutton & Co. Inc., 1939

Burgess, Ebenezer. Translation of the Sûrya-Siddhânta. New Haven: American Oriental Society, 1860. 23 Feb. 2011 <http://books.google.com/books?id=jpE7AAAAcAAJ>

Chidbhavananda, Swami. The Bhagavad Gita.
Tirupparaitturai: Sri Ramakrishna Tapovanam, 1972
Chinmayananda, Swami. Sreemad Bhagawad Geeta: Hinduism at a Glance.
Bangalore: N. M. Sirur, 1958
Chinmayananda, Swami. The Holy Geeta. Mumbai: Central Chinmaya Mission Trust, 1996
Coomaraswamy, Ananda K. Hinduism and Buddhism.
Mountain View: Golden Elixir Press, 2011
Coulson, Michael. Sanskrit: An Introduction to the Classical Language.
Gomrich, Richard & Benson, James, eds.
London: Hodder & Stoughton Publishers, 2001
Datta, Amaresh. The Encyclopaedia Of Indian Literature. Volume One (A To Devo).
Sahitya Akademi, 2006.
8 Apr. 2011 <http://books.google.com/books?id=ObFCT5_taSgC&dq=The+Encyclopaedia+Of+Indian+Literature&source=gbs_navlinks_s>
De, Soumen. "The Historical Context of The Bhagavad Gita and Its Relation to
Indian Religious Doctrines." Exploring Ancient World Cultures: Essays on
Ancient India. 1996. 14 Oct. 2008 <http://eawc.evansville.edu/essays/de.htm>
De Riencourt, Amaury. The Soul of India. Honeyglen Publishing Ltd, 1986
Debroy, Bibek. The Bhagavad Gita. New Delhi: Penguin, 2005
Desai, Mahadev. The Gospel of Selfless Action or The Gita According to Gandhi.
Ahmedabad: Navjivan Publishing House, 1956
Dharma, Krishna. The Great Spiritual Epic of All Time: Mahabharata.
Badger: Torchlight Publishing Inc, 2005
Dowson, John. A classical dictionary of Hindu mythology and religion, geography, history,
and literature. Calcutta-Allahabad-Bombay-New Delhi: Rupa & Co., 1987
Durant, Will. The Case for India. New York: Simon and Schuster, 1930
Dutt, Guru K. Hindu Culture. Hind Kitabs, 1951
Easwaran, Eknath. The Bhagavad Gita: Translated for the Modern Reader.
Tomales: Nilgiri Press, 1985

Fosse, Lars Martin. The Bhagavad Gita. 1st ed. New York: YogaVidya.com, 2007
21 Oct. 2008 <http://www.yogavidya.com/Yoga/BhagavadGita.pdf>

Freke, Timothy. Lao Tzu's Tao Te Ching. London: Piatkus, 1999

Galav, T. C. Philosophy of Hinduism - an Introduction: Universal Science-Religion.
T. C. Galav, 1992

Ganguli, Kisari Mohan. The Mahabharata of Krishna-Dwaipayana Vyasa.
Calcutta: Bharata Press, 1883-1896.
19 Oct. 2008 <http://www.sacred-texts.com/hin/maha/index.htm>

Giri, Swami Nirmalananda. Srimad Bhagavad Gita: The Holy Song of God. Atma Jyoti
Ashram. 2004. 10 Oct. 2008 <http://www.atmajyoti.org/pdfs/gita_full.pdf>

Gopalacharya, Srinivasa Chakravarthy. Samskrita-Kannada Dictionary.
Bangalore Press, 1997

Goswami, Satsvarupa Dasa. Readings in Vedic Literature: The Tradition Speaks for Itself.
Bhaktivedanta Book Trust, 1985

Goyandka, Jayadayal. Śrīmad Bhagavadgītā. Trans. Editorial staff of the
Kalyana-Kalpataru. 1st ed. Gorakhpur: Gita Press, 1969

Griffith, Ralph T. H. The Hymns of the Rig Veda.
17 Jan. 2010 <http://www.sacred-texts.com/hin/rigveda/index.htm>

Gundappa, D. V. *Jeevana Dharma Yoga*.
Bangalore: Directorate of Kannada and Culture, 1990

Gupta, Prashant and Gupta, M. D. The Bhagawad-Gita.
New Delhi: Dreamland Publications.

Harrison, Paul. "A history of pantheism and scientific pantheism."
Bhagavad Gita – the Song of God. 1996.
13 Oct. 2008 <http://members.aol.com/Heraklit1/gita.htm>

Harshananda, Swami. All About Gītā. Bangalore: Ramakrishna Math, 1993

Hawley, Jack. The Bhagavad Gita – A Walkthrough for Westerners.
Novato: New World Library, 2001

Hegde, Krishnananda. Bhagavad Gita: The Dialogue.
Udupi: Rashtrakavi Govinda Pai Research Centre, 2006

Hooker, Richard. Bhagavadgita. 15 Oct. 2008 <http://www.wsu.edu/~dee/TEXT/gita.rtf>

Hubert, Paul. Histoire de la Bhagavad-Gîtâ: ses diverses éditions de 1785 à nos jours.
Adyar-Paris, 1949

Huchzermeyer, Wilfried & Zimmermann, Jutta. The Bhagavad Gita as a Living Experience.
Herndon: Lantern Books, 2002.
11 Oct. 2008 <http://books.google.com/books?id=CiGSLOJPBz4C>

Iyengar, Masti Venkatesa. Srimat Bhagavadgita: A Study.
Bangalore: Jeevana Karyalaya, 1978

Jackson, Carl T. The Oriental Religions and American Thought (Nineteenth-Century Explorations). London: Greenwood Press, 1981

Johnson, W. J. The Bhagavad Gita. New York: Oxford University Press, 2008

Johnston, Charles. Bhagavad Gita: "The Song of the Master".
New York: The Quarterly Book Department, 1908

Jyotirmayananda, Swami. Srimad Bhagavad Gita. Vishva Hindu Parishad of America, 1986

Kaushik et al. *Srimanmahaabhaarata*. Volumes 13 and 14.
Bangalore: Bharata Darshana Prakashana, 1977

Keay, John. India Discovered: The Recovery of a Lost Civilization.
HarperCollins Publishers Ltd, 2001

Kosambi, D. D. Myth and Reality: Studies in the Formation of Indian Culture.
4 Jan. 2009 <http://vidyaonline.org/arvindgupta/mythandreality.pdf>

Krishnananda, Swami. A Short History of Religious and Philosophic Thought in India.
Sivanandanagar: The Divine Life Society, 1970

Lal, P. The Bhagavadgita. New Delhi: Roli Books, 1994

Maeterlinck, Maurice. The Great Secret. San Diego: The Book Tree, 2003

Maharshi, Ramana. Sri Maharshi Gita.
10 Oct. 2008 <http://www.atmajyoti.org/gi_bhagavad_gita_maharshi.asp>

Mascaró, Juan. The Bhagavad Gita. Middlesex: Penguin Books, 1962

Merton, Thomas. Thoughts on the East.
New York: New Directions Publishing Corporation, 1995

Miller, Barbara Stoler. The Bhagavad-Gita: Krishna's Counsel in Time of War.
New York: Bantam Books, 1986

Mitchell, Stephen. Bhagavad Gita. New York: Three Rivers Press, 2000

Mohanraj, V. M. The Warrior and the Charioteer: a Materialistic Interpretation of the Bhagavadgita, Including a New Translation of the Poem.
New Delhi: Leftword Books, 2005

Mookerji, Radha Kumud. Ancient Indian Education: Brahmanical and Buddhist.
Motilal Banarsidass, 1990

Munshi, K. M. Bhagavad Gita and Modern Life. Bombay: Bharatiya Vidya Bhavan, 1947

Nabar, Vrinda & Tumkur, Shanta. The Bhagavadgītā.
Hertfordshire: Wordsworth Classics, 1997

Narale, Ratnakar. Gita As She Is – in Vyasa's Own Words. Volume 1 – Chapters 1, 2 & 12.
Toronto: Hindu Institute of Learning, 2007

Natarajan, S. Main Currents in India Culture.
Hyderabad: Indo-Middle East Cultural Studies, 1960

Nath, D. History of the Koch Kingdom 1515-1615. Mittal Publications, 1989

Nehru, Jawaharlal. A Discovery of India. New Delhi: Oxford University Press, 2002

Osho. Inner War and Peace: Timeless Solutions to Conflict from the Bhagavad Gita.
Watkins, 2006

Osho. Krishna: The Man and His Philosophy. New Delhi: Jaico Book House, 2004

Parthasarathy, A. Bhagavadgita. Bombay: A. Parthasarathy, 2008

Patri, Umesh. Hindu Scriptures and American Transcendentalists. South Asia Books, 1987

Paz, Octavio. In Light of India. Trans. Eliot Weinberger. Orlando:Harcourt, 1995

Piparaiya, Ram K. The Bhagavad Gita: Your Charioteer in the Battlefield of Life.
Mumbai: Aridhi Indusvista, 1999

Powell, Barbara. Windows into the Infinite: A Guide to the Hindu Scriptures. Fremont: Asian Humanities Press, 1996

Prabhavananda, Swami & Isherwood, Christopher. The Song of God: Bhagavad Gita. New York: Mentor Books, 1951

Prabhupada, A. C. Bhaktivedanta Swami. Bhagavad-Gita As It Is. Los Angeles: The Bhaktivedanta Book Trust, 1983

Prasad, M. G. Garland - An Anthology of Vedic Hinduism. Flushing: Foundation for Arts and Sciences from India (ARSI), 2001

Prasad, Ramananda. The Bhagavad Gītā. New Delhi: Motilal Banarsidass, 1996

Radhakrishnan, Sarvepalli. The Bhagavadgītā. London: George Allen and Unwin, 1948

Raghavachar, S. S. Ramanuja on the Gita. Calcutta: Advaita Ashrama, 1998

Rajagopalachari, Chakravarthi. Bhagavad-Gita. 4th ed. Madras: Federation of International Fellowships, 1941

Ramachandra, Magdal. Shashvata Dharma in Srimad Bhagavad Gita or The Lord's Science of Eternal Religion. Bangalore: Magdal Ramachandra, 1954

Ramanujam, Saroja. Srimad-Bhagavad-Gita. Volumes 1-3.
16 Mar. 2011 <http://www.srihayagrivan.org/html/ebook057.htm>
<http://www.srihayagrivan.org/html/ebook058.htm>
<http://www.srihayagrivan.org/html/ebook059.htm>

Ramanujananda, Swami. Divine Nectar (Gita in Verse). Trissur: Ramakrishna Math, 1994

Ranade, R. D. The Bhagavadgītā as a Philosophy of God-Realization. 3rd ed. Bombay: Bharatiya Vidya Bhavan, 1982

Ranganathananda, Swami. The Charm and Power of The Gita. Calcutta: Advaita Ashrama, 2001

Rao, P. Nagaraja. Introduction to Vedanta. 2nd ed. Bombay: Bharatiya Vidya Bhavan, 1960

Rao S. R. The Lost City of Dvaraka. New Delhi: Aditya Prakashan, 1999

Ravindra, Ravi. Yoga and the Teaching of Krishna. Chennai: The Theosophical Publishing House, 1998

Renou, Marie-Simone. The India I Love. New York: Tudor Publishing Company, 1968

Revel, Louis. The Fragrance of India: Landmarks for the world of tomorrow. Allahabad: Kitabistan, 1946

Roy, Dilip Kumar. The Bhagavad Gita: A Revelation. New Delhi: Hind Pocket Books, 1993

Ryder, Arthur W. The Bhagavad Gita. Kessinger Publishing, 2004

Sargeant, Winthrop. The Bhagavadgita. Albany: State University of New York Press, 1984

Sarma, D. S. The Bhagavad Gita. Mumbai: Bharatiya Vidya Bhavan, 2003

Sarma, D. S. What is Hinduism?. Madras: G. S. Press, 1939

Sastry, Alladi Mahadev. The Bhagavad Gita: With the Commentary of Sri Sankaracharya. Madras: Samata Books, 1979

Schweig, Graham M. Bhagavad Gita: The Beloved Lord's Secret Love Song. 1st ed. New York: HarperSanFrancisco, 2007

Schweitzer, Albert. Indian Thought and its Development. London: Rodder and Stougkton, 1936

Singh, H. L. The Treasury of Hinduism. Robin Books, 2002

Singhal D. P. India and World Civilization. Pan Macmillan Limited, 1993

Sivananda, Swami. Bhagavad Gita. Shivanandanagar: The Divine Life Society, 2000 17 Oct. 2008 <http://www.dlshq.org/download/bgita.pdf>

Somanathananda, Swami. *Gitaabhaavadhaare*. Mysore: Ramakrishna Ashrama, 1993

Stanford, Ann. The Bhagavad Gita: A New Translation. New York: Harder and Harder, 1970

Swami, Purohit. The Bhagavad Gita. 10 Oct. 2008 <www.thebigview.com/download/bhagavad-gita.pdf>

Swamiji, Sugunendra Teertha. *Srimadbhagavadgita*. Udupi: Suguna Samsath, 1991

Swarupananda, Swami. Srimad Bhagavad Gita. Almora: Advaita Ashrama, 1909.

Tadatmananda. Bhagavadgita: A Lyrical Translation for Singing, Chanting, and Recitation. Saylorsburg: Arsha Vidya Gurukulam, 1997

Tapasyananda, Swami. Bhagavad Gītā: The Scripture of Mankind. Madras: Sri Ramakrishna Math

Telang, Kâshinâth Trimbak. The Bhagavadgîtâ: With the Sanatsugâtîya and the Anugîtâ. Volume 8, The Sacred Books of the East. Oxford: The Clarendon Press, 1882. 11 Oct. 2008 <http://www.sacred-texts.com/hin/sbe08/index.htm>

Thompson, George. The Bhagavad Gita: A new translation. New York: Northpoint Press, 2008

Thoreau, Henry David. Walden; or, Life in the Woods. Stilwell: Digireads.com, 2005

Tilak, Bal Gangadhar. Srimad Bhagavadgītā Rahasya or Karma Yoga Sastra. Trans. Sukthankar, B. S. 10th ed. Poona: Tilak Brothers, 2000

Tokunaga, Muneo. The Mahabharata in Sanskrit. Smith, John D., ed. 20 Oct. 2008 <http://www.sacred-texts.com/hin/mbs/index.htm>

Tomlin, E. W. F. Great Philosophers of the East. London: Arrow Books, 1959

Van Buitenen, J. A. B. The Bhagavadgītā in the Mahābhārata. Chicago and London: University of Chicago Press, 1981

Vedavyasa, E. Astronomical Dating of the Mahabharata War. Delhi: Agam Kala Prakashan, 1986

Veerabhadrappa, B. V. The Bhagavadgita: A Rational Enquiry. Trans. Sastry, D. K. Seetharama. Bangalore: Navakarnataka Prakashana, 2004

Versluis, Arthur. American Transcendentalism and Asian Religions. New York: Oxford University Press, 1993

Vireśwarānanda, Swāmī. Śrīmad Bhagavad Gītā: With the Gloss of Śrīdhara Swāmī. 3rd ed. Madras: Sri Ramakrishna Math, 1972

Vivekananda, Swami. My India, the India Eternal. Calcutta: The Ramakrishna Mission Institute of Culture, 1996

Wadiyar, Sri Jayachamaraja. The Gītā and Indian Culture. New Delhi: Orient Longmans, 1963

Yardi, M. R. *Jnaneshwari*. Pune: Bharatiya Vidya Bhavan, 1995. 18 Oct. 2008 <http://www.bvbpune.org/contents1.html>

Yogananda, Sri Sri Paramahansa. God Talks With Arjuna: The Bhagavad Gita. Volumes 1 & 2. Kolkata: Yogoda Satsanga Society of India, 2002

Yogi, Maharishi Mahesh. Maharishi Mahesh Yogi on the Bhagavad-Gita: a New Translation and Commentary: Chapters 1-6. New York: Viking Penguin, 1990

Zaehner, Robert Charles. The Bhagavad-Gītā: With a Commentary Based on the Original Sources. New York: Oxford University Press, 1973

Gitaartha Sangraham of Yamunacharya. 16 Mar. 2011 <http://srivaishnavism.yuku.com/topic/466>

Kailasam Krithigalu: Collected Works of T. P. Kailasam (1884-1946). Mysore: Institute of Kannada Studies, 1987

Mahabharata in Oriya – Sarala Mahabharat. 8 Apr. 2011 <http://www.hindu-blog.com/2008/05/mahabharata-in-oriya-sarala-mahabharat.html>

The Bhagavadgītā or The Song Divine. Gorakhpur: Gita Press, 1975

The Call of the Gita. Madras: Sri Ramakrishna Math, 1983

The Complete Works of Swami Vivekananda. 18 Feb. 2011 <http://www.ramakrishna vivekananda.info/vivekananda/complete_works.htm>

The Wisdom of India. Ed. Lin Yutang. London: Michael Joseph, 1948

Vedanta Deshika's Prabandham on Bhagavad-Gita. 16 Mar. 2011 <http://www.freeonline book.net/Others/28029/Gitartha-Sangraham>

Audio tapes

Bhadragiri, Sant Keshavadas. Shrimad Bhagavadgeetha.

Saraswathi, Swami Dayananda. Ten essential verses of the Bhagavad Gita.

Shankar, Sri Sri Ravi. Contradictions in the Bhagavad Gita.

Sukhabodhananda, Swami. Gita Talks.

Documentaries

Joseph Campbell and The Power of Myth. Episodes 1-6. Feat. Campbell, Joseph. Exec. Ed. Moyers, Bill. Public Broadcasting Service, 1988

Root of All Evil?. Dir. Barnes, Russell. Feat. Dawkins, Richard. Prod. Clements, Alan and Kidd, Deborah. 2006.

The Naked Truth: Exposing the Deceptions About the Origins of Modern Religions.
Feat. Partridge, Derek and Maxwell, Jordan with Jenkins, Bill.
Writ. Maxwell, Jordan. International Research and Educational Society, 1991

Websites

About.com: Hinduism. <http://hinduism.about.com>

Hindu Website. <http://www.hinduwebsite.com>

Hindu Wisdom. <http://www.hinduwisdom.info>

Śrīmad Bhagavad-Gītā: For Everyone In All The Worlds. <http://www.bhagavad-gita.org>

The Bhagavad Gita: The Divine Song of God. <http://www.bhagavad-gita.us>

Wikipedia: The Free Encyclopedia. <http://en.wikipedia.org>

Others

<http://www.atomicarchive.com/Movies/Movie8.shtml>

<http://wikimapia.org/1025255/Niranam>

<http://www.vnn.org/world/9804/07-1732/index.html>

Harijan 24-8-1934

Sathya Sai Speaks II

The Telegraph, Calcutta - 14 Nov. 2002

Typefaces used in the book

Calibri, a humanist sans-serif typeface designed by Lucas de Groot for Microsoft to take advantage of their subpixel rendering technology.

Garamond, an old-style serif typeface named after punch-cutter Claude Garamond that remains one of the most eco-friendly typefaces when it comes to ink usage.

Georgia, a transitional serif typeface designed by Matthew Carter.

Tallys, a one degree slanted serif typeface designed by Jos Buivenga.

Times New Roman, a serif typeface created for *The Times* by Victor Lardent under the guidance of typographer and designer Stanley Morrison.

ABOUT THE TRANSLATORS

KOTI SREEKRISHNA, PhD (b. 1953, Bangalore) studied biochemistry and worked as a research fellow with the Baylor College of Medicine and the University of Kentucky. After working with Phillips Petroleum Company and Marion Merrel Dow, he is currently a senior scientist in the Global Biotechnology division at the Procter & Gamble Company. His interests include philosophy, inter-religious dialogue, and studying the Hindu scriptures. He has previously authored a translation of the *Purusha Suktam*, a Hindu creation theme. He has served in the executive council of Hindu Society of Greater Cincinnati (HSGC) for several years and contributes articles to HSGC-Temple magazine. He is a distinguished Toastmaster.

HARI RAVIKUMAR, BE (b. 1984, Bangalore) studied mechanical engineering and then trained and worked as a software engineer with Infosys Technologies Ltd. Now he works as editor and content manager of the Melton Foundation and as administrative director of the Subramaniam Academy of Performing Arts (SAPA). His interests include Eastern wisdom, *carnatic* music, mathematics, films, martial arts, learning languages, *yoga*, comic books, travel, and design. He has earlier co-authored a book 'Roots and Wings' on the significance of human values.

Proof

8438488R0

Made in the USA
Charleston, SC
09 June 2011